CW00521036

278/48

JOHN VAUGHAN AND HIS FRIENDS;

OR,

MORE ECHOES FROM THE WELSH HILLS

JOHN AND SHADRACH'S LAST VISIT TO HUGH ROBERTS.

John Vaughan and his friends;

OR,

MORE ECHOES FROM THE WELSH HILLS.

BY

REV. DAVID DAVIES,

BRIGHTON,

Author of "Echoes from the Welsh Hills," "The New Name," "Talks with Men, Women, and Children," "Christ Magnified," "Sacred Themes and Famous Paintings," "Vavasor Powell," etc.

ILLUSTRATED BY J. HARMSWORTH, T. H. THOMAS. R.C.A.
AND OTHERS.

TENTMAKER PUBLICATIONS
STOKE-ON-TRENT
2002

Tentmaker Publications
121 Hartshill Road
Stoke-on-Trent
Staffordshire, UK
ST4 7LU
www.tentmaker.org.uk

ISBN: 1 899003 40 1

Originally published in London 1897
This edition retypeset and published 2002

TO

MY WIFE

AND CHILDREN

I LOVINGLY DEDICATE

THESE PERSONAL REMINISCENCES

OF MY COUNTRY

AND PEOPLE.

Contents

Preface 9

I.   Christmas Eve at the Smithy 15

II.   John Vaughan and his friends on Preaching 32

III.   John Vaughan and his friends at Llandrindod Wells 54

IV.   John Vaughan and his friends at Llandrindod Wells

      (Continued) 76

V.   John Vaughan and his friends at Home 92

VII   John Vaughan and his friends at the Fellowship

      Meeting 104

VII.   John Vaughan and his friends Haymaking 132

VIII. Caleb Rhys' return from "The Hills" 154

IX.   John Vaughan and his friends in the Cornfield 168

X.   A Lecture at Horeb Chapel 188

XI.   A Service at Carmarthen 206

XII.   John Vaughan and his friends on the Eisteddfod 217

XIII. Kitty Vaughan at Llanstephan 233

XIV. John Vaughan on "The Lad with the Barley Loaves".... 243

XV.   The Closing Scenes of Hugh Roberts' Life 255

Preface

THIS book, like my "ECHOES FROM THE WELSH HILLS," aims at presenting a picture of peasant life as it has existed for generations in the heart of Wales. The villages for the last fifty years have been gradually, but effectually, depleted of their inhabitants, in favour of the large towns and busy commercial centres. The result is, that the primitive customs, which once prevailed in Welsh hamlets, are gradually dying out. My earnest hope is that they will, at least, be not altogether forgotten. The memory of the simple faith and quaint customs of Welsh villages, are so sacred to me, that it is with a positive pang that I think of the possibility of their ever ceasing to exist, and still worse, of their being ever forgotten.

I have also the further aim of giving our English friends a better conception, than they even now have, of the power of the pulpit and the Sunday School in Wales. In the first place, I would say just a word about the latter institution. Men and women of all ages attend the Bible Classes in Welsh Sunday Schools, and of late the probability of this happy state of things continuing is greatly enhanced by the very valuable help supplied to teachers and scholars by our Welsh Sunday School literature.

With regard to the preachers of Wales, I can only mention here six typical representatives, all of whom have recently passed from us; while I am obliged to pass over others who were almost, if not quite equally, gifted and blessed.

Nine years ago there were not two finer men, physically and mentally, in Wales than Revs. J. R. Kilsby Jones and Benjamin Thomas. Men of magnificent physique and towering intellects, they stood head and shoulders above their fellows for originality of thought and sparkling utterance. They were great friends in life, and in death they were not long divided. I personally count it among the greatest privileges of my life to have known the two intimately enough to become eternally their debtor. The two men had much in common.

They had the defects of their grand qualities. They were fallible, and, what was more, they knew it: which is a rarer gift than fallibility. They were children of Nature, and, great as they were, they in one sense never outgrew their boyhood. To the last they had the charming transparency of childhood, and the playful mirth, exuberant life, and effervescing spirits of their boyish days.

Gloriously free, as they were, from suspicion, and possessing a confiding, trustful nature, they were perhaps too easily led by far smaller men than themselves. Their splendid judgment was at times held in check by an over-generous sentiment or friendly preference. Sociable and companionable to a fault, they had their besetments. Had they, indeed, possessed less volume of humanity, and, therefore, had they been less susceptible to the emotions of joy and sorrow, rapture and depression, they would have lived a more even and peaceful life. Withal, both were richly endowed with an imagination which in its wild play startled, and almost shocked, prosaic and commonplace, but very proper men. Thus, more empty heads were shaken, and more whites of eyes turned up, in regard to these two preachers than perhaps any two in Wales. Little men, who could not reach their ankles, and were never within sight of their towering heads, occasionally offered Holy Willie's prayer, and uttered pious slander over these great heroes. All the while Wales was proud of her two great sons.

In this work sufficient reference is made to each, to supply a glimpse into their style, although Mr. Thomas appears as a lecturer only. In "ECHOES FROM THE WELSH HILLS," he has already been described as a preacher. His lectures and sermons had much in common. The last time I heard Mr. Thomas in his own pulpit at Narberth was on a Sunday evening. A thunderstorm had suddenly visited the district. The preacher was so moved by the terrible aspect of things that within half-an-hour of the service he changed his text, and, when the time arrived, preached from the words, "God thundereth marvellously with His voice." The preacher proceeded to speak of the different voices of God. Among others was the voice of thunder. The heavens were meanwhile ablaze with lightning, and the welkin was rent with the crash of elements. Catching the spirit of the storm, the preacher spoke in words of surpassing eloquence, and overwhelming force, of God's voice in the storms of life. At length, as if the elements without competed with the preacher in the pulpit, in giving due and adequate emphasis to the truth, there came in quick succession deafening claps of thunder, and blinding flashes of lightning; which grew in force and intensity until at last, by one terrific outburst of power, the building was shaken to its very foundations. Immediately that manly form stood erect and unmoved in the pulpit. He looked like one of the ancient prophets, or the lawgiver amid the thunders and lightnings of Sinai, and instantly from the lips that are now silent in death there came the reverent, intensely solemn and prophetic words, which thrilled all who heard them, "Hark! when the Master speaks, it behoves His servant to be silent." With that he sat down!

Within the last decade, too, there were four other great preachers in Wales who were specially endowed with popular gifts. The first was the Rev. R. D. Roberts, of Llwynhendy, Carmarthenshire. He was unquestionably the most popular preacher of the day with the masses. He was a perfect Master of assemblies. The moment he stood up every eye was fixed on him, and from that hour until the close of the service he appeared to mesmerise his audience. We have never witnessed such splendid natural oratory, blended with burning zeal, as he exhibited. His eye and mouth betokened a mighty orator; and he unstintingly expended all his fine powers of voice and utterance in the preaching of the Gospel. He always began his sermon with vigour and precision of speech. Every word had its place, and every tone and movement their significance. As he proceeded his words glowed more and more with intensity of feeling, and his fine voice assumed a greater compass; until finally, during the last five or ten minutes of his discourse, he would chant his sentences in the strongest and most triumphant tones in music, viz., those of the major common chord in its normal position. Having given the leading tone, he would lightly touch the intervening ones, but only to give greater effect and prominence to the Tonic, Mediant, and Dominant. Beginning on the Tonic with a few words, he would smoothly ascend to the Dominant which was emphasised, then slowly glide to the Mediant, or he would leap to the Super-tonic and pause on the following Mediant softly. This he would do repeatedly, but on coming to *the end of his paragraphs* he invariably burst into a loud victorious shout on the note marked *forte* below. The effect as a rule, was electrifying. Having a strong bass voice, and an excellent resonator (mouth), and being full of Welsh fire, he could keep the congregation spell-bound for any length of time. His themes also were without exception grand, joyful and triumphant; hence the triumphant tones used suited them perfectly.

He was himself quite ignorant of the theory of music; yet he instinctively gave expression to what musicians affirm were the most appropriate notes possible for making his words overwhelmingly effective.

The following are two different strains which Mr. Roberts often adopted in the delivery of his discourses. The former was when he spoke in a condensed style toward the middle of his discourse; the latter, when he gave fullest scope to his oratory, in extended periods and fervid perorations, especially as he drew near the close.*

Another great preacher of the age, to whom reference has been made in this volume, as well as in my former "Echoes,"—is the Dr. E. Herber Evans. He was so well known in England that only a few words are required with regard to his power as a Welsh preacher. Endowed as he was with a very exceptional gift of speech, and a voice as resonant as a bell, he was, moreover, a perfect artist in the presentation of his theme. He was a man who took infinite pains in preparation. He was

---

* These notes, together with a description of Mr. Roberts' "hwyl," have been kindly supplied by Rev. W. Evans, of Tredegar, whose retentive memory, and intimate knowledge of music, have enabled him to reproduce these tones perfectly.

absorbed in his subject, and fairly quivered with the thought of the importance of every opportunity. He was often as nervous as a child, and in that respect was very much like Mr. Roberts, of Llwynhendy, to whom I have just referred. He was also an omniverous reader of Welsh and English books, ever apt at an illustration, especially of a pathetic nature. He could tell a touching story, or give expression to a tender sentiment, with overpowering effect. His manly tears, and his genial glowing countenance, so full of human feeling, added greatly to the effect of his utterances. Those who were present at the Metropolitan Tabernacle, at one of Mr. Spurgeon's Memorial Services in connection with the funeral of that greatest of all preachers, will never forget how Mr. Evans first subdued himself, and then his vast audience into tears. They, too, will readily understand with what irresistible power he overcame an emotional Welsh audience, as he spoke to them on the best of all themes in his native tongue, which, like himself, was full of fire and feeling.

Another to whom I must make a brief, but appreciative reference, is the Rev. Joseph Thomas, of Carno. He was a perfect master at a story or quaint, homely illustration, which never failed to impart charming freshness to his theme, and great incisiveness to his appeal. He made his points stick like burrs in the memories of men, women, and children. Thus his sayings are to-day repeated ever and anon amid the mountains and valleys of Wales, and the name of Joseph Thomas is gratefully associated with unique naturalness, and charming quaintness and appropriateness, in enforcing the teachings of the Gospel.

Just a word, too, about another gifted and genial man, Rev. John Evans (Eglwys-bach), who has very recently gone to his reward. He stood for many years shoulder to shoulder with Herber Evans, as a popular preacher in the strength of life. He had less pathos it may be than "Herber," but probably greater mental vigour. Of late years he had suffered much physically; and he had, moreover, devoted himself largely to the English ministry—a fact which detracted somewhat from his power as a Welsh preacher. Like all the others whom I have mentioned, his genius was peculiarly Welsh, he was therefore never seen at his best, except when he proclaimed "the wonderful work of God" in his mother tongue. Then the effect was often overwhelming.

And what shall I more say? Time would fail me to tell of men like Dr. T. C. Edwards, of Bala, whose culture and contact with the literatures of other nations, have taken from them some of the peculiar characteristics of pure Welsh preachers; but yet none of the fire and thought and pathos. I can also only refer in passing to men of the type of Dr. Owen Thomas, Dr. Saunders, Dr. John Thomas, and Rev. Evan Thomas, who have within the past ten or twelve years gone to their reward; as well as to the eloquent evangelical preacher of the Established Church—still vigorous, though also contemporaneous with them—namely, Dean Howell, of St. David's.

Space, too, forbids my dwelling upon the impression which is still made by the younger generation of Welsh preachers on the present age. The Welsh pulpit has lost none of its power. The customs of the people change, and often, alas, for the worse, as commerce extends; but, thank God, the pulpit (allied now to the religious press, as it never was before) still remains as the great dominant force, which, under God, moulds and fashions the thoughts and destiny of the Welsh people, as nothing else does.

I hope in another volume to give a picture of the rising generation in Wales in its commercial centres, and in relation to its increasing educational, social, and religious advantages, which may cast additional light upon the hopes and prospects of my country and people.

I present this book, as the companion volume to "Echoes from the Welsh Hills," to the kind consideration of my readers; and I can only hope that it will receive some measure of the exceptionally generous treatment which was accorded my former work on all hands.

David Davies

63, Wilbury Road,
        Hove, Brighton,
Dec. 20, 1897.

CHAPTER I.

Christmas Eve at the Smithy

IN the little hamlet among the Welsh hills, whose "Echoes"* have already been given in part few events take place which ruffle the placid surface of its quiet and peaceful life. The villagers, for the most part contented and unambitious, are blissfully ignorant of the conflicting passions and restless plottings of the great world without, save as they catch snatches of information from their various denominational papers.

The news that thus reaches them is mellowed by distance, and comes to them as if from another realm. Old Testament records of

---

* *"Echoes from the Welsh Hills."* By Rev. David Davies. (Stoke-on-Trent: Tentmaker Publications)

victories and defeats do not seem to come to them from a much
greater distance than these accounts of the struggles and diplomacies
of modern kingdoms; while the New Testament narratives of
persecutions and martyrdoms are so fresh in their memories, that
nothing in modern history, outside their own native land, is more
familiar to them than these.

The increased facilities for travel have of late years largely depleted
the village of its most vigorous and ambitious youths, whose occasional
visits to the old scenes of their childhood familiarize the villagers with
much that is going on in "the works"* of Glamorgan and Monmouth;
still the most vigorous thoughts and tender emotions of their life even
now gather round Horeb, Jerusalem, Bethlehem, Nazareth—and their
own village "sanctuaries" called by the same, or similar Scripture names.

Thus life moves but slowly among these lowly peasants. Most of
their dwellings are still thatched and whitewashed, as they were in
days of yore. The only buildings which show marked improvement
are the sanctuaries where they worship the God of their fathers. The
very seclusion of these villagers protects them from the spirit of change
which prevails nearer the large centres of commercial enterprise.
Although they understand politics far better than their fathers did,
all political questions become interesting to them only so far as they
bear upon those religious and civil liberties withheld from their fathers,
and only obtained by them gradually and at great cost.

Although Christianity has left its mark indelibly upon all the
institutions and customs of the village, yet old traditions linger on,
and are fondly cherished by its inhabitants, and some of the quaint
and time-honoured customs in connection with festive seasons,
especially Christmas and the New Year, die a hard death.

The day before Christmas in 18— was one of exceptional brightness
in this little Welsh hamlet. With the dawn the heavens flung open wide
the cloudy gates which had closed upon the previous day, now to reveal
a serene sky, from which the sun shone forth with sparkling brilliancy:
insufficient, indeed, to melt the snow which had fallen the night before,
and thus to transform the thick-set hedgerows and the thousand twigs
on tree and shrub into a network of liquid diamonds; yet just enough to

* "Y gweithiau"—this is the general phrase applied in agricultural counties
to the busy centres of activity in Glamorganshire and Monmouthshire.

JOHN RHODERICK COLLECTING HOLLY AND MISTLETOE.

transfigure the crisp snow with its light ethereal touch, and to convert the whole landscape into one of transcendent beauty.

In the early morning, John Rhoderick, the village "ne'er-do-well" and "Jack-of-all-trades," had taken his donkey and cart into the country, and had been busily engaged during the day, with his worthy wife, in collecting holly and mistletoe, hoping to earn an honest penny on his return by the sale, at modest prices, of those seasonable commodities among his neighbours.

As the afternoon wore on, and the shadows of evening began to steal over the charming scene, softening down every detail and giving to the whole a mellowing hue of indistinctness which possessed a kind of dreamy beauty all its own, Shadrach Morgan's smithy began to assume its usual appearance on wintry nights; not only because of the ruddy glow of the village forge and the silvery symphonies of Shadrach's anvil, which were seen and heard respectively by all passers-by; but, also, because just then the old friends who were wont to meet there began to assemble for their evening's chat.

Just as the twilight was deepening into darkness, Farmer Hugh Roberts' aged and saintly face appeared at the door of the smithy. Shadrach and his son Jenkin, being busy at work, did not notice his approach until they heard his mellow and tremulous voice.

"Shadrach, my son," said the veteran, as he entered, "this has been a glorious day, hasn't it?"

"It has, Hugh," responded the stalwart smith "it reminds me of the Beatitudes, 'White is the world to the poor in spirit, etc.'"*

"Yes," added Hugh, "the old earth is in her best white to-day, and she looks beautiful in it. I'm not surprised that white is the favourite colour in heaven—'the great white throne,' and so on—and that the highest blessing promised to the poor in spirit and the pure in heart is that their world shall be white. Shadrach, the older I get, the more I like the pure white."

"Ah, Hugh," replied Shadrach, as a tear moistened his eye, "you'll have the colour you like by-and-by, and all without the coldness. 'They shall walk in white,' Hugh; and you'll be one in that grand procession, that's certain."

---

* "White is the world" is the literal rendering of the Welsh translation for "Blessed" in the Beatitudes or elsewhere—a beautiful conception.

"Yes, my son," responded the aged farmer, "and I don't care how soon. Your father, and most of those who began the Christian life with me, have stolen a march upon me. They are called up higher. My turn is long in coming, and I have to wait patiently, I suppose; and that's what I am trying to do. But it's hard work, Shadrach, now that all my early friends are gone, yea, and my wife, and last of all, the only one that God seemed to have left for me in my home, my poor daughter. Maybe my turn will come soon now. Who knows?" Here the old man s voice faltered, and his face assumed a half-expectant, half-perplexed look.

Shadrach had not bargained for this when he began. He had heard Hugh speak to the same effect before, and had generally managed to give a lively turn to the conversation by telling him that he was wanted on earth that there were plenty of good people in heaven: and that he must not be selfish. But this time, either because he was more susceptible, or there was something specially touching in the old man's voice, and in his allusion to the departed, Shadrach was overcome unawares. He felt a strange lump in his throat, and coughed, but could not remove it. Then there was perfect silence for a few moments.

Just then, John Vaughan, the village shoemaker, Shadrach's cousin, entered in company with David Lewis, the village shopkeeper.

"Hard at work on Christmas Eve!" said David Lewis, playfully, in a half-tone of surprise.

"We have almost finished now, David," replied Shadrach. "We'll go into the house in a few minutes, and have a chat round the fire."

"Good," said David, "such chats as your father and Hugh used to have in days gone by."

"Ah, many an hour have we spent together there," interjected Hugh, as if aroused out of a dream, his countenance meanwhile revealing much of its former youthful vivacity, "before you were born, Shadrach, and many more since then, but all now long ago. I really think I'll come in with you for a while, for the sake of old times."

"Of course," replied Shadrach; "and you must tell us something about them too."

"First-class," ejaculated Jenkin, as his face lit up with a broad, good-natured smile, and his hammer went down with unusual force upon the glowing iron on the anvil.

"Many of these meetings, especially those we had when we were young, are not worth talking much about, I'm afraid," murmured Hugh, with an air of misgiving.

"We'll have them as they were," said John Vaughan.

"Yes, just as they were," added David Lewis.

"Go, Jenkin," said Shadrach, "tell your mother that we shall all be coming in soon, and that Hugh Roberts is going to tell us something about the old times. Tell her also to be sure to put an extra log on the fire to make it cheerful."

CHRISTMAS EVE IN SHADRACH MORGAN'S KITCHEN

Shadrach had no sooner spoken than Jenkin rushed out of the smithy full of glee, and a minute later returned saying, "Mother told me to say that she has a blazing fire to welcome us, as good as any Christmas fire you ever saw, and that the sooner we go the better she will be pleased."

To anyone who may have watched Shadrach and Jenkin's movements after this, it would appear quite plain that the work was despatched with more than ordinary alacrity. With a few parenthetical remarks to the effect that this job and that could be left till after the holidays, father and son, with one consent came to the conclusion that there was nothing more to do, and the company left for next door.

Upon entering the house they received the cordial greeting of Mary Morgan, Shadrach's better half. Hugh Roberts was invited to the post of honour—the old oak arm-chair. The two next positions of honour—the large chimney-corners on each side of the fire, and beneath the wide open chimney—were devoted to John Vaughan and David Lewis. Indeed, one corner was always recognised as John Vaughan's by the sacred right of custom. Shadrach and Jenkin sat on the settle opposite the fire, and Mary upon her favourite stool near Jenkin, her hands meanwhile being busily engaged in knitting a fancy pair of ribbed stockings for Shadrach, bearing his initials, as a New Year's present.

"How homely this looks!" exclaimed Hugh, as he cast his eye upon the old oak beam, as black as ebony, which divided the open chimney from the room and reflected the kindly rays of the blazing fire. "How homely this looks," he repeated, as he looked upon the chimney-corners, then the settle, the dresser, and the old eight-day clock, with its long oak case. "I can see scarcely any change, Shadrach, since the days your father and myself used to chat here with our friends, practically *no* change, except (here the aged man suddenly pulled himself up)—*except in the faces,* Shadrach. But there, Jenkin looks the very picture of his grandfather as I knew him over sixty years ago. Ah, I hope he'll turn out to be as good a man as he was," added Hugh, in an emphatic tone, and with an equally emphatic nod.

"I hope so," replied Shadrach earnestly. Here Mary Morgan nodded her head: then her lips moved silently, and an expression of placid satisfaction rested for a few moments upon her countenance, which seemed to tell that she knew he would.

"Come, Hugh," exclaimed David Lewis from the chimney-corner, "tell us something about the Christmas Eves you used to spend here when you were young."

"Well, there wasn't much to be proud of in those times," replied Hugh. "Like others of our age, we were young and foolish. There were strange customs then. I'm glad that most of them have passed away; though some of them were harmless enough."

"But let us hear all about them, Hugh," exclaimed Jenkin. Hugh looked into the fire as if lost for the moment in a reverie.

"Why, *I* remember 'Mari Lwyd' ('Gray Mary') coming about at

Christmas-time very well, and so do you, John and Shadrach,"
interjected David Lewis, after a brief silence, by way of prompting
their old friend to tell a story he had heard before, but which he was
anxious to hear from Hugh's own lips. "You, Hugh," continued David,
"must have had a good deal of interesting experience in your early
days with 'Mari Lwyd.'"

"Of course I've had 'Mari Lwyd' at my door many a time," replied
Hugh Roberts, "and I had something to do with getting one up once,"
he added quietly. "It was as nearly as possible sixty years ago. One of
my father's horses had died during the winter; and I, together with a
few of my young companions—your father, Shadrach, and yours, John,
among them—decided to make a 'Mari Lwyd' of the skeleton of the
horse's head. We took the skeleton, when it was properly bleached,
covered it with calico, and dressed it up as they used to do in those
times, with ribbons; and having fixed it upon a pole, joined to it a long
sheet, beneath which one of our number was to go, in order to carry it
and work the mouth by means of a string fastened to the lower jaw.
Your father, John, acted that part, and the rest of us accompanied
him, intending to go to the farmhouses to sing 'wassail.' The first place
we went to—I remember it as if it was last night—was 'Ty-mawr,'
and we began by singing the well-known words:—

> "Wel dyma ni'n dywad
> Gyfeillion diniwad
> I ganu, &c."
> (Here we are meeting,
> Dear friends, with a greeting
> And song, &c.)

Unfortunately for us, the people at Ty-mawr had received a hint
that we were coming, and they had called in 'Ifan Talcen Slip,'* who
knew no end of verses, and besides could rhyme by the yard, and cut
it off at any length, as you, David, would tape. We had no sooner
sung one verse than 'Talcen Slip' and his friends answered us by
singing another. We had a good stock of verses by us; we sang a
second, and a third, and so on, but only to be answered as quick as

---

* "Talcen Slip" is the Welsh nickname given to doggerel rhymesters; "Ifan"
is the Welsh colloquial form of "Evan."

thought by those within the house. We could hear 'Talcen Slip' singing, and knew there was no chance of defeating them while he was there, and thus of entering the house to partake of bread and cheese and beer and other bounties; so we gave up and left, and, as we were coming down the road towards this place, we decided to come in here; and, having thrown 'Mari Lwyd' with disgust into the smithy, and shut the doors, we came to this very room, to amuse each other with stories, and an occasional song. That was my first and last experience with 'Mari Lwyd,' and I often wish I had never had that. It's nothing to be proud of."

"MARI LWYD" GREETED AT THE DOOR

"But you often met after that to spend Christmas Eve here and at your house, didn't you?" asked David Lewis.

"Yes," continued Hugh, "for many years after that we met on Christmas Eve. They called those meetings, in many places, 'Watching for the Dawn'; but it was only on one occasion that we stayed long enough to see the dawn, and then having previously sat down to a very hearty meal at that long table by the window, we went to the 'Dawn Service' at six o'clock on Christmas morning; but

I confess that the amusements and storytelling all the night through, followed by a big feast, were not very helpful to devotion. I remember, however, that we went, each one taking a 'mould candle,' some of which were used at the service, but most of them were kept in stock for future services during the winter months. Indeed, we used to supply enough candles for all the winter in that way. We managed to keep awake, but that was with great difficulty, and I for one made up my mind either to give up in future 'Watching for the Dawn' or 'The Dawn Service' on Christmas Day."

"That is, you couldn't do the *watching* and *praying,*" interrupted Jenkin, jocosely. David Lewis rather enjoyed the remark; but Jenkin caught his mother's eye and looked a little self-condemned.

"No, Jenkin," responded Hugh, gently; "not *watching* of that sort. Yet we did not give up meeting for a few hours on Christmas Eve. We used to invite our best friends. The colder the night the bigger the faggot or log we put on the fire, and, therefore, the brighter it burned, and the more genial was the circle and the heartier the laugh. Poor fellows, they are all gone who used to be so full of fun then."

"Tell us about the night Griffith Prys, the harpist, was with you," said Shadrach.

"Well, he was an extraordinary man," replied Hugh. "He was always a welcome visitor, especially on such occasions as 'Watching for the Dawn.' He was the best harpist in the whole neighbourhood. I never heard his equal. He was a good singer too. His delight as a young man was to sing the songs in the interludes at church. He was sought on special occasions by the great and small, but never did he despise or overlook the poorest. Ah, he was one of the kindest that ever trod shoe-leather. Many poor widows and orphans had reason to thank Griffith Prys for collections he got for them when he had charmed people at the Christmas Feasts,* which were held in those days in public-houses. I am not sorry they have passed away: there was very little good that came out of them except now and then in the way I have mentioned; but they encouraged a great deal of drunkenness and revelry. Well, I was speaking about Griffith Prys. I remember well the Christmas Eve he spent with us. That was fifty-eight years ago this very night. Your father, Shadrach, and I had not much thought

---

* Pastau Nadolig.

about religion or anything else that was serious then. I remember that Griffith Prys sat in this chair, and on this very spot. Your father sat in the chimney-corner, where David is now, and I on that one, where John is sitting. Jack Roland, the fiddler, sat on the settle just there. He was not much of a fiddler; but he thought he was, and as far as he was concerned that answered the same purpose."

"The Lord is very kind," ejaculated John Vaughan, the shoemaker, who was naturally gifted, and was looked upon by all as an oracle in theological matters—"the Lord is very kind, Hugh; what is wanting in brains in a man is often made up for him in self-conceit. That's the great law of compensation, Hugh. Were it not for that, some men would hang themselves." All smiled: Jenkin laughed.

"I'm afraid that for once your theology is rather at fault, John," replied Hugh, kindly, and with a smile; "however, it applied in *this* case. Griffith Prys, who never thought very much of himself, asked Jack Roland to play. But what a fuss he made before he began! The candle had to be put in a dozen places before he could see his music, although all knew that he could no more read music than the man in the moon. He lost his resin, too, with which he used to rub the bow. At last he found it melted on that hob, where he had put it. John's father, who was present, had to hurry to his workshop to fetch some of the resin he used for making wax before Jack could play. By-and-by Jack was ready and there he sat on the settle, playing 'Poor Richard,' and everybody was delighted; but not so much with the music as Jack's swagger. Griffith Prys then took his harp, and played, as few but he could, 'The March of the Men of Harlech,' 'Hob y Derri Dando,' 'The Ash Grove,' 'The Rising of the Lark,' and 'David, the White Rock.'"

"Ah, yes," said John Vaughan, "tell us the story he gave about 'David, the White Rock.' I've often heard my father speak of it."

"He said," replied Hugh, "that 'David, the White Rock' was the author of 'The Rising of the Lark,' and of the air called after his name; and then he told us the story of his life. It was something like this:—His name was David Owen, but he was called 'David, the White Rock,' because 'The White Rock' was the name of the small farm where he lived with his parents. Early in life he became a very clever musician, and his name was known throughout Wales. Early one summer morning he was returning home before dawn from a gentleman's house, where he had been playing his harp to the invited

THE BARD EXTEMPORISING "THE RISING OF THE LARK"

guests. David sat down on a mossy stone by the wayside, and, leaning his head wearily upon his harp, he fell asleep. Soon the lark rose from its lowly bed and poured forth its sweet song to awakening day. In an instant David awoke, and snatching the cover from his harp, he struck out of that instrument one of the sweetest songs we have, 'The Rising of the Lark.'"

"I never knew that before," exclaimed Shadrach.

"Nor did I, my son, till Griffith Prys told us on that occasion," replied Hugh earnestly.

"He gave us, too, the history of the other air, called 'David, the White Rock.' It seems that David's long travels and frequent engagements proved too much for his frail constitution. He became the prey of consumption; his strength ebbed fast, until at length he was forced to lay aside his harp. Still, amid the pauses of his disease, when he felt a little stronger, he would go to his harp and play some of those tender and pathetic airs which were so suited to his gentle disposition, and which have soothed thousands of our countrymen in sorrow. He became weaker and weaker. At last he scarcely left his bed. One day he was very drowsy, and fell asleep. In his sleep his mother noticed a sweet smile pass over his countenance, and his hands move as if he were playing the harp. His face, too, seemed all at once to recover its former ruddiness and plumpness. She became terrified: so sudden and strange was the change—but at that moment he opened his eyes, looked eagerly, and said, 'Oh, mother! I have seen a wonderful sight, and I never in my life heard such music as I did just now. Oh, mother! give me my harp. I *do* think I can play the music I have heard.' Again he fell back into a swoon, but awoke again speedily, and said, 'My dear mother, let me have my harp *once* more.' She brought the harp, raised her son gently in his bed, and at his request helped him to sit upon the edge of the bed, bolstering him up to enable him '*once* more' to play his harp. He then played one of the sweetest airs she thought she had ever heard—he played it again and again, till she remembered every note. When tired out he was placed back on his bed. After resting awhile, he told his mother the whole secret. He said, 'I have been in another world. I found myself in a beautiful land, with luxuriant forests, rich pastures, and broad, clear, and gentle-flowing rivers. I stood near a fine mansion, in front of which was a beautiful garden. In a summer-house—a kind of booth—in the corner of the garden, I heard, as I thought, someone play the harp. I went quietly but quickly to the spot; but, to my surprise, there was no harp there. Still, the music continued, and lo, at length I found it was the breeze that made the music, as it rushed through the plaited twigs which divided the garden from the booth. How earnestly I then wished you could have heard it! I looked still more carefully, and then saw two doves near. Upon this I awoke, and saw you, mother. I shall never hear music like that again; but there, you must sing it for me mother.' With this he finished speaking; his strength had failed him. During the brief time he still lived, amid much weakness and suffering, nothing pleased him so much as to hear his mother sing the air which he himself had snatched, as he loved to say, from 'another and a better world than this.'

"His mother told the story to her friends, and when he died, she expressed the wish that this air might be sung at his funeral. It was sung all the way from the house to the grave; but, strange to say—so Griffith Prys assured us—two doves appeared as the procession started from the house, and followed all the way, while the people sang the song; and not until the clergyman came to the words, 'Earth to earth, ashes to ashes, dust to dust,' did those strange visitors take wing, never to be seen again. That is the story as I heard it, and though I am old, and my voice all but gone, I'll try to sing the song to you."

DAVID OF THE WHITE ROCK.

Hugh's aged and tremulous, yet exceedingly sweet voice, in addition to the exceptional circumstances of the occasion, gave a strange and weird expression to the air, which made Shadrach say that he never heard music that seemed to come from another world like that.

Jenkin mischievously whispered to his mother that it certainly was weird enough to come from any world except this.

His mother gave him a reproachful look, which only very imperfectly disguised the amusement which had set her lips quivering. She, however, continued knitting, and looking intently upon the stocking she had in her hand, gave a sharp jerking cough, as a further attempt to divert attention.

"Well, there it is," added Hugh, "as I heard it, and there is the story very much as Griffith Prys gave it that night. Dear me, how much better I can remember what I heard when I was a young man, about sixty years ago, than what I have heard of late; but there, that's always the tale of old men."

"They were good old times when you were young, Hugh," exclaimed David Lewis. "There was a great deal of poetry about the stories they used to tell. I like those old legends; they are so touching, and then you know the people didn't leave the village as they do now for other parts, and neighbours could meet, Christmas after Christmas, in the same houses, without anyone absent except by death, or any new comer except the children who were growing up, and were admitted for the first time into the circle."

"That's quite true," responded Hugh. "When I was a boy, very few went outside our own county, and those who went to Merthyr Tydvil and 'the Hills' were looked upon as wonders, and were questioned quite as much as those who return from Australia now-a-days. Then, again, the same house was the home of the same family for generations. But these are changeable days; and what with railways, telegraphs, and newspapers, we have all our old customs taken away from us. As I have said, it is well that some of them are gone. They were never any good; but I confess there were some old customs that were very homely and harmless, far more harmless than many new ones that I can see. The old proverb is very true: 'Better an old custom than bad conduct.' ('Gwell hen arfer na drwg fuchedd')."

"I remember the services held at dawn on Christmas Day, which they called 'Plygain,'" said David Lewis. "They used to charm me when a boy. You know they were held in the chapels as well as in the old parish church. But I used to like to go to church to hear old David Lloyd, the tailor, who was clerk at that time, and who used to pitch the tunes as well as give the responses. Why, he would pitch one tune sometimes very much after the fashion of pitching hay, right up through the ceiling somewhere among the rafters; we were all on tiptoe, vainly trying to reach it. He then would try to make up for that in the next tune, and would pitch that right down in his boots somewhere, and we could feel it rolling and rumbling under the joists. Poor old David, he was a far better tailor than a singer; although that is not to say much. He could make a suit of clothes to fit sometimes, but a tune never. It was always also up with the sparrows or down with the mice."

"He was just such another as Richard Jones, at Horeb Chapel," said John Vaughan, "with the difference that Richard always pitched the tunes too high. Many years ago, when the chapel was enlarged, 'Silly Billy' one day went up the ladder during the dinner-hour, and when the men returned to work, they found Billy up among the rafters looking eagerly for something. They asked him what he was looking for. 'Hush,' said Billy in a whisper, and looking very mysteriously, 'I'm looking for the tunes Dick Jones, the singer, pitched up here; there are thousands of them here, somewhere.'"

"That's good," said Jenkin, in high glee.

"Billy was not as silly as people thought he was," said David Lewis.

"Well," said Hugh, as he took out his huge watch from his fob, "I must be going; I see the time has passed quickly. After all, the former days had their drawbacks, and these days as a whole are far better, though it isn't always that you can get an old man to confess it. The spread of the Gospel during the past sixty years has done more for Wales than tongue can tell. Christmas feasts in public-houses, Mari Lwyd, Watching for the Dawn, and other customs have passed away. We have now sobriety, peace, and goodwill; and on Christmas Day, as indeed on other holidays, we have large religious gatherings, not to say anything about Eisteddfods here and there all over the country. Besides, the less *superstitious* we are about Christmas, the more likely we are to honour Him whose name the day bears. May you all have a very happy Christmas, my children!"

"And you, Hugh!" responded all, as they stood to shake hands with the aged man whom they all loved so much.

It was not long before David Lewis and John Vaughan returned also to their homes, leaving Shadrach, Mary and Jenkin in full possession of that hearth, made sacred by a thousand reminiscences, to compare the present Christmas Eve with those spent in bygone years, and amid very different conditions.

CHAPTER II

John Vaughan and his Friends on Preaching

JOHN VAUGHAN
IN A MEDITATIVE MOOD

THE great theme of conversation among the villagers is still pre-eminently religious, although it is not as doctrinal as it was one or more generations ago; and the Bible is the recognised infallible text-book in all debates. The great events, too, which stir the life of the village to its depths are the Association and Anniversary meetings, which are periodically held in the surrounding chapels. Long after the meetings have been held, echoes of spoken words reverberate in the humble cottages, and especially in the shoemaker's and blacksmith's workshops.

Hitherto we have repeated the conversations which took place in Shadrach Morgan's smithy. It would be very erroneous, however, to suppose that all, or even the great majority, of the talks among those friends, took place in that familiar resort. John Vaughan's workshop maintained a friendly rivalry with the smithy. It would be hard to tell at which the friends met more frequently, although now one, and then the other, appeared to enjoy almost exclusive patronage.

JOHN VAUGHAN'S COTTAGE

John Vaughan was not the only shoemaker in the village. There was another who lived near, of whom we shall hear only occasionally, as he was of a more retiring disposition. William Owen, the other shoemaker, was a Calvinistic Methodist of the old type, and had two sons "working at the trade," whose hearts were set upon the Christian ministry, and whose thoughts often wandered into theological regions, while their hands were busily engaged with stirrup and clamps, brad-awl and bristles, lapstone and leather. John, too, had an apprentice who had resolved to devote his life to preaching the Gospel.

It is from such places and surroundings that the pulpit in Wales has drawn its mightiest occupants. It will be remembered that John himself, early in life, had his dream about future usefulness in the Christian ministry: a dream, however, which the sudden death of his father and the consequent responsibilities which rested upon him as the eldest son of a large family, brought rudely to a close. While John was thus permitted in early days to cherish the joyous and inspiring thought that he might yet become a messenger of Jesus Christ to his fellows he had frequent chats with his pastor, the Rev. James Davies, about the ministry. John well remembered what he had then learnt at the feet of that old divine, whom he had well-nigh worshipped in earlier days, and whose memory, now that he had long since vanished out of sight, imparted a pathetic mellowness to John's voice, and a strange tearfulness to his utterance whenever he spoke of him. In addition to this early training, John had gained a great deal of intimacy with the ordinary work of the ministry by a life-long and sympathetic intercourse with preachers and pastors, and thus had acquired very clear and emphatic views of ministerial efficiency and success.

One evening, early in the New Year, a few of John's old friends—namely, Hugh Roberts, Shadrach Morgan, David Lewis, Caleb Rhys, and Llewelyn Pugh—met in his workshop. During the preceding week a new minister had been "recognised" as the pastor of a neighbouring church. John and his apprentice, Thomas, as well as most of the friends present, had attended the services. John had been greatly impressed by them, and the apprentice was full of enthusiasm, especially in view of being probably admitted to Carmarthen College the following summer. Indeed, Thomas had for many months regularly visited Mr. Llewelyn Pugh, the learned schoolmaster, and the oracle of the village in all matters pertaining to scholarship; and had spent his evenings in diligent preparation for the entrance examination. Besides, he was to have three months of day schooling before the examination came on.

The talk for a while was somewhat discursive, regarding the services and the prospects of the new pastorate; but all at once John turned to the apprentice, who sat on the bench on his left, and said, in his own emphatic and intense fashion: "Thomas, my boy, shoemaking is child's play compared with the work to which you hope to devote your life. If there is any man in the world who must needs toil hard and constantly, it is the Christian minister. We work in leather—the tanned hides of dead creatures; but he works in the hearts of living men and women and this is the work that lasts! It's no wonder that Paul said to Timothy, 'Study (or 'give diligence') to show thyself approved unto God, a workman that needeth not to be ashamed, rightly dividing the word of truth.' You see, Timothy was to show himself approved unto God as a *workman.* The most vehement supporters of the Church of England in Wales have sometimes boasted that in sending clergymen to our country they have placed a *gentleman* in every parish. That's rather an insult to the squire. But be that as it may, it is worth remembering that Paul wanted Timothy to be a *workman,* let who would be a gentleman; and after all he considered that the only true gentleman was the one who did his work so well that he had never any need to be ashamed of it.

"Now, the only hopeful thing possible about any bad workman is—what you seldom, if ever, find in him—that he *is ashamed of himself.* I can generally tell by that one thing whether an apprentice of mine is going to make a good shoemaker or not. If he is not ashamed of bad work, I soon tell him that he had better go and start for himself, as I have no more to teach him. But if he is a little ashamed of himself now and then—and I confess I have found you, Thomas, always so when you have done a thing badly—I say: 'That's poor, certainly; but you will be able to do something better by-and-by.' And, depend upon it, that's the only kind of apprentice over whom the Lord Jesus Himself will take any trouble, and of whom he will make a decent workman for His first words were, 'Blessed are the poor in spirit'—that is, those who don't think too much of themselves. There were those Pharisees of His day who cobbled up a bit of morality of their own, and like all poor cobblers, covered over the

JOHN VAUGHAN'S WORKSHOP

bad work and gaping cracks with blackball and polishing irons; but, bless you! the first rainy day told the tale! Now, Jesus would have none of them, and He will not to-day. He will have workmen that *need not to be ashamed.* Not that they are *satisfied* with their work— no good workman ever is—but they are *not ashamed* of it, or even if, in their humility, they are, they *need not be."*

"But surely," said Thomas, "there are times when you need be ashamed, even after you have done your best."

"That will not be long, if you keep well in view of the standard and continue to do your best. Now what takes all need of shame from the Christian minister is that he *rightly divides the word of truth,* or, as our dear old Mr. James Davies used to translate it, *'cuts it straight.'* I cannot help thinking—although I do not find one Welsh commentator agree with me—that Paul here uses what was a very homely figure to him as a tentmaker, namely, *cutting the canvas straight.* You may depend upon it that Paul had learnt his trade thoroughly, cutting included. He well knew how many tents had been utterly spoiled by bad cutting. Why, it is exactly so in our trade. There was dear old Shem Thomas, to whom I was apprenticed. He was as good a man as ever trod shoe-leather, and there never was a man who put better leather or tighter stitches into a pair of shoes than he did; but he *never could cut* properly. The result was that half the boots he ever made were thrown on his hands for a time, till they could by a thousand shifts be made to fit some other customers; and even the other half never fitted properly. So much depends in our trade upon good cutting.

"It is just so in the highest and best work, Thomas. The true Christian minister must give every truth its right place and its right proportion. To do that he must have a straight eye—'a single eye' is the Scripture phrase—and a steady hand. It is only then that his sermons fit the hearers, and his ministry suits their needs. What a blessing it is when a minister makes his people feel that his message exactly fits them, so that they are bound to put it on and wear it! Some men think that they can make a sermon fit with a bit of application at the end. They are exactly like poor old Shem, who used to think that all misfits would be made right when the boot was laced up—especially a few times—and the leather, as he used to say, had 'come to the foot'; whereas he ought to have made the leather come to the foot at first, in the fit."

"Poor Shem" exclaimed Hugh Roberts, "he is gone, and therefore we will say as little as we can of his failings; but there are some of us who will limp to the end of life's journey through his misfits."

"You are quite right, Hugh," responded John, "no one can tell how far poor Shem was responsible for the corns on good people's feet in his time. Why, you could scarcely see any of his customers who didn't limp hopelessly along, and complain of the ruggedness of the way. There are some Christian ministries like old Shem's boots: they produce any amount of corns. The people get very touchy because they have been pinched instead of fitted; and they pass for very conscientious people as they walk along the path of life so cautiously and tenderly, and talk about the roughness of the way, whereas all the while its not their consciences but their feet that are tender; and it is not the way that is rough but their toes cramped. They suffer from spiritual corns; and once people have them it is a long time before they get rid of them. Indeed, I have never yet seen any one *perfectly* cured of them. There is always a tenderness, and something very much like a corn left. Ministers, like shoemakers, will have much to answer for in that direction. Remember, Thomas, *nothing can make up for a bad cut,* and that is as true of the ministry as it is of shoemaking, tailoring, or tent-making, every bit."

Hugh Roberts, although he agreed with John thoroughly about Shem Thomas's misfits, showed some signs of perplexity as he listened intently to John's exposition of Paul's words to Timothy, and, true to his instincts as a farmer, now interjected the remark: "I have always understood that the words 'rightly dividing the word of truth,' or 'holding a straight course in the word of truth,' was a figure taken from farming, namely, 'ploughing the furrows in a straight line.' Of course I will not try to discuss the matter, but Mr. Pugh knows what it is in Greek."

Llewelyn Pugh—who always remembered his University career with pleasure and some pride, although he had conscientiously departed from his early purpose of becoming a clergyman, and had subsided into a quiet village schoolmaster, and the companion of humble peasants—immediately responded to Hugh Roberts' polite hint, and said—"Well, the truth is, that the Greek word may mean what John understands by the passage, or what you have given as its meaning; or, indeed, this may be a figure derived from cutting a road straight through a country. It is hard to decide."

"I am glad to hear you, Mr. Pugh, say that," replied John with emphasis. "Now that you have told us *the possible* meanings of the words, we must use our common sense to decide which is *the most likely* meaning. Now, if Paul had been a farmer, like Hugh Roberts, I should have thought, after what you have said, that he referred to a straight furrow; or, if Paul had been a road surveyor, I should have thought that he used the figure of making a straight road; but, as he was a tent-maker, I believe he used the illustration with which he was most familiar. I rejoice to have your opinion, Mr. Pugh, for I suppose you could have chatted with Paul in Greek, as you do with us in Welsh." [Mr. Pugh shook his head and smiled, but John Vaughan took no notice of this disavowal.] "And now that you say the words *can* mean what I say, I intend to stick to my opinion."

"Well," said Hugh Roberts, "I mean to stick to mine, too, John. This isn't the first time that the figure of the plough is used in the New Testament."

"Just so," said Mr. Llewelyn Pugh, "and I don't blame either of you. Paul's words are wide and deep enough to include both illustrations and a dozen more, for no illustration can exhaust the whole truth. At best, it only helps us to understand it better."

"That's it," said John; "but thank God for such helps, and we ought to make the best use of them. Well, I understand cutting better than ploughing, and so do you, Thomas; and, therefore, that's the figure that suits us best; and we'll let Hugh Roberts stick to his illustration of ploughing straight, and I have no doubt he'll get any amount of meaning out of that," John added, as his eye twinkled mischievously, "especially when his man John some day fails to plough a straight furrow. He will then be sure to have an eloquent exposition on the words of Paul."

"I can see how you apply it to a minister's work in a general way," interjected Thomas; "but I don't see how a minister could carry that idea out in every part of his work."

"I cannot see the difficulty," quickly responded John Vaughan. "Take public worship, for instance. Now, I think that in every service held in the house of God the Christian minister is engaged in dividing—cutting out—the Word of Truth. He gives out a hymn to sing. Old Mr. James Davies used to say that a great deal depended upon giving out the first hymn. It was that which broke upon the silence of God's house, and gave the keynote to the whole service. I believe that thoroughly. Much depends upon how the minister announces the opening hymn. Sometimes you have heard the words jerked out one over the other, as Hugh Roberts would toss turnips out of a sack; at other times they have been muttered lazily, and in the same tone from beginning to end, just as we used to repeat the multiplication table at school when we were sick of the whole business. Thomas, if you ever become a minister, pray that you may never throw a wet blanket over a service by mumbling out a hymn as if you were not quite awake yet, or, if awake yourself, did not want to wake others. But there, 'Physician heal thyself.' I am not rightly dividing the Word of Truth; but taking up all the time in speaking about the hymn. The same thing applies, of course, to all the other parts of the service.

"We ought never to begin a service hurriedly, as if we wished it was already over, or lazily as if we wished it had never begun. A tone of indecent hurry at the outset sends away the Holy Spirit; and a service that is begun without any heart is not likely to improve as you go on. A service ought never to begin in a low flat tone. If it does, there's no knowing where it will finish—most likely down somewhere in our boots, or probably under the joists. Now, like minister like people. If there's no fire in the pulpit, you will look in vain for it to the pew. A minister should enter the pulpit—hard as it is to do so often, I have no doubt—with enthusiasm for his work. I think that the preparation needed is more in this direction than in the sermon. Bless you, if the minister is prepared, the sermon is sure to be. And if he is prepared, he will begin the service as if he meant to make the best use of it, God helping him. There will be a ring of heartiness from the first moment that he lifts up his voice to the last; and he *will* lift it up, and not be afraid."

"Now come, John," said Hugh Roberts in kind, paternal tones, "you make no allowance for the minister being frail and mortal like the rest of us. You do not pull the stitches always as tight as you might. Your liver may be wrong, or you may feel tired and jaded, and find it very difficult to put heart into your work."

"I quite agree with you, Hugh," replied John. "I am speaking of what should be aimed at, and not what is always reached. Besides, all the work and responsibility by no means rests with the minister.

A hymn given out well ought to be sung well. What a burst of thanksgiving ought to go up to God from the congregation because they have been permitted once again to appear in Zion! We are all often guilty of missing these grand opportunities."

"Quite right, John," exclaimed Hugh Roberts.

"Thus, I am afraid we have something almost as bad in some chapels in the reading of the Scriptures in an assumed tone, and without any special regard for the meaning of the passage read. In other places there is an evident slovenliness in reading the Bible, which I think is very harmful. Now we believe as Protestants in having the Word of God read to the people. The fact that they have it in their homes is not enough. It is too often kept there with the cups and saucers on the dresser, or on the chest of drawers in the little parlour; and people show their reverence for it by keeping it well dusted; but in too many instances it is, I fear, seldom read, except a few verses at family worship.

"Now, there are some ministers who make it impossible for this sort of thing to continue, for they read God's Word in public in such a way as to create an appetite in their people for reading it at home. Well a true minister's desire is to let the good Old Book speak for itself to the congregation. For the time being, like John the Baptist, he desires only to be 'a voice.' But in such a glorious service as telling out the message of his King, in the King's own words, he desires to do it to the best of his powers.

"I like to read the account given by Luke of our Lord reading from the Book of the Prophet Isaiah in the Synagogue at Nazareth for the first time after His baptism. The Evangelist tells us that when Jesus closed the book, 'the eyes of all in the Synagogue were fastened on Him.' That was one of the results of His reading. The word 'fastened' ('craffu,' Welsh) is a strong word. Those eyes couldn't help it. There was a power that fixed them so that they could not move. There was more than a mesmeric power that held them. Now, securing people's eyes is a long way towards securing their hearts. A minister has won more than half the battle when, in a congregation of five hundred people, one thousand eyes are fixed upon him. Our Lord's reading on that occasion at the beginning of His great ministry had riveted attention, and had stirred up a keen expectation that the exposition which would follow such a reading was one which

would well reward them for listening. What an example is this to all
His servants not to neglect the public reading of God's Word!"

"Ah, that's true, Mr. Pugh," said John, "Old Mr. James Davies used
to say: 'John, if some good folks who give running comments—if,
indeed, such feeble things can be supposed to run, except it be out of
sight for very shame—did but *read better* and *comment less,* what a
voice of rejoicing would be in the tabernacles of the righteous!'

"Then, as to preaching," added John, "I should think that every
preacher must often turn to our Lord's Sermon on the Mount. The
first thing that we read about the Great Preacher is, that 'He went
up into a mountain.' He did not wait till a carpenter had made a
pulpit for Him, or until He had been invited to occupy the pulpit of
one of the synagogues. God had, in ancient times, made a pulpit of
Sinai. Jesus now made a pulpit of another mountain. The grand old
preachers of Wales followed His example, and preached from the
rugged hill-tops and mountain slopes of our native land to the
thousands gathered at the foot. They did that in the days when there
were no pulpits, except those occupied by men who themselves
couldn't preach, and who would not let others do so. In those good
old days God seemed to give His servants extra lung-power. Preachers
were men of the Boanerges sort, true sons of thunder, who scarcely
ever knew what a cold on the chest was, or only as something which
lent a little more thunder to their voices. They could preach in the
storm without any inconvenience; thus they could keep a
congregation together in the roughest gale that ever blew. Why, grand
old Francis Hiley never had such *hwyl* as when the wind was
boisterous. With his mighty voice he rejoiced to hurl his message on
the shoulders of the storm, and the wings of the wind, and thus make
them the bearers of good news from God to man."

"Ah, yes!" said Hugh Roberts, "I remember him well in his best
days. His voice was like that of a trumpet which sounded higher and
higher while he was carried away in the *hwyl* as in a fiery chariot."

"I remember hearing him once," said Caleb Rhys, who had been
sitting quietly listening until now, "and I shall never forget it."

"No, you are not likely to forget such preaching," continued John.
"Now, that there is less open-air preaching, preachers' lungs get very
sickly and weak, and men whisper the message of the Cross as if they
were speaking through a pipe stem. Our Lord, when on the Mount,

no sooner sat, as the old Jewish teachers used to do, than in that
homely attitude He opened, not His sermon case, but *His mouth!* The
preacher who makes a pulpit of a mountain must 'open his mouth,'
or the pulpit will soon be too big for him and his congregation. What
an example as a speaker Jesus was! With what ease and naturalness
He spoke! What do they call those professors they have now in our
colleges, who profess to teach the young men how to speak?"

"Elocutionists," replied Mr. Llewelyn Pugh.

"Yes, that's the word," responded John. "It is such a grand name
that I always manage to forget it. Well, they have 'elocutionists' now
in our colleges to teach the students how to speak. They tell me that
the first thing those men say to the students is, 'If you would speak
well, *open your mouths.'* A great deal of money, I am told, is paid
every year to those gentlemen for the repetition of that valuable hint.
Why don't the young students open their Testaments, and read the
account of our Lord's first sermon? There they would find at once
that when He began to preach 'He opened His mouth.' Instead of
that they must have a man with a grand name to teach them what
they would long since have learnt from their Testaments if they
would but read them. Besides, there is no shepherd, or cowboy, in
the neighbourhood here who doesn't know that if he is to be heard—
especially among these old mountains—he must *open his mouth."*

"Yes, that's true enough," said Hugh Roberts with a kind smile.
"But the simplicity of the thing seems to be against it."

"I heard that noted preacher from England the other night in
Carmarthen," interjected John Vaughan; "I walked there and back. It
wasn't worth it. Another minister read and prayed, and then the
stranger got up, a clever looking man—all head and spectacles. He at
once took out of his breast pocket a huge bundle of papers, and put
them on the Bible. He never so much as opened the Bible. I suppose he
thought it too ancient and old-fashioned, although his papers, too,
seemed to look uncommonly ancient. He read the text and the sermon
alike from this bundle. I suppose he had his prayer there as well, if
there had been need of it. Everything the man had or wanted seemed
to be in that bundle. In that he lived and moved and had his being. He
stooped and buried his face in it all the while he spoke, so that all I
could see from the gallery was a bald patch on the top of his head, and
his hand working like a crank about twenty strokes to the minute. His

voice seemed to come from behind a wall, or from the distant ages—
before the Deluge, I should think; and for all of Christ that I heard in
the sermon it might have been preached then; only he said nothing
about sin, so I suppose it was meant for the days before the Fall."

"Perhaps you could not understand him thoroughly, John?"
queried Llewelyn Pugh, half apologetically.

"Well, you know I don't understand English as well as I should
like," replied John; "but if a man talks English—*English,* Mr. Pugh,
and not what you call Latin—and opens his mouth so that his words
may have a fair chance of coming out alive, without being stripped of
all their limbs, I can make out a sermon pretty well, and enjoy it; but
that great man went on sending his words tearing through his teeth,
so that we couldn't catch one in three that was not torn to tatters and
therefore beyond all recognition. Oh it was a terrible massacre of the
innocents! I could not help thanking God that all were not like him;
but that we have some ministers who open their mouths."

"Very true," responded Caleb Rhys; "it was pitiful!"

"Opening one's mouth isn't a very difficult task," responded
Thomas. "There are plenty who can do that who can't preach."

"Quite so, Thomas," replied John; "yet no man can preach who can't
open his mouth. But there is another thing said about Jesus on the
Mount that I want you to notice. It is said that 'He opened His mouth
and taught.' What an important addition that is! How many there have
been who have opened their mouths, as compared with those who have
opened their mouths *and taught!* Even apart from our Lord's divinity,
what wonder that He *taught* men after such a long and patient silence
in the carpenter's shop at Nazareth. Thomas! there is a glorious
preparation possible by patient waiting for the right hour in a
shoemaker's shop, as well as in a carpenter's. The teachers of men ought
not to open their mouths too soon. Speech comes to us but slowly. What
a mercy to our mothers that we could only coo and laugh, or, at most,
cry, in our earliest days; and that we could not then twaddle endlessly
as some of us have done ever since! The man who speaks to purpose is
the one who, first of all, has learnt how to be silent. The grandest
discipline in God's school for the ministry is enforced silence. Some of
us have never learnt that lesson, hence the weakness of our talk. Oh,
for the grace to keep our mouths shut until God gives us something to
say! Then when we open them, we shall *teach* men."

"Our colleges are capital things for that: they soon teach you there to think more before you speak," exclaimed Thomas with a new-born admiration for colleges, which every candidate for admission possesses.

"True, Thomas," replied John, "and I hope that by-and-by you will be admitted to college. Our colleges are glorious institutions; but a college will not do everything.

"In the first place, if a man has no grace before he goes to college, he is not sure—I was going to say, likely—to have it while there. Indeed, he'll need all there that he can take with him. Then, again, he must have brains before he goes to college. If he enters that institution an ass, any amount of clipping with the president's shears won't make an Arab steed of him. There's one thing that tutors—clever as they are—cannot do, that is, give brains to a man. Indeed, the good Lord Himself does not do this for us after we are once started in life. He gives to every man a new heart who asks for it, praise Him! but He does not give us new heads. We have all to make the best use of the one He has already given us with which to begin life. Now, college does not make up for this want of special provision in the Divine economy of things. If a man has brains when he enters, he will be all the better for a good college course; but if he hasn't—well, as it says in the Prayer Book, 'As it was in the beginning, is now and ever shall be, world without end.'"

"One thing the college ought to do for men preparing for the Welsh ministry," said Llewelyn Pugh, "is to teach them to write and speak Welsh accurately. I know that much attention is paid to English, Latin, Greek, Hebrew, and other languages, and that some little men try to forget their mother tongue in order to show that they are very learned in those tongues. But it requires very silly people to be duped by that kind of thing. Welsh churches which contribute to the funds, and to whom the students are to minister in the future, have a right to expect that they are taught to speak Welsh accurately and well. It is well to remember that the offers of salvation are none the less Divine, and need not be any the less acceptable, because they are given in pure Welsh."

"There is so much to do in the few years given that it is hard to see to everything," exclaimed Thomas, who had recently been reading the annual report of Carmarthen College, and had been greatly impressed by it.

"That is very true," replied John, "but I quite agree with Mr. Pugh. If a man ought to know any language thoroughly, it ought to be the language in which he is to preach the Gospel to his fellows. Besides, college preparation should be followed by hard study through life. Old Mr. James Davies was a wonderful student. I asked him once what was the best time for preparation. 'Always,' answered the old man; 'blessed is the man who is always in a preparing mood; who, without being fussy, catches every moment as it passes, and makes it supply something for his work.' I have often noticed since then how true that was. There are some folks who, without any great effort, have the knack of turning everything to good account. Why, whenever I take up a pair of boots to the Squire's, I see a pot simmering on the hob in the kitchen. Mary is a grand old cook, and if you ask her whether that is broth in the pot, she'll tell you, 'No, but it's something that would soon make good broth or soup. I always keep the bones and the odds and ends of meat, and put them in here to simmer. The result is, I am never without stock for a basin of broth, or soup, or gravy that they may want in the house.'

"Believe me, good preachers are like old Mary, never without good stock simmering on the hob—a Scripture passage or two, which they can turn to good account on the shortest notice. I am not now speaking of direct preparation; but a sort of general readiness for the good work. The great aim of every minister, indeed of every teacher, should be to understand his Bible. The first step toward that is to be on good terms with its Author. The secret is in speaking often to Him, and on your knees. How frequently He will open up some of His hidden treasures to us. At other times He will let us plod on. All the Scriptures are not easily understood even in our most spiritual moments. It is by prayer and much fasting that the dumb spirit is cast out of some passages. Now, there are some verses like Welshmen: they tell out well nigh all that is in them at once. There are others like the reserved Englishman who will say next to nothing to you till you have gained his confidence, and then he'll tell you a good deal worth hearing. Now, what you have to do with those verses is to become well acquainted with them. Talk to them as often as you can, and tell them all you think; and by-and-by they'll begin to tell you their thoughts, and all you have to do is to let them speak through you to others. Ah, I have found that often true even in my Bible class."

"Quite right," said Llewelyn Pugh; "I also think that every teacher—and that includes the preacher—ought to learn more than just enough for his lesson or sermon. It is pitiful when a man has to go on from hand to mouth in that fashion. A teacher, according to Paul, ought to be 'throughly furnished.'"

"Ah, it is so!" ejaculated John; "but the worst of it is that most of us have only enough stock to keep up a respectable appearance. My little lad the other day went for a pennyworth of nuts to David Edwards' shop. He had seen them in the window, and his mother had no rest till he got the penny she had promised him for fetching water in order to buy some nuts. He went full of expectation, and

"THE NUTS IN THE GROCER'S WINDOW"

ran most of the way. But he came back crestfallen and disappointed. It seems that he rushed into the shop, and, putting the penny upon the counter, said, 'A pennyworth of nuts, if you please.' David Edwards looked at the lad, and said, 'I haven't any to sell.' 'But,' answered the boy, 'I saw them in the window.' Then David had to explain that there was a board behind the nuts which he had put into the window for show, and that if he took any away the timber would appear. Poor boy, how disappointed he felt! Now that represents what is too often the case with teachers, and, I fear, sometimes with preachers. They keep all their nuts in the shop window, and cannot spare very many without showing the timber behind. A man ought to think and read so as to enrich his own mind, and not merely just enough for a particular lesson or sermon."

"That's rather hard, John, but sometimes true," said Llewelyn Pugh in a philosophical tone. "I remember a minister once saying to me that he had just been reading a large volume, and had been boiling it down into a sermon."

"The man who said that," interjected Jenkin—Shadrach Morgan's son, who had just entered the workshop—"deserved to be boiled down himself, only I am afraid there wouldn't be much result."

"Well, I should be sorry to say that," replied John Vaughan, half reproachfully; "but I am perfectly sure that is not the proper use to make of books; besides, such sermons as are got from boiling down books must be very hard and indigestible. If every teacher and preacher would only read more of men and women, and less of books, it would be a blessing. Next to knowing God and His Word, I think it is most important that a minister should study and know men. A shoemaker must understand the nature of leather—its tannage and its grain—before he can know how to deal with it. How important it is that minister who has to deal so much with man should know what is in him! Our Lord needed not that any should testify to Him of man: for He knew what was in man. He knew as God; but He also knew as man. A minister, Thomas, depend upon it, should be well able to read character. And remember, he should know man so as to sympathise with him. A minister can get on, and do a good work, without a big brain, but not without a big heart.

"Besides, I think it is a grand thing when a minister knows something about people's trades and callings. The first thing that gave me confidence in old Mr. James Davies was that he thoroughly understood leather. I had greater faith in him as a teacher ever after that. This is unreasonable, I know, but we are all unreasonable sometimes. Old Shem Thomas lost confidence in his minister because one day he found that he knew nothing about boots. Shem used to say, 'Why, the man who has worn boots all the days of his life without learning anything about them cannot know much of anything. How can a man who doesn't understand his boots understand his Bible?' Of course, that was extreme; but yet every minister is sure to gain power over his people by being interested in their trades and occupations. Moreover, he thus becomes practical in his teaching, and there is nothing done without that."

"I like practical sermons," said Shadrach; "I can always do my work with better heart after hearing them."

"Talk about practical sermons," interjected Caleb Rhys; "there is an old minister near Llandrindod who is noted for being very practical in his discourses. He is the Rev. John George, of Gravel*— a grand character. He is a Baptist minister, and for nearly forty years has been working hard upon his holding during the week, and on Sundays has generally walked ten or twelve miles to preach the Gospel to his people. He is now over eighty years of age, and has only recently had a co-pastor. On one occasion, not long ago, he baptized a master shoemaker and his workman. 'Now then,' said Mr. George, 'just a word to you both. To-day you acknowledge Christ before the world. It will henceforth be in your power to honour or dishonour your Lord as you have never yet done.' Then, turning to the master shoemaker, he said, 'Mind you put good leather in the poor man's boots as well as in the rich man's—be sure to put your religion always into your leather.' Then, addressing the workman, he said, 'And you, John, mind you wax your threads well, and take care of the stitches, pull them home tight—put your religion into every stitch.' Then, speaking to both, he added, 'Now remember, good leather and tight stitches in the future, and God bless you!'"

"That is grand teaching," said Shadrach, "but it isn't always easy to come up to it, is it John? How do you find it with the boots?"

---

* Mr. George has since died, and has left behind him a memory which will not soon be forgotten.

"Hard enough," replied John; "one has to be always on the watch. The devil is long in letting go his hold of us. He comes to the workshop if he possibly can. The least pretence is enough. He says, 'Other people do so and so, and you *used* to do it—why not now? He knows that it is hard to get rid of old habits. When he comes in that sneaking fashion, I begin to offer the prayer of old Billy Pugh, of Rhayader: 'Oh, Lord, Thou hast long since dethroned the devil, and cast him out of my heart; but he has left some of his old furniture behind and he still often comes and wants to see it! Good Lord, help me to throw his old furniture out for ever.'"

"That's the sort of prayer I like," said Shadrach; "so true to experience, and a prayer that no one could forget."

"That is almost as quaint," said Hugh Roberts, "as what James Thomas, the carpenter, once said when he was converted during his short stay in Glamorganshire. He was then a journeyman, working in the same workshop as some would-be infidels. They heard by-and-by of his conversion, and therefore, when he went to his work the following morning, shouted, 'Hullo, Jim, so you believe in the Carpenter of Nazareth'? Jim looked straight at them, and calmly said, 'Yes, I have every reason for believing in Him, for He has already planed a lot of rough stuff out of me. He'll do the same with you, too, if you only come to Him; and you know you have much need of it.'"

"Ah," ejaculated Jenkin, "that's what I call proper teaching— simple, homely, and to the point."

"Yes, Jenkin," said John Vaughan, "but the difficulty is to teach or to preach in that style. There is a story told about Dr. William Rees (Gwilym Hiraethog) once sitting in his study in the twilight; and, looking out, he saw Mr. Kilsby Jones trying to open the gate, but, owing to the darkness, failing to find the latch. At last Dr. Rees opened the window and said, 'The latch is lower down; you'll find it if you only stoop a little.' That is just it in teaching and preaching. How often men fail to find an opening to the heart, just because the latch is lower down than they think, and they must needs stoop. Blessed is the teacher who can be simple, just as Jesus was, and like Him touch the latch that opens to the heart of the humblest hearer."

"Very true," said Llewelyn Pugh; "and Jesus Christ was the simplest preacher that the world has ever seen. He loved to speak of His discourses as 'These *sayings* of Mine.' 'Did not our heart burn within us while He *talked* with us by the way?' was the exclamation of the disciples who walked with Him to Emmaus after His resurrection. It was by talking to them that He 'opened' to them the Scriptures. It is *simple talk,* and not high sounding sentences, that generally *opens* the Scriptures. Our Lord always talked in the language of the people—that of the farm, the fishing boat, and the market place—and yet He talked all the while of the divinest things. The result was that they could put His teaching into practice. He exclaimed, 'Whoso heareth these sayings and *doeth* them.' I like that. No man *does* an oration except the man who gives it. Our Lord's sayings, on the contrary, could be *done* because they were so simple and practical. I am quite sure the Gospel was never intended to be preached in a language which the poorest and most ignorant hearer cannot understand. The offers of mercy should be made known in the simplest words, because so much depends upon whether they are understood or not."

"Quite right, Mr. Pugh," said John; "and in all teaching there should be 'line upon line and precept upon precept.' I think that speaking to children helps preachers and teachers to be simple. There might be more for the children in our services than there is. Children should be made to feel that the service is theirs as well as ours. I think that they ought to be specially addressed, and not in a few words of application at the fag end of the service, when everybody else has been tired out; but, just as we do in the Sunday-school treats, the children ought to have their little bit first, and then the older ones have theirs. Besides, after talking simply to children, the preacher is more likely to talk simply to the older folk. Children help us to be simple and bright in our talk at home, and I am sure they ought to help us in simplicity and brightness in the house of God."

"Then you don't believe, John," asked Mr. Llewelyn Pugh, "in having a separate service for the children as they do in England and in some of our larger towns?"

"Well, you see, Mr. Pugh," replied John Vaughan, "that is not possible in our villages, for there are no schoolrooms. Besides, if we had schoolrooms, I should say that the afternoon school ought to be enough for the children to be alone, except, perhaps, a few minutes in the schoolroom before the morning service. But I think that in the house of God there ought to be one spiritual meal a day when young and old should meet at the same table, and parents have their

children by them. This would make the little ones feel an interest in
the services and the house of God. I don't believe in keeping the
children in—what they call at the squire's—'the nursery,' but believe
in letting them be oftener with their parents. That is one reason
why the squire's children don't turn out as well as the children of
poorer folk in the village. And in the house of God, if you keep the
children in 'the nursery,' and make them have all their meals there,
instead of having a feast of good things now and then with their
parents in the sanctuary, depend upon it they'll suffer for it. But
then, of course, those who carve ought to remember when they are
carving for the young, and when for the old. That is one of the difficult
tasks which preachers have to perform."

"Ah, the minister's position is very solemn and difficult, and must
often cause great anxiety," exclaimed old Hugh Roberts. "Just think
of his standing up before a congregation at the beginning of a service,
knowing that there are so many hungry ones there, and yet, realizing
that his store, like that of the little lad of old, is but five barley loaves
and two small fishes. What are they among so many? The preacher
may well tremble and fall back upon his Master, and we may well
pray for him."

"Yes, Hugh," replied John Vaughan, "I suppose no moment can
bring with it such a weight of responsibility as that—except it be,
perhaps, the time when a congregation is about to separate. It is
much easier to draw a congregation than it is to meet its needs after
it has been drawn, and then to dismiss it so that no one need go
unblessed. Jesus, on the occasion to which you referred, Hugh,
attached great importance to the way He dismissed the multitude.
The disciples would send them away before they were fed. Not so
the Master. He fed them first, and then bade the disciples go to the
ship while he sent the multitude away. Many of us at that late hour
would have dismissed them with a wave of the hand, or by hurriedly
giving out the doxology to be sung. But Jesus took the greatest care
in dismissing that throng. What if some one who had been fed had
some hungry ones at home? What think you became of the twelve
basketsful? Think you that Christ did not distribute every crumb
before that multitude had departed! And what if there was some
one in that crowd who was troubled, and had a question to ask?
Would not Jesus remain behind with that inquirer there and then?

Jesus felt that the congregation had a claim upon His service until the last and feeblest had been dismissed safely. Oh, I sometimes think that the dismissing time must be the moment when the minister becomes most watchful that no needy one should leave unblessed. That is why we in Wales believe in the fellowship meeting (*'cyfeillach'*) at the close of the public service. Much depends, too, upon the way in which that meeting is announced, and how it is conducted. It is a meeting in which Jesus loves to have a few last words with anxious, needy, and trustful souls before they leave."

There were general signs of agreement on the part of those present with the sentiments just expressed by John, and all felt that there could be no better ending to their meeting than this. It was, moreover, late, and the shoemaker and his apprentice had brought their day's task to a close. The little company therefore dispersed, each for his home and his night's rest, better and happier for having had the chat in John Vaughan's workshop.

CHAPTER III

John Vaughan and his friends at Llandrindod Wells

LANDRINDOD WELLS were known to John and Kitty only by repute. Consequently, an advertisement of "A Cheap Excursion to Llandrindod Wells and Back" arrested their attention on their way to market. John had not been well, and Kitty strongly urged him and Shadrach Morgan to go for the days advertised—"from Saturday to Tuesday." What with change of air and "taking the waters," she felt sure that John would return as well as ever.

Besides, June had just begun with charming weather. John and Shadrach, she argued, could be well spared for a few days. That evening the matter was discussed and settled enthusiastically in the affirmative in Shadrach Morgan's kitchen, Mary Morgan having vigorously supported all Kitty Vaughan's arguments. Mary further urged that her son Jenkin should accompany them. The boy—she still called him "boy"—had not seen much of the world, and it might be many years before he would have the opportunity of going so far again; besides he would see more of the preachers, and other great men of Wales, there, than he would at home all his lifetime.

There were great preparations for starting early on the following Saturday. The morning at length arrived. Hugh Roberts, of Pentre-mawr Farm, sent his conveyance to the smithy before the break of day. It was an antiquated vehicle, made by old Cadwaladr Jones, the carpenter. The springs were made by Shadrach's father; but he had, by some strange perversity of fate, forgotten to put any spring in them, for they were as rigid as the axle itself. Just as the first streaks of dawn shot upward from beyond the horizon, the start was made, and Kitty and Mary bade the three departing travellers a fond good-bye.

They soon arrived at the summit of the hill outside the village, from which they could command the surrounding country. The mists of night were still lingering in the lowlands. Just then the sun peeped over the hill-top, and John Vaughan, ever responsive to every touch of natural beauty, exclaimed, "Look, Shadrach, there's the great sun, 'like a bridegroom coming out of his chamber, and rejoicing as a strong man to run a race;' but we have had the start of him to-day. He looks at us slyly over the hills, as if to say, 'What has taken possession of you this morning?' And it won't be long before he will have something to say to the mists in the valleys beneath us. Do you remember hearing Rev. Rhys Prys, Cymllynfell,* preaching at Peniel, yonder, from the text, 'The path of the just is as the shining light, that shineth more and more unto the perfect day?' It was a wonderful sermon. In it he gave a

---

* Formerly a weaver by trade, who never had any College training, but who became one of the most distinguished preachers of his day.

description of sunrise. He first spoke of the dim grey light, the forerunner of the glowing dawn. Then he described the shaft of light appearing above the eastern hills, and preparing the slumbering world for the glance of the full-orbed eye of day. 'As yet,' he added, 'a haze covers the earth, and thick mists lurk in the valleys. But the sun steadily mounts the steep ascent. Soon you see his upper eyelash resting on the eastern horizon—then a small section of the eye appears—then half—then the whole, and the lower lash fringes the mountain top, while that all-seeing eye pours forth a flood of light over all the land. The darkness has vanished; yet still some mists linger sleepily in the wild ravines and deep hollows but they are under notice to quit. Up he mounts with giant strides the steep ascent of heaven; looks down with piercing and burning glance into every gorge, chasm, creek, and cranny. See! the mists awake out of their dull sleep; they are startled they flee away in battalions. See! they are going—gone—over the battlements of the west: not one is left—*It is perfect day:* "The path of the just is as the shining light, that shineth more and more unto the perfect day."'"

"I well remember that sermon," said Shadrach, "but couldn't repeat it like you, John, for all the world. What wonderful powers of description he had!"

"Yes," replied John. "Did you ever hear his description of the miser?"

"No," answered Shadrach.

"Let us have it!" ejaculated Jenkin.

"Well," said John, "I can't remember it all; but, among other things, he said: 'The miser's sickle is so keen that he leaves not a single head of corn for the weary gleaner; his knife is so sharp that he leaves not a solitary crumb for little robin-red-breast; and he keeps his dog so thin that he has never been known to cast a shadow, but only a dim haze.'"

"That's quite as keen as the miser's sickle," exclaimed Jenkin, "and cuts as clean, too."

This was the staple of the talk while four miles and a half were covered. The railway station was at length reached. The train started punctually and sped its way along the lovely vale of Towy. The train soon arrived at Llandovery, the place made sacred by having been the birthplace and, for the greater portion of his life, the dwelling-place of Rev. Rees Prichard (1579—1644), who, in his *"Welshmen's Candle"*

THE VALE OF TOWY

(Canwyll-y-Cymry) denounced the evils and vices of his day, and especially those of the Welsh clergy, with scathing power; and whose memory is thus lovingly cherished as that of one of the grand apostolic men, who, at infinite cost to themselves, delivered Wales from the depths of degradation into which the Popish Church, and the licentious clergy of the subsequent Protestant Established Church, had unitedly hurled it. Much indeed had John and his friends to say about old Vicar Prichard, and many were the favourite stanzas repeated by them from the *Welshmen's Candle*. John Vaughan, indeed, seemed to know it all by heart; and oh! how his eyes shot fire, and then became suffused with tears, as he repeated the burning denunciations, and then the earnest warnings and tender appeals, of the man who centuries ago lived and died in the service of his God and his countrymen.

By this time the train had reached Llanwrtyd Wells, which John and Shadrach had visited some years before. John pointed out to Jenkin the mountain which the Rev. J. R. Kilsby Jones owned, and on the further slope of which he lived. "On the other side of the mountain," said John, who was in one of those poetic and descriptive moods into which he occasionally lapsed, "he lives in a house commanding a very beautiful valley, through which a river goes singing on its way, a river which is the home of many a merry trout, and the resort of many a cunning angler. Beyond his house is a charming little glen, where he ordains that he shall be buried, without a stone to mark his resting-place; but only the touch of nature to beautify the spot, and the lonely wild flower to send forth its fragrance like incense o'er the grave of that child of Nature, who, having revelled on her bosom, desires at

VICAR PRICHARD'S RESIDENCE, LLANDOVERY

length to sleep upon her lap, until his Lord shall wake him.* He is as stern as a giant; and as tender as a woman. He is passionately in love with his mountain. I well remember meeting him once on that peak. I said to him, 'This is a splendid view, sir.' 'Almost panoramic,' was his prompt reply. 'Besides,' he added, 'it is classic ground. In that farmhouse

---

* The Rev. J. R. Kilsby Jones died in April. 1889 but, contrary to his oft-repeated wish, was buried in "consecrated ground."

John Penry, our great apostle, was born and bred; there in that little church by the river side, and at the juncture of the valleys, William Williams—the Isaac Watts of Wales—spent the earlier years of his ministry; and there Charles Wesley—wise man! found a wife.' That and much more he told me. He talked like a prophet. To have met with him is a great treat never to be forgotten."

As the train entered Llandrindod Wells, the platforms were crowded; and John, who was of a nervous temperament, concluded that there must have been an accident. Jenkin jocularly suggested that the crowd had come to meet him. There was more truth in this than was at first apparent, for "meeting the train" is an ancient and sacred institution at Llandrindod. The great bulk of visitors attend the train arrivals as regularly as they do their meals, and, it is to be feared, more religiously than their prayers.

Lodgings were soon obtained, and before an hour had passed John and Shadrach were in eager search for the "waters." Jenkin was greatly amused at the amount of water—sulphur, saline, and chalybeate—that people consumed; and as time advanced he became more and more intolerant of the habit. He vowed that if a regiment of them were in the region of the Dead Sea they would soon drink it dry, and that that historic sea would no longer exist. The Dead Sea, he firmly believed, was a strong mixture of sulphur and saline, half and half. He affirmed that people of Llandrindod Wells were drowning themselves by inches; the more offensive the taste and the more foul the smell of the water, the greater the charm it had over them, and the more efficacious it was supposed to be. He never knew that there were so many lunatics in the world till he came to the Wells. Drinking a glassful, then repeatedly going the same orthodox walk round a field before the next glass was taken, and meeting the same people, whom they accosted after the first greeting with the same insane nod, was, he held, abundant proof to any unprejudiced mind of hopeless imbecility. No creature but man, fallen from the pedestal of reason, would do this. Every other animal would be struck with the comicality of it.

Yet, there they were, members of Parliament—"Lords and Commons"—bishops, deans, canons, ministers of all denominations, aldermen, musicians—in short, representatives of all professions and trades, going the same round, tramp, tramp, like prisoners on a treadmill. He would not, however, complain if they only did this at

JOHN PENRY'S BIRTHPLACE

their own cost and inconvenience. But it was a part of the craze that they should get up with the daylight, and in so doing wake everybody in the same house by throwing their boots about, and banging the doors, as if to say, self-complacently, "We are up, you see, and off to the waters." He had never known anything that made such Pharisees of men as this early rising for the waters. Now, if all were moved to get up at the same time it would be bearable; but no, they seemed to agree to keep the house moving from dawn to breakfast time every morning. Then, when they returned to breakfast, they were like a plague of locusts. They swept the tables, and devoured everything within reach. Those who got up in reasonable hours, and paid due regard to their toilet, had no chance of competing at the morning meal with those who had been "out getting an appetite," as they termed it.

Jenkin further affirmed that all those who drank the waters ought to be lodged together, and be made to pay double fares. Were it not for those who stayed at home, the proprietors of hotels and boarding-houses would be eaten out of house and home. Talk about drinking intoxicants to excess! That wouldn't compare with the drinking of saline and sulphur that was going on at Llandrindod. Some one should move for a Parliamentary inquiry into the matter. His father, if he continued as he had begun, would soon drink enough chalybeate—provided there was *any* iron at all in it—to make a horse-shoe; and as for John Vaughan, he promised well to drink enough saline to turn him into a pillar of salt.

By the evening John and his friends had got into the way of going with the multitude to meet the train. As the last train came into the station that Saturday night, Shadrach observed the Rev. Joseph Thomas, of Carno, and Dr. Saunders, of Swansea, in one of the compartments. "There," said he, "there's more theology in that compartment than in all the train besides."

"It depends who are in the other compartments, I suppose," added Jenkin laconically.

LLANDRINDOD PARK AND PUMP-HOUSE

"Dr. Saunders is a very substantial man, and one of the best theologians in Wales," exclaimed John.

"Yes, he is a very deep preacher," responded Shadrach.

"Well, I don't know what Dr. Saunders* may be as a theologian or preacher; but give me Mr. Thomas for a lively speech," said Jenkin. "That was fine, what he once said at Liverpool. It was the centenary of Calvinistic Methodism there, and there were great meetings held. Almost every speaker had been claiming some great-grandfather or great-great-uncle who had something to do with founding Calvinistic Methodism in Liverpool. At last Joseph Thomas spoke, and his lisp as usual added greatly to the effect of his speech. He said: 'It is easy to see that Methodism has been a success in Liverpool, because we are all very anxious to have some share in the concern. I once heard of a farmer near Cerig-y-Druidion, who, together with his men, had one summer day made a very fine haystack. He stood on the hedge, admiring it, at the close of the day, when a neighbouring farmer passing by, said, "What a beautiful haystack! Who made it?" Mr. Jones stood upright, and proudly said, "I did, Mr. Williams." That night a great storm blew the stack down, and on the following morning another farmer passing by, as Mr. Jones looked sadly upon the scene of desolation, said, "Dear me, was *that* ever a haystack? I never in my life saw anything like it. Whoever made that stack, Mr. Jones?" Mr. Jones scratched his head, and said bewilderingly, "Oh, there were several *of them* about it." My friends,' added Mr. Thomas, 'the Methodist haystack must look well at Liverpool, for we are all anxious that the world should know that we have had a leading hand in making it.' That was pricking the bladder with a vengeance," concluded Jenkin.

"Very good," said John. "He is very fond of illustrations taken from farming. I recollect him preaching once upon the duty and privilege of helping others. He said, 'I remember once hearing of a farmer in Merionethshire, who went out with his servant man one morning after a very heavy fall of snow. The snow had drifted, and had buried many of the farmer's sheep in the corners of the fields. They went in search of the sheep, and dug out many. At length they

---

* Both Dr. Saunders and Rev. Joseph Thomas have died since the visit recorded here.

REV. JOSEPH THOMAS, OF CARNO

came within sight of one which the farmer did not recognize as his own. He immediately asked his servant, "Whose sheep is that?" "So-and-So's," replied the man. "Oh, come along," answered the farmer impatiently, "his sheep often wander over my land, and he shall find it out now." Thus, leaving the neighbour's sheep, both went in further search of the farmer's own sheep. But the servant was more tender-hearted than his master. So when the search was over he returned quietly to the spot where the neighbour's sheep was buried and dug it out; but shall I tell you what he found behind it?—one of his own master's sheep. Thus,' added Mr. Thomas, 'when we seek our own sheep they are often found behind our neighbour's, and the best way to rescue them is to be ever ready to rescue other sheep also.'"

"Splendid!" exclaimed Shadrach. "That, I suppose, was what Jesus Himself hinted at when He said to those who were only anxious about the sheep which belonged to their little fold, 'And other sheep I have, which are not of this fold, them also I must bring.'"

"Yes," replied John, "that is exactly it. Jesus would have men think of other sheep as well as their own, by reminding them that He did not overlook even those, but was determined, at every cost, to gather them in."

"Mr. Thomas is also very witty, and always quite equal to the occasion," said Jenkin. "Did you ever hear what he once said at a meeting where there was a discussion about long and short sermons? One or two ministers, who were guilty of preaching other people's sermons, strongly urged that some of the long sermons which were preached should be cut in half. It is well known that Mr. Joseph Thomas preaches somewhat long usually, but he always preaches his own sermon. His name was repeatedly called to take part in the discussion, but for a time he remained silent. At length he said, 'I have just been thinking about Solomon and the two women who came to him to settle their dispute. One woman's child had died, and she had robbed the other of her living babe, placing her own dead child in its stead. A dispute arose. Both mothers claimed the living child. At length they came to Solomon. Finding the difficulty of getting at the truth, he sent for a sword and proposed to settle the quarrel by cleaving the living babe in two. The mother who had stolen the child readily consented—the plan seems to have suited her—but the real mother protested with tears. Thus Solomon easily concluded whose the child was. It is something like that with sermons,' added old Mr. Thomas significantly, as he glanced sideways at the two ministers who had so much to say about dividing long sermons, 'those who, under pressure of Providence, have to take other people's sermons, are, as a rule, quite willing to have them cut in half, but those who own them, and have a parental love for them are loth to consent to the mutilation.' That ended the discussion on that subject."

"He can say some *very solemn* things, too," added John. "Did you, Shadrach, ever hear of him once presiding at a Communion Service one Sunday evening? People began to move, and make ready to go out, before singing the last hymn. Mr. Thomas rose up, and said earnestly: 'My friends, do not leave now; we read of only one who left the Lord's Supper before "they sang a hymn," and we all know who he was. Let none of us be like him.'"

"Ah, yes, how that thrilled all present!" exclaimed Shadrach. "No one could go out after that."

As the train left the platform, John Vaughan caught sight of the Rev. J. R. Kilsby Jones, who had just arrived for the Sunday. There he stood, head and shoulders above his fellows. John was disappointed in finding that the flowing white beard of former days had been cut short, in some fit of remorseless clipping. "It's a pity he wears a moustache," said Shadrach, who had a little objection to such adornments. Jenkin suggested the previous question, by asking whether it was a pity that God had ever given it him to wear?

Nothing could be less ministerial than Mr. Kilsby Jones' appearance. He wore a straw hat with a wide brim; and a large loose collar, revealing the foundations of the neck and its sinewy strength. His countenance was stern and tender in its rapid alternations. His eye darted light with every piercing look, and yet it was tremulous with merry glances that played hide-and-seek in every corner. The central ornament—the nose—which gave character and individuality to the whole, was long, straight, and firmly fixed; and, by an occasional dilation of the nostrils, asserted supremacy in royal fashion, and shot upward a threefold furrow, dividing into two counterparts the towering forehead above, that had braved many a storm and thought many a noble thought. A fine mouth, powerfully set, but indulging occasionally in a playful pout, completed the picture of forehead and face. It presented an index of the man, who was as stern as a judge, yet frolicsome as a schoolboy. The transitional expressions of righteous

REV. J. R. KILSBY JONES

indignation, withering contempt, and melting tenderness, and
especially the relaxation of that face in the presence of woman, child,
or congenial spirit, were a study. The head and neck were upheld by a
large expanded chest and a pair of shoulders, which in the days of
physical prowess would have alone asserted his pre-eminence among
his fellows. Altogether he was a man who at once claimed attention
by his commanding presence and movements. Had he not feared God
he would have been terrible for he never feared man in his life. He
was fearless in war, and, at such times, as erratic as Samson in wielding
his strength. The huge practical jokes immortalised in the story of
the foxes, and of the carrying away of the gates of Gaza, found repeated
counterparts in the history of Kilsby's attacks on the Philistines of
Welsh squirearchy. He was terrible in his grim satiric onslaughts, laying
low his opponents with weapons which, like Samson's, were suggestive
of grotesque irony and irrepressible mischief.

"There is Mr. Kilsby Jones," said John, "like Saul among the
prophets, towering high above all the rest."

"He's an original character," replied Jenkin.

"Yes," said John. "You can never mistake him for anyone else, and
he never panders to anyone, but speaks out his mind like a prophet.
There is a very striking story told about him. About thirty-five years
ago he was walking through Haverford west, arm in arm with Mr.
Rees, the late well-known solicitor of that town. As they walked along
the leading street, a poor man recognising Mr. Rees, took off his hat
repeatedly, and bowed and cringed slavishly as he passed by. Mr. Kilsby
Jones could not bear the sight, and at last, straightening himself to
his full height, said to him, 'Put on your hat, my man, and stand on
your feet; worship God—not Mr. Rees the lawyer.'"

"Did you ever hear of him," added Jenkin, "meeting Dr. R——,
who, in a conceited fashion, looked at Mr. Kilsby Jones through his
eye-glass? Mr. Jones was at the time on horseback, and, quick as
lightning, he took his foot out of the stirrup, through which he, in
return, stared at the Doctor."

These and many other stories were repeated in quick succession
about "Kilsby," ere the three retired for the night all showing that
he was no respecter of persons, but "an honest man of God."

Sunday morning was exceptionally bright, giving promise of a
happy and cheerful Sabbath. The three friends decided to go in the

morning to the Baptist Chapel, about a mile distant. There they enjoyed the service, and listened to a substantial sermon—sixteen ounces to the pound—from the Rev. John Jones, the pastor. In the afternoon two *Welsh* services had been announced, one at the Methodist Chapel and the other at Mr. Kilsby Jones's. John regretted that they had a Welsh service in the afternoon only, and repeated the saying of the Rev. William Howell, of Trevecca, at the opening of an English chapel in Cardiff—"It must be admitted that the Welsh language is gradually dying in Wales but it will die a religious death. It will die like the old woman who died on her knees at the foot of Cader Idris, saying, 'I know that my Redeemer liveth.'"

As John Vaughan and his friends reserved for the evening the pleasure of hearing Mr. Kilsby Jones, they went to the Methodist Chapel, to hear a "stranger" preach. This service proved as enjoyable and profitable as the morning service had been—perhaps more so, because it was in their native tongue.

The time for the evening service soon arrived. John and his friends understood English sufficiently well to appreciate an English service, especially if a Welshman conducted it. They entered Mr. Kilsby Jones's chapel just as the preacher entered the pulpit. A short prayer was followed by a hymn. Then came the reading of the Scripture—the fifth chapter of the Epistle to the Romans. When the preacher had read the seventh verse he paused, and said, "I think this is a verse that will pay exceptionally well for knocking at its door. I think it will open, if we persist. This world would be better than it is if all were righteous; yet it would be but poor if all were only righteous—those who only did what was in the bond. Have you seen the funeral of a righteous man? Yes; the chapel was full, but a handkerchief of the same length and breadth as a gnat's wing would have been quite big enough for the tears shed. Mount Gilboa was quite dry. Not one widow sighed; no orphan was the poorer that day—save the man's own children, *possibly.* But no other orphan. When the father of a family died, this righteous man never pressed the orphan's hand, saying, 'Do not weep my little man, you shall not want; you shall still have a roof over you, and bread to eat.' No; when the child's father died, the cold earth was warmer than this righteous man's heart, though he was scrupulously honest. Will anyone die for him? 'Scarcely'—'scarcely.' I know no one who would. But for the *good* man? 'Perchance.' Ah, yes! Job says,

'When the ear heard me, then it blessed me: and when the eye saw me, it gave witness to me: because I delivered the poor that cried, and the fatherless, and him that had none to help him. The blessing of him that was ready to perish came upon me; and I caused the widow's heart to sing for joy.'

"I think I can see Job passing by, when he was in prosperity. Some one says to a cripple, who has received good at his hands, 'Job is passing.' 'What did you say?' is the prompt response—'Job passing by? Where's the crutch? Give it me quickly. Ah, yes; I see him, good soul—God bless him.' 'The blessing of him that was ready to perish came upon him.' One asks the poor cripple, 'You would do a great deal for Job?' 'Yes, indeed.' 'But to die?' *'Peradventure.'* But Christ died for evil men just what men have found most difficult to do for their friends."

There were very many additional comments on other verses: all similarly forcible and striking. Then came the prayer—such a prayer! so natural and refreshing, without a borrowed expression or tone. It was the outpouring of the gratitude and yearning of a child who dared tell out all he thought and felt, without fear of being misunderstood by his heavenly Father. Nor were the many and varied wants of that crowded congregation overlooked. Everyone present must have found his own experience faithfully mirrored in one part or other of that wonderfully comprehensive, though brief, prayer. Then followed a hymn from a small "Selection" of fifty or so, compiled by the minister for the use of his congregation. In all these the powerful individuality of the preacher sufficiently asserted itself to impart a refreshing naturalness and reality to the whole.

The preacher took for his text John xii. 24: "Except a corn of wheat die, it abideth alone." It was a timely text, and must have proved a preparation to John and his friends for the harvest activities in which they would be engaged on their return home. The speaker was in his best mood. Standing erect, with commanding mien, and in authoritative tones, he projected for the space of half-an-hour, incisive, thoughtful, stimulating sentences, that stuck like burrs in men's hearts and consciences.*

---

* The following is an outline of the discourse.—"It is the law of *cereals* that they never see their parents, and never see their offspring. An oak may

The service throughout, although conducted in English, was greatly appreciated by John and his friends. There was a simplicity of style, a terseness and force of diction, and an originality of thought about the preacher's utterances, which were as refreshing as the morning dew.

"I shall never forget that service," said Shadrach as he left the building. "No," said John, "it is difficult to forget anything that Mr. Kilsby Jones says. His comments in reading are as striking as his sermon."

"That was good about Job," exclaimed Jenkin.

"Yes," replied John. "When he spoke about the power to lay down one's life for another, I was reminded of what I heard him say once about love. He said, 'Love throws the whole of a man's nature into

---

live long enough to see itself surrounded by a happy family of young oaks, but a 'corn of wheat' must *die* before it can reproduce itself. But does it die? Is there such a thing as death in the world? If by death you mean annihilation, there is no such thing; if change—it is a constant occurrence. What part of a corn is it that dies? Only the envelope. The germ of life, placed in the first corn of wheat, has passed on through an endless series of wrappages, and thus has been perpetuated until now.

"There are a great many things we call death which are simply changes. That young man had once a baby face, then pouting lips and fat cheeks; another face at twelve; at eighteen the beard came on, the shadows of promising manhood. Follow him on from forty to sixty: the black, raven hair is being gradually blanched by frosts, or the storms of life are blowing a great deal of the thatch off. All the past stages of being are dead, but *he* lives.

"To what extent is the Kingdom of Nature the counterpart of that of Spirit? Not in many very important respects. There is no atonement in Nature, and there is no forgiveness. Was this reproductive law of cereals designed to teach us the essential service of death, and the great though unwelcome doctrine of self-sacrifice? Death is the feeder and nourisher of life. What poet has not celebrated its praises? In point of friendly service to a believer, death stands next to Christ.

"I. Let us just glance at the wide Kingdom of Death. Certain forms of matter must *die,* to prepare the way for other forms.

"1. The supposed gaseous first form of the earth: then a gradually hardening envelope, which we call the crust.

"2. The surface of this crust must die in the form of rock, and become, through the influence of various agencies, pulverised into soil.

"3. Huge trees and other gigantic forms of rank vegetation must die, in order to produce coal fields.

every task. Think of its transmuting power. The poor mother scrubs the floor on Saturday, washes the children, irons the linen; but on the following morning the children are like so many bouquets of flowers in the house of God and round the table at home. Love has converted the prose of hard toil into the truest poetry. Think, too, of its burden-bearing power. No one has so strong a back as love. I met a mother at Llanwrtyd Wells the other day. She carried a child on her back, a bag of meal on one side, and sundry articles on her arm, and withal she was knitting. I asked her, "Mary, would you do this in service?" "No." "But your master was a good master, was he not?" "Yes, Sir," "And your mistress a good mistress?" "Oh, yes," "Then why do this now?" "Oh, I do it for the sake of John and the baby. Expect me to do this for wages! Never—but for John—*John*—I would *die* for John! and what

---

"4. The present grasses and vegetables must die, to support man and beast. The ox eats the grasses, and man eats the ox. *All* flesh was *once* grass.

"II. Men must die in a variety of senses, before they can be of any real service to Church or State.

"1. *Agriculturally and commercially* they must *die* to sloth and self-indulgence.

"2. *Educationally.* He who would be a scholar must be *dead* to everything, except the burning desire to cultivate and *bring out* of his mind all that it potentially contains.

"3. *Patriotically.* He must be *dead* to the praise of the favoured few, who live on the sweat of those who toil and moil. Dead to misrepresentation and abuse—dead to the verdicts of the short-sighted present.

"4. *Religiously.* The apostles and all their *true* followers are glorious instances of men dead to all influences, except such as harmonised with the master-passion of life—the love of Christ. Dr. Livingstone and other missionaries are splendid examples.

"Christ, by dying, *killed* death, which was the only possible way of 'bringing life and immortality to light.' To *live* in the full grand sense of the word, we must *die*—that is, the body, our first schoolmaster, *must* die; but the soul cannot die, and, unlike the corn of wheat whose *germ* of life passes from one envelope to another of the same material and fashion, the *next,* and perhaps finer, envelope of the soul will be made out of matter in one of the most ethereal forms which it is capable of assuming. It was not of His life—though the only example of the highest ideal of human life translated into actuality—that the Saviour said it would "draw *all* unto Him," but of His death, by crucifixion—that death being only a preparation for His speedy resurrection, the *'power'* of which to sustain the whole fabric of Christianity the apostle longed to 'know.'"

would I *not* do for *the baby!*" Ah, my friends,' added the preacher, 'things have to be done in life which cannot be accomplished but for the love of Christ. But the apostle says, "I can do all things through Christ, who strengtheneth me." Aye, aye—that explains it.'"

"Ah, he is a great believer in having the motives right, and the heart pure," exclaimed Shadrach. "Do you remember him expounding at Peniel, when he said that in ancient countries people used to put out the eyes of the adulterer; but that the Gospel did nothing of the kind: for it put into him a new mind—the old windows would do very well."

"That is just his style," replied John.

"It was then," added Shadrach, "that he spoke about our Lord's talk with the woman of Samaria, and showed how even one listener was enough to kindle the enthusiasm of Jesus. Then, he added, 'but this woman was a listener of the right sort, for at the close she forgot her water pot. Just like the mother who has gone out shopping; but has met the postman, or received a letter left at the shop, from her son in Australia, and runs home shouting to her husband, "I have a letter from William." "But what about the errands?" "Oh, I forgot the errands when I saw William's letter." So the woman of Samaria now forgot her pitcher. But was it at all likely that any earnest soul would remember her pitcher after seeing Jesus Christ? Or, even if she remembered it, could she, think you, be detained by having to lug that, when she wanted to run to tell the news to others?'"

"That's very good," said John. "He once said something like that about Christ's talk with the disciples on the way to Emmaus. He said that Jesus had only two hearers, and yet His talk with them was divine. I forget much that I heard Kilsby then say, but I remember one thing: 'In travelling the mind grows tired sooner than the body. The experience of pedestrians largely points in this direction. I remember the time when my feet carried me many a mile, because I was too poor to hire and too proud to borrow. Now and then I met with men of extraordinary conversational powers. I then forgot all about my feet and the roughness of the way but when we came to the parting of the ways, and I lost them and their exciting conversation, I soon received telegrams again from my poor feet. There are some men who talk to you so charmingly that even if you were an alderman you would forget your dinner. On this ever-

memorable journey, seven miles soon passed. It was now getting late.
The shadows, which were cast deep and wide over the quiet glens
and hillocks, told the travellers that they resided there, and had
retired to rest, and that it was time for man to wend his way
homeward for the night. The disciples arrived all too soon at their
destination, and Jesus made as though He would have gone further;
but they constrained Him, saying, "Abide with us, for it is evening,
and the day is far spent."'

"Having spoken of the eyes of the disciples being opened, so that
they recognised their Lord in the breaking of bread, Mr. Jones
proceeded to read, 'And He vanished out of their sight.' 'What a
blank' said the preacher, 'when he vanished! I remember well the
visits of my old friend—the Rev. J. P. Mursell—many years ago.
Whenever he came he filled every nook with light; but when, after
an hour's brilliant talk, he used to leave me in my room alone, the
light vanished all too rapidly with him. I used to gather the lingering
gleams of his presence, and indulged the fond imagination that he
was still in the arm-chair. On one occasion a small brother called
upon me, and broke upon my reverie. He was about to sit in the
chair just vacated by my great friend. I said, "Pray, sit in this chair,
not that." "But that is empty," responded the visitor. "No," said I,
"it isn't empty; it will be *if you sit in it.*"' These words of scathing
satire were followed by words of thrilling tenderness, for shrugging
his shoulders and looking bewildered, the preacher added, 'Ah me,
that was a dark room when Jesus vanished out of it! But the reflection
of His presence still shone in their memories and hearts, and they
said one to another, "Did not our hearts burn within us while He
talked with us by the way and opened to us the Scriptures?"'"

"Ah," said Shadrach, "that story of the resurrection and of the
risen Lord never wearies us. As Dr. Lewis Edwards, of Bala, used to
say, 'every grave becomes old except the grave of Jesus Christ; that
never will.' It tells of life for evermore. Because He lives, we shall
live also. Death has lost its sting, and the grave its terror."

"Very true," replied John. "That reminds me of what Gwilym
Hiraethog* said, by the grave of his brother—the Rev. Henry Rees—
when he compared his brother dying to a patient undergoing an

* Rev. William Rees, D.D.

operation. He described, in a few graphic touches, the kind surgeon giving chloroform to the patient, thus enabling him to pass unconsciously through the crisis which he had so much dreaded. At length, when all was over, the patient awoke, and asked in astonishment, 'Is that all! Is that amputation?' 'So,' added Mr. Rees 'when my brother Henry bade farewell to this old earth, some kind angel brushed his pallid face with its wing so that he fell asleep, and passed through death without feeling it, and when he awoke on the other side, he said in infinite surprise, 'Is that all! Can that be death?'"

"Grand," ejaculated Shadrach.

"Did you see that arm-chair in the corner of the chapel, on the left side of the pulpit as we entered?" interjected Jenkin. "That is the chair in which Gwilym Hiraethog used to sit at the services when he came to Llandrindod for his holidays. The highest compliment which Mr. Kilsby Jones can now pay a friend is to ask him to sit in that chair. It is sacred for his departed friend's sake! On one occasion, a man who had a big waistcoat, but required only a small hat, walked pompously up the aisle, and seated himself in the arm chair. It must be confessed that so far as body was concerned he filled it well. Mr. Kilsby Jones's eyes, however, were restless. During his sermon, he cast an occasional glance at the intruder, and noticed the evident disproportion between the man's head and his stomach. Memories of a more welcome and inspiring presence rushed upon him, and, recalling a reminiscence by way of illustrating the subject of his discourse, he began, as he cast another significant look at the chair, with these words—'There sat a *man* in that chair *once.'* The preacher proceeded to say something, in his own brief vivid style, of his departed friend; but every eye was fixed on that chair, and all wondered who the pompous individual was who occupied it just then."

"He deals hard blows more directly than that sometimes," said Shadrach. "On one occasion he was reading that passage in which Paul mentions, among other dangers through which he had passed, 'perils of robbers.' He no sooner read the words than he looked as if he had been shot, and said, 'perils of robbers.' What, rob an apostle! It is no doubt possible to rob a modern so-called successor of the apostles—£5,000 a year or so, I can understand that there would be some plunder in that case. But rob an apostle! They must have been hard up before they would ever entertain such a thought. They could not have known Paul, and how poor he was, or the robbers would have relented; and instead of entertaining the mad thought of robbing him, they at once would have made a collection for him, and would have put in something better than the coins we get here— coppers or at most threepenny bits."

"That's just like him," replied Jenkin. "He is a rare one at a collection. In this morning's service he seems to have given them a short speech about it. He said, 'The collection will now be made, don't make it quite *so heavy* as usual. The market in copper will soon become depressed if people will persist in bringing it to us at the rate they do. Take a turn to-day at the silver—if not at the gold—and then give a coin that can be seen and felt, and not the invisible threepenny bits. I would rather see even a bold honest penny than one of those sneaking coins, which ought never to have had an existence.'"

"Mr. Jones, the Baptist Minister, is every whit as rich in his collection announcements," said John. "Don't you remember how he said this morning that in former days in Wales men were fined many pounds each time they were found guilty of worshipping God according to their own convictions; whereas some of their descendants almost fell into a swoon if, from sudden enlargement of the heart, they gave sixpence extra at a collection?"

"Yes, that was rather sharp," ejaculated Jenkin.

"Well, after all," said John, "the collection is often the test of our practical Christianity. The religion of Jesus Christ is not a mere sentiment: it has backbone in it. It teaches us to use temporal gifts for the highest purposes. Did you ever hear of Mr. Kilsby Jones's sermon on 'Religion, and bread and cheese?'"

"No," said Jenkin. "That's a queer subject. 'What on earth could he say about that?'"

"He preached from Matthew vi. 33," replied John.

"'Seek ye first the kingdom of God and His righteousness; and all these things shall be added unto you.' I can only tell you how he began. He said, 'My text shows the connection between religion and the necessaries of life, or between Christianity and bread and cheese.' It was a wonderfully striking and practical sermon."

"He is a downright practical preacher," responded Shadrach, "and goes right to the root of things. He has no patience with preachers who talk about everything in general and nothing in particular, especially with those who never venture to say a single word, even in a whisper, about hell or the devil. 'You would think,' said Kilsby Jones once, 'by the blank silence on the part of some Christian teachers, from one year's end to the other, that there was no devil; or if there ever had been that he had died years since, and had been buried at night, or on the sly; whereas, believe me, the devil is alive, and is nearer some of you than you think.'"

"Talk about the devil being dead!" said Jenkin, "did you ever hear the story of two young fops meeting the Rev. Lewis Powell, of Cardiff? They had agreed to have a joke at the old minister's expense. When they met him they pretended to be very solemn, and said, 'Well, Mr. Powell, have you heard the latest news?' 'What is it?' answered Mr. Powell. 'The devil is dead,' replied the two. 'Well, well,' said the old man, as he looked at them intently and tenderly, 'I pity you from my heart. Sad news! Two more helpless orphans in the world! Here is a shilling for you.'"

The time had quickly passed as the three chatted together. It was now late; with a smile, therefore, at Jenkin's story, they retired to rest at the close of a bright and happy Sunday, although far from home and from their beloved "Horeb."

CHAPTER IV

John Vaughan and his friends at Llandrindod Wells.

(continued)

THE TOWER OF OLD CEFNLLYS CHURCH

ONDAY was the last day for John and his friends at Llandrindod, and they were determined to make the best of it. The surrounding country had a special charm for John and Shadrach. From the summit of the hill above the lake they had almost a panoramic view. The distant horizon, jagged with innumerable hilltops and declivities; the intervening country abounding with an infinite variety of undulation and a charming combination of light and shade; and at the foot of the hill, just on the other side of the lake, the uncultivated common, revealing a striking contrast of yellow gorse and purple heather, all combined to present a perfect picture of pastoral and rustic beauty. The wood at their feet, which dipped toward and skirted the lake, had many a shady nook and quiet seclusion. John and Shadrach, like lovers, fondly walked arm-in-arm along its rugged paths, and talked together of other days, when they were boys.

They were anxious to visit the Shaky Bridge and Cefnllys Church, from the tower of which a luxuriant shrub had been growing for years, and was said to be fast assuming the proportions of a tree. There were many ways to that quaint and secluded spot, but the path John and Shadrach chose was that which skirting the lake led to the wood, from which they at length diverged, crossing the hill and descending almost opposite the frail structure which in that lonely spot is suspended across the river, and which, when John saw it, he would not cross for the wealth of the Indies. He and Shadrach therefore contented themselves with looking at the bridge, and taking such a distant view of the old church as they could get on their return journey from the road which ascended the opposite hill and led them out at length near Llandrindod Wells.

Meanwhile, Jenkin was otherwise engaged. He remembered the wholesome proverb, that while the gorse blossomed kissing was in fashion. Thus the yellow bloom had a sentimental—not to say a poetical—significance for him, which it had not for his elder companions. This sentiment was heightened by the fact that among the excursionists from Carmarthen were William Jones, the miller, and his charming daughter, Margaret. Jenkin had cherished a kindly feeling and more than a brotherly solicitude for Margaret in bygone days, when he had taken wheat to her father's mill to be ground. While the miller was taking his toll for grinding the wheat, Jenkin had on one or two occasions taken his toll out of the miller for waiting, by abstracting a kiss from his daughter. Jenkin thought on such occasions that he had the best of the bargain. Whether by chance, or as the result of a gentle hint given among the flour bins, we cannot tell, but it is a historic fact that Jenkin and Margaret had gone by the same excursion to Llandrindod Wells; and now, while the older folk were eager in search of fresh scenes and pastures new, the two young friends, by the force of a law which is well known, but which it will be among the triumphs of future science adequately to define, were found

BIRD'S-EYE VIEW OF LLANDRINDOD AND SURROUNDINGS

wending their way to the same spot, at the same time, and responding to the same irrepressible desire to go out on the lake at the same moment, and, *mirabile dictu,* in the self-same double canoe.

Not having been accustomed to paddle their canoe together, they found themselves most of their time either among the rushes in the centre of the lake, or at its southern extremity. It was so very difficult to keep in the open expanse the breeze was rather strong, and the

THE SHAKY BRIDGE

current very powerful; besides, they *might* be run down if they did not seek shelter. So they were generally found among the numerous creeks skirting the lake, having in utter despair given up paddling. On the principle, however, that "good is the goal of all ill," they meekly subsided into a quiet and confidential chat, as the best that could be done in the circumstances. Indeed, Jenkin had noticed that he and Margaret were not the only two who had sought the kindly refuge of the rushes from those hostile forces which they vainly attempted to resist for he had seen one or two curates, in the exercise of what appeared to be semi-pastoral functions, drift with the fair objects of their charge into one or other of those treacherous inlets—so powerful was the current and he had further observed that weightier and older people, as well as robuster divines of different denominations, including dignitaries of the Established Church, had occasionally with great difficulty kept out of those alluring recesses, as if by a prevenient grace granted them in exceptional measure.

OLD CEFNLLYS CHURCH

What with the Scylla of rushes at the centre of the lake, and the Charybdis of nooks on its outskirts, it would seem as if all the boats and canoes which had only two in them—but, after the manner of the ancient ark, having both sexes represented—were doomed!

Could the rushes but speak, they would tell a thrilling tale of the confidence exchanged in that canoe between Jenkin and Margaret. The narrator can only guess, and leave it to those who have been in similar circumstances to conjecture. Suffice it that at length Jenkin and Margaret, after a supernatural effort to reach the land, found *terra firma;* and as the dinner hour had arrived far too soon, and

William Jones, the miller, had an unfortunate fad of insisting upon punctuality with regard to meals, they, not without a few fruitless regrets, brought a very enjoyable outing to a close.

Meanwhile, John and Shadrach had completed their perambulations, and were awaiting Jenkin's return. The afternoon—being the last they had at Llandrindod—was spent by the three in visiting the Alpine

CORNER OF LAKE, WITH SWANS

Bridge. This is about four miles distant, and, when reached, is one of the most romantic spots in miniature which can be found in Wales.

On their way they met a vehicle, occupied by two gentlemen, and drawn by a white pony with whose peculiarities Jenkin had become familiar during his brief stay at Llandrindod. As old age had advanced, early habits had secured an increasing hold upon that very interesting animal. By a long process, extending over many years, evil communications had corrupted his whilom good manners. The result was that this venerable pony never by any chance passed a public-house. With a thoughtfulness and precision which could be gained only by years of careful training, this noble creature, however great the

speed at which he might be going—though that was never dangerous—
stopped short opposite every public-house door with a resoluteness
suggestive of "grandfather's clock," which "stopped short, never to
go again." This nag occasioned intense amusement to Jenkin, who
affirmed that he had heard of only one steed more provoking in its
persistent habits than this. That animal he had shod once. It appeared
that it had been hired almost from time immemorial by the Wesleyan
ministers of the district. On one occasion, however, a commercial
traveller, who represented a firm of wine and spirit merchants, and
who therefore was anxious to visit the public-houses of the
neighbourhood to obtain orders, hired that horse. To his great
astonishment and vexation of spirit, the illustrious creature rushed
by every public-house, and insisted upon stopping opposite every
Wesleyan chapel in the neighbourhood, and occasionally, if the gate of
the stable or yard adjoining the chapel were open, would run him in
safely and there remain. Jenkin thought that that commercial traveller
would do well to buy the white pony of Llandrindod renown, as it
would stop instinctively at every customer's door.

"Horses soon form habits," said John. "I remember hearing the Rev.
Joseph Thomas, of Carno, speak once on Temperance. He had been in
turn an old-fashioned Teetotaler, Good Templar, and Blue Ribbonite.
He justified this by saying that he was like the Duke of Wellington's
charger. Wherever in later years that charger saw a standard or banner
he went up and stood beneath it. Mr. Thomas said that he himself was
very much the same wherever he saw the Temperance flag unfurled,
whether it bore the distinctive name of 'Teetotal,' 'Good Templar,' or
'Blue Ribbon,' he instinctively went up and stood under it."

"That is something like what the Rev. David Davies, of Aberporth,
once said, although the figure he used was a very different one,"
exclaimed Shadrach. "He, too, had joined the Teetotalers, Good
Templars, and Blue Ribbonites. Some people had said that he was
therefore changeable. 'No, indeed,' replied Mr. Davies. 'When, many
years ago, I used to court Mary my wife, she used to wear a tall hat, a
flannel gown and petticoat, a pair of shoes and pattens. Now she wears
a bonnet, a French merino dress, and a pair of elastic-side boots *but
she is the same Mary still.* So is it with Temperance at one time she
wore a very simple garb, then she wore Good Templar regalia, and last
of all the Blue Ribbon, or Blue Cord, *but she is the same Mary still.*'"

"He was a great man on Temperance, wasn't he?" responded Jenkin. "Do you remember him once giving an amusing illustration? He said that near Aberporth there were large caves into which the sea rushed high tide. There a large number of seals hid themselves. When the tide receded, men used to go after those seals, and often they had a lively time of it. At length the seals would try to escape, and they did it very cleverly. One braver than the rest volunteered to be the leader, then each of the others hid his head between the hind legs of the seal before him, and if the men did not cripple the first by knocking him on his nose, it was impossible to stop the others. 'It is precisely so with the drink,' added Mr. Davies; 'if you do not stop the first glass, it is generally hopeless to prevent the rest.'"

"His illustrations generally were very pointed," responded John. "I remember him speaking once about tippling. He said that an occasional bout of downright drunkenness, bad as it was, was not so dangerous as constant tippling. He added, 'If you put a piece of good oak furniture out in a heavy shower of rain once or twice, although it may be damaged by the downpour, it will not be nearly so badly injured as if you put it into a damp corner of the house, where the rain drips from the thatch above, and oozes from the damp walls around; for there it will gradually but certainly become rotten through and through. So is it with drink. One or two bouts of drunkenness, while bad enough, are not so injurious as constant soaking in drink, although a man may never be said to have much at a time. That enters as a rot into his nature, and he becomes depraved throughout."

"Ah, Mr. Davies was a very wonderful old character," continued John. "He was one day at a fair, trying to sell his horse. Someone looked at the horse's knees, and thinking, or pretending to think, that the animal had been down, said to Mr. Davies, 'I see your horse has been saying his prayers.' 'Perhaps so,' replied the old patriarch, calmly 'but he is an awful old Pharisee, for he always says them *standing!*'"

"Very good," exclaimed Jenkin; "tell us more about him."

"There's a very good story told about him" added John readily. "One day a ship carpenter was repairing a vessel at Aberporth, near Cardigan, where Mr. Davies lived. The man had been for some time driving in a bolt. The bolt was hard to move, and the man was very exhausted and out of patience. Seeing Mr. Davies draw near, he said, half in mischief and half in bad temper, 'Why, the devil is in this hole.' 'Is he indeed?' exclaimed Mr. Davies very earnestly, 'then keep him in; hammer the bolt well; I have never got him into such a corner though I've tried all my life; hammer away, my son, and give the old fellow close quarters.'"

"Glorious," exclaimed Shadrach. "First rate," added Jenkin.

Meanwhile the three friends had almost reached their goal. They

THE ALPINE BRIDGE

had already turned from along a path that passed by a quaint mill, and had now only to cross a few fields to reach the Alpine Bridge. This is the name of a rustic structure, consisting of one half of the trunk of a tree sawn through the centre, and having on each side a wooden railing. This is thrown over a narrow defile, through which a river, compressed on each side by the rocky ribs of the deep ravine, rushes in its devious course between the huge boulders, which seem here to claim an almost complete monopoly of the river-bed. Just beneath the bridge, however, is a deep pool, excavated out of the solid rock by the constant rush of the river during past millenniums, as it has persistently forced its way through the narrow gorge on its journey seaward. The steep slopes—save where the narrow irregular zigzag paths have furrowed, and where the winter torrents have recently scarred them—are covered in summer with rich foliage, mosses, and ferns, while overhanging all are the arching branches of the trees on each side of the river, as they play "touch" with their fellows on the opposite side.

It is one of the most secluded and, on a small scale, most alluring spots which can be found anywhere, John, as soon as he caught a glimpse of this miniature chasm, paused, and would not go a step further. Being of a highly nervous temperament, and having an excessive dread of dizzy heights, he would not for the wealth of the Rothschilds cross that rustic bridge. Who knew? He might slip between the rails and the bridge; besides, the timber looked quite rotten, and would probably snap like match-wood if he but stood upon it! It gave him a shudder to see Shadrach and Jenkin cross, and he was profoundly grateful to see them return safely. He had, meanwhile, however, gained enough confidence to enable him to step sufficiently forward to catch a glimpse of the wild defile, and no one could appreciate such a sight

REV. E. HERBER EVANS, D.D.

more enthusiastically than John. It was to him a rich reward for walking
so short a distance. He would have gladly remained there for an hour
and have talked awhile with the river, when no one else—not even
Shadrach—was present but time was pressing.

The three friends, after repeated attempts, gave the spot a final
look and a parting greeting, and then, following the path by which
they had come, they soon reached the highway. When nearing
Llandrindod, they met, to their great surprise, the Rev. J. R. Kilsby
Jones and two friends, who had arrived that day, and in honour of
whom "Kilsby" had delayed his return to Llanwrtyd until night.
Those friends were congenial spirits, or he would not have paid them
this high compliment. They were the Revs. Benjamin Thomas, of
Narberth, and E. Herber Evans, of Carnarvon.*

The three looked like giants, and were nearly the same height,
but varied in width and thickness, from the comparatively athletic,
sinewy figure of "Kilsby," to the soft rotundity of the woolsack, as
exemplified in the person of "Herber." Between these two stood the
Baptist, who in his person struck a moderately fair average of the
dimensions of his two friends, but yet showed a slight bias in favour
of "Herber." Long before they appeared at a spot where the road
takes a sudden turn, their voices and ringing laughter were easily
heard, and just as they appeared in sight of John and his friends,
"Kilsby" was relaxing from a stern erect attitude and breaking out
into frolicsome gaiety; "Thomas" was bursting into a wild hurricane
of merriment; and "Herber" was heaving like a volcano. They were
evidently telling tales which were only intended for the initiated few.
"Kilsby" looked the liveliest of the three.

"Mr. Jones wears marvellously well," said John Vaughan, as he
caught a glimpse of him in the distance.

"How old is he?" asked Jenkin.

"I forget," replied Shadrach; "but he tells it out freely when
asked."

"He is not like Ishmael Jones," added John. "He was an old
bachelor; and in his later years he would never tell his age. Many
were the efforts made to get at the secret, but the old man could not

* Since the above was first written, these three great men have passed
away, and left a terrible gap behind them.

be caught. At last, he fell in love, and had to give notice of his marriage. The Registrar was one of Mr. Jones's friends, who had tried in vain to find out his age. He was delighted with the thought of getting at the secret at last, and of being the means of extending the news to others. In the form which had to be filled there was a column for 'age.' The Registrar did his utmost to conceal his emotions; but his voice quivered slightly as he asked, 'What is your age, Mr. Jones?' The old patriarch looked him through, then a twinkle played bo-peep in the corner of his eye, as he said in a round sonorous voice, 'Full age, sir.' It seems that this is all that the law demands: the old man knew it, and thus still kept the secret, much to the disappointment of his friends."

"That is a valuable hint for old bachelors," said Jenkin. "I heard David Lewis tell a story the other day about the Rev. Griffith Jones, of Tregarth. He was always annoyed at references made to his age, and on that account some of his friends were very fond of reminding him that he was getting old. On one occasion he was suffering keenly from pains in one of his legs. He complained to a friend, who replied, 'Ah, well, Mr. Jones, old age is beginning to tell upon you.' 'Old age, indeed!' replied the old man indignantly, 'the other leg is quite as old, and there isn't a pain in it.'"

Just then "Kilsby" and his friends drew near, and, according to the free and genial custom of Welsh salutations, accosted the strangers. In passing them, Mr. Thomas instantly recognised them. He had preached often at Horeb Chapel, where the three were wont to worship. During his visits to the village, he had called at the smithy and John Vaughan's workshop. He recognised Jenkin as the smith's son, who, in the exuberance of boyish mischief, a few years before, used occasionally to place hobnails with points upwards on the seat which was generally occupied by the visitors to the smithy. He well knew John as an able expounder of Scripture and a vigorous disputant on doctrinal subjects. Besides, Kitty, John Vaughan's wife, was a lateral descendant of David Evans, of Ffynon-henry, whose biography Mr. Thomas had written. During the preparation of this book—one of the most popular biographies ever published in the Welsh language—Mr. Thomas had repeatedly conversed with John and Kitty about the quaint old patriarch of Ffynon-henry. He, therefore, on this occasion stepped aside, and cordially greeted the

shoemaker and his comrades; then, after a few enquiries concerning
themselves and their friends at Horeb Chapel, he hastened to
overtake his companions.

He was barely beyond ear-shot when John, turning round and
looking after him and those who accompanied him, said: "There, we
should have to go a long way in Wales before we could find three
other such men as those. They must be having a rich time together."
Shadrach and Jenkin smilingly nodded assent.

"I shall never forget Mr. Thomas's sermon at Horeb on 'The
Chariots,'"* said Shadrach.

"No, never," replied John. "I should very much pity the memory of
the man who could ever forget that. But I remember one sermon he
preached even better than I do that. It was on a very stormy Sunday
evening in August. It thundered terribly before and during the service,
and the lightning almost blinded us at times. We learned afterwards
that Mr. Thomas changed his text for the evening just before the service,
as the thunderstorm began. I noticed that as he proceeded with the
service there was a strange searching look about his eye, and a wild
play about his countenance. At last, he took his text—I shall never forget
it, it so struck everybody. He read it calmly and impressively: 'God
thundereth marvellously with His voice.' He proceeded to speak of the
different voices of God, one being the voice of thunder. As he proceeded
with his theme, the thunder grew louder and louder, and the lightning
flashed at times as if it were a glance from the eye of God. At last there
came a flash of almost blinding brilliancy, and a crash that shook the
building to its foundations; the preacher then paused, and said, 'Hark!
when the Master speaks it behoves His servant to be silent.' With this
he sat down: the sermon was over. God gave the rest."

"John," said Shadrach earnestly, "I couldn't have stood that!"

Jenkin was solemnised, and said nothing.

After a pause, during which no one cared to speak, John gave a
characteristic short cough, and proceeded, "You were talking just as
we met those ministers, Jenkin, about the Rev. Griffith Jones, of
Tregarth. Did you ever hear his remarks about conversion?"

"No," replied Jenkin; "tell us."

---

* See "Echoes from the Welsh Hills," by the same Author, pp. 35-44 (pp.
33-43 in the original edition).

"Ah, they are very good," said Shadrach; "tell Jenkin that story."

"Well," responded John, "Griffith Jones was a shoemaker before he entered the ministry; he was one of the great men who once handled the lapstone, and of whom we shoemakers are justly proud, I think. In his later ministerial years he was present at a conference where 'Conversion' was the subject under consideration. Some of the ministers urged the importance of people being able to relate the time and circumstances of their conversion. At length he was requested to speak. He got up and said, 'Before I entered the ministry I was, as many of you are aware, a shoemaker. My father was a shoemaker before me. Many of the Tregarth lads were, at different times, apprenticed to him. In their cases indentures were drawn up, giving their names, the time they commenced, and the dates on which they would close their apprenticeships. But I was never apprenticed; and I cannot tell when I began working at the trade. My earliest recollections are that as a little boy I used to run from my mother's apron strings into my father's workshop, and putting an odd piece of leather into the clamps, sew it with the ends of wax-threads which my father had thrown aside. In that way I began to learn my trade. I know not when; but I went on, and learnt the trade as thoroughly as any of my father's apprentices ever did. It is, I think, just like that with conversion. Some have very sudden and decided conversions; they can always produce their indentures, bearing the exact date on which they began their apprenticeship. Saul of Tarsus was one of those; he often used to talk about the time; yea, the very hour and place he began his:—"As I went to Damascus at mid-day." On the other hand, I don't think that Timothy could produce his indenture. He somehow began to learn of his grandmother and mother without realising it, just as I learnt my trade; but who will doubt that he was converted?'"

By the time they reached Llandrindod, the sun was setting over the western hills, and, as if by a conscious supernatural effort, flooded the land with light. Long after it had disappeared beneath the horizon, the clouds that arched over its setting reflected the gorgeous hues with which its light transfigured them. Gradually, as the King of Day withdrew, the Queen of Night modestly appeared over the eastern hills, and began her nightly pilgrimage across the sky. It was difficult to withdraw from such a scene, but John and his friends were hungry and weary with their journey, and supper time had come; thus, quitting with reluctance that strange transitional scene from the warm golden glow of a summer sunset to the bright weird silvery hue of a moonlit night, John, Shadrach, and Jenkin betook themselves to their lodgings for a refreshing wash and a hearty meal.

On the following morning the excursionists from Carmarthen arrived in full force upon the platform, awaiting the arrival of the train on the return journey. Again, by a strange coincidence, as it would appear, Mr. William Jones, the miller, and his daughter Margaret, found themselves in the same compartment as John, Shadrach and Jenkin. Jenkin and Margaret, too, chanced to sit opposite each other. It matters little where the others sat; nor does it matter much how often and how sweetly Jenkin and Margaret glanced at each other during that most pleasant journey.

Suffice it to say, that the presence of Margaret seemed to give piquancy and zest to all Jenkin's remarks. The train had not long started before he saw a farmer who, with oats in the hand which he stretched out in front, and a bridle in the other which he kept well concealed behind his back, was trying to catch a horse in an adjoining field. "Look there," said Jenkin to the company, as he cast a side-glance at Margaret, "that is a rare dodge." "Yes," said William Jones, who was rather suspicious of Jenkin's motives regarding Margaret, "that's like many young men when courting: they show nothing but corn till they secure their wives, and, after that, there is nothing but bridle."

"I say," said Jenkin, "that's rather startling, and yet you married folk ought to know. The affair reminds me of what the Rev. R. Thomas (Ap. Fychan), the late theological tutor at Bala, once said. He affirmed that was just the way some churches did with ministers—all oats at first, and all bridle and hard work afterwards. That was a wonderful sermon that he preached at the ordination of a neighbouring minister many years ago. Tell us that other bit you gave us in the smithy the other day, John: it gives a gentle hint to millers."

"I am afraid you are a little spiteful, Jenkin," replied John, with a smile; "but I will gladly repeat what I then said. Mr. Thomas urged the church to give well toward their minister's salary, and then proceeded to say, 'The preachers of God, in former days, were often maintained without human help: Elias was fed near the brook Cherith for months by ravens; but there are no such ravens to be found in our country. The woman of Sarepta had an invisible mill, in which her flour was constantly ground, and she could go to the bin whenever she pleased: the flour increased according to the demand; but I do not know of any such mill in our day. The preacher now must take the wheat to the mill before he can get anything out of it, and the miller will be sure to take his toll from him for grinding as well as from anyone else.'" (Here Jenkin smiled, and Margaret blushed. John proceeded.) "'Peter and his Master, when they had no money wherewith to pay the tax, got it from the mouth of a fish; but there are no such fish in any of our rivers, and even if one chanced to pass up this way, and your young minister caught it, he would be sent to prison for a month for his trouble.'"

"Very good," said William Jones, "I hope they gave that minister a good salary after that; because it strikes me that the miller is not the only one who takes the 'toll' out of him."

"Do you see that chapel yonder, John?" asked Shadrach, evidently anxious to change the theme. "There I heard, many years ago, Mr. Robert Fornos, of Festiniog, preach. I don't recollect his sermon, but I remember well that he was greatly annoyed with the coughing. At first he made a pathetic appeal, but the coughing continued, and, at last he said impatiently, 'My dear people, don't cough; or, if you must cough, go to cough at that place where you caught the cold.'"

"That was well put," said Jenkin; "but he didn't take it as easily as old Parson ——. While he was preaching—that is, if reading other people's sermons can by any stretch of charity be called preaching— the people got restless, and coughed a great deal. At last the old parson said, 'You all seem to be enjoying a cough uncommonly well. I think I'll join you, and have a cough too,' and he coughed vigorously. That was about the only original thing, they say, he ever said or did in the pulpit."

Such was the staple of the talk during the whole journey. The train at length arrived at Carmarthen. William Jones and his daughter drove home in their trap, Hugh Roberts sent his old man-servant and his still older vehicle to fetch John, Shadrach, and Jenkin. The welcome home by "Kitty" and "Mary" was more gratifying than any of their holiday experiences; yet the recollections of that trip long lingered in their memories, and supplied material for many a reminiscence in after days.

CHAPTER V

John Vaughan and his friends at Home

N the day following the return home of John, Shadrach, and Jenkin from "The Wells," many were the greetings which they received from those who called at the smithy and the shoemaker's shop.

Early in the evening Hugh Roberts, of Pentre-mawr Farm, and Caleb Rhys, the weaver, called at the smithy. As Shadrach had finished his most pressing work for the day, and had not quite recovered from his holiday feeling, he felt indisposed to do more, although work had greatly accumulated during his absence. Consequently the three resolved to go to John Vaughan's workshop, and Jenkin gladly joined in the company.

John, too, had found a heap of work awaiting his return, but, like his cousin Shadrach, he had no enthusiasm for it. The advent of his old friends was therefore even more welcome to him than usual. Once more, the story of the holidays was repeated by John and Shadrach, with an occasional interjection by Jenkin; and as they had never before been so far from home, they enlarged upon the details of the journey, the powerful engines and long trains, and especially upon the long delay which had been occasioned on the way by the dropping of a pin from one of the finest engines they had seen. John, amid all his surprise at the immense power of a steam-engine, was greatly impressed by this incident as a proof of its helplessness if only a pin or screw chanced to be misplaced. What helpless things, he thought, even the strongest are in some circumstances! Just imagine an engine failing to proceed for want of a small iron pin!

Caleb, who had traversed the greater part of Wales in his periodical journeys with his flannels, was familiar with such delays and their various causes, and now among other things affirmed in a playful style, that the steam-engine was a very thirsty creature, and had now and then to stop on the way to have a drink.

"Ah," responded John, "I remember Rev. Griffith Jones, of Tregarth, once giving an account of such an incident. He was going from Carnarvon to Avon Wen. He travelled with another minister, who soon after was excluded from the ministry for intemperance. When the train had reached Pen-y-groes Mr. Jones' friend alighted; but soon returned to the carriage, with a strong odour of brandy which he had just been drinking from a flask he carried in his pocket. The train proceeded, but before Brynkir Station was reached the engine stopped. The minister who carried the flask asked why the train stopped, Mr. Jones replied: "The engine is only taking water; it never requires brandy to do its work."

"That reminds one of what old Rev. David Davies, of Cowarch, once said," responded Shadrach. "When speaking about the murmuring of the children of Israel for water he said: 'Fair play to the Israelites. Although they murmured when in a great thirst, it was for water that they clamoured; instead of peering to see if they could find a public-house round the next corner.'"

"A public-house in the wilderness was a scarce commodity. I should think," interjected Jenkin, in a saucy tone.

"It would be a good thing if it had been a scarce commodity in our country, too," replied Shadrach.

"There were not any cook-shops in the wilderness either," answered John, "and yet they sighed for the flesh-pots of Egypt. Wherever there is a drunkard he will sigh for a public-house anywhere, wilderness or no wilderness. It is very evident that the weakness of the Israelites was in the direction of gluttony rather than drunkenness. I fear that in this age men are given to both excesses. But whatever may be said about that, old Mr. Davies was a wonderful man. He attached great value to a consistent character, and often used to speak to the young about the importance of beginning well. I remember him, many years ago, speaking to young people, and saying, 'Seek true religion at the outset, if you do not begin aright in your religious life, you are not likely to be up to much as Christians later on, unless something extraordinary befalls you. It is just the same as when we mark the sheep. If we do not succeed in making a good letter at first, any amount of mending later on will not make it better. Just so, if you do not begin your religious life aright, there is little hope of you later on.'"

"I well remember that sermon," exclaimed Caleb, "and especially that illustration which you have just given, John, as well as another that was quite as striking. You no doubt remember that when he had shown how important it was to begin aright, as every wrong act weakened a man for life, he added that those who had gone astray needed to be exceptionally watchful. He said, 'It is very important that you should keep a constant watch on those places where you have before now broken over the bounds. I notice that on the banks of the River Dovey they construct dams of twice and thrice the ordinary thickness and strength just at the places where the river has previously made breaches and overflowed the meadows. They are the places where it is most likely to break through again. See to it that you, too, set double watch over your old excesses and follies, or they will long continue to be the sins which will the most readily beset you.'"

"How very true," responded Shadrach.

"Mr. Davies was a wonderfully practical teacher," added Caleb. "I well remember what he said once at Cowarch, at the close of a prayer-meeting held while a low fair was being carried on very near the chapel. He said, 'our prayer meeting is now about to close. The children of this world are holding a fair in the street outside. Go straight home from this place without mixing with them. There is a river in America—It is the great river Amazon, I think—which flows with such force as it enters the sea that it goes out in a straight line into the sea for miles without mixing with the briny waters. Go and do likewise. Go home in a straight, undeviating course, right through the fair, without mixing with the current of sin that is in it.'"

"That bit of advice to go straight on reminds me," said Jenkin, "of what Mr. Williams of Aberduar once said. He took for his text, 'What is that to thee? Follow thou Me'; and then proceeded to say, 'The motto of my text is, *Let everyone mind his own business.*'"

"Yes," said Hugh Roberts; "but Mr. Davies gave it also a wider application—namely, that we should always abstain from having any fellowship with the children of this world, because it can only result in disappointment and misery. We can make no compromise with worldlings. 'The light of the wicked shall be put out, and the spark of his fire shall not shine. The light shall be dark in his tabernacle, and his candle shall be put out with him.'"

"Quite true, Hugh," responded John; "and when that light goes out there is no hope. As Mr. Jones, Holywell, once said, 'The valley of the shadow of death is a poor place in which to try to exchange the vanities of a godless course for the realities of the godly life. The market price of all that is good and holy rises greatly, and the market price of all that is worldly and unholy falls terribly, there.'"

"Ah," replied old Hugh Roberts, "it behoves us to 'purchase' (Welsh translation) 'the time, for the days are evil.' Life is so short, and yet so important; and the older we get, the more we feel this."

"Yes, Hugh," responded John, "I remember hearing Rev. John Ffoulkes Jones, of Machynlleth, preaching once from the words you have just repeated. It was at the Methodist Chapel; and you were there, and so were Caleb and Shadrach."

"I remember it well," said Shadrach.

"So do I," exclaimed Hugh.

"And I," said Caleb.

"But go on, John," added Shadrach, "for you can recall everything, while my memory is like a sieve."

"It's not so bad as that, Shadrach," replied John, "for you very often remember what I forget. I do, however, recollect what Mr. Jones then said, for it impressed me much. He said: 'Some islands in the sea constantly get smaller. As the waves beat upon the shore, the cliffs crumble and fall in pieces gradually, until at length the last sod goes, and nothing remains but sea. My friends, the waves of the eternal sea wash against the shores of our lives every moment, and as that sea beats and surges, some part of our life crumbles and falls away constantly. Oh, what huge portions have already gone! And they represent the best and most fertile parts of our life—the rich meadows of childhood and youth! Some sod or other drops constantly into the restless waves, and is swallowed up by the limitless ocean. Every step, every breath, and every time the clock strikes—one part after another falls; and before long the last inch will give way beneath our feet, and nothing but the great sea, and its boundless outlook, will remain with us!'

"Then he went on to tell us that this contrast between us and our present dwelling places is that which gives such importance to life. Everything on earth passes away, but our inner selves will remain. 'It is this,' said he, 'that gives such great importance to the day of our birth. It began what will never end. Probably, no bells rang on that occasion; our birth was not registered in any public calendar; but it was a day that will be noted on the last judgment, and be remembered for ever. I have before now stood and looked eagerly into the eye of a bubbling spring, on the slope of one of our mountains, and have asked it, "Dost thou, youthful spring, think of going to the sea some time or other?" "Yes," replied the spring in its own language; and, lo, it began to start on its pilgrimage, and danced down the mountain slope, and leapt over the rocky precipice; and gathering strength and resolve as it advanced, it urged its way through the meadows and along the valleys and plains. Many beautiful things grew upon its banks; but it only gave them passing notice and a hasty greeting. It never paused or delayed in its course: to the sea it went. Every drop within its bed; every twig and leaf upon its surface, felt the mighty resistless attraction that drew it to the sea. Oh friends," he continued, "there is an urgency in your life consider whither you are going, with all your idle words, vain thoughts, and prayerless lives. Remember that all go sweeping on ceaselessly to the eternal world.'""

"Ah! Mr. Jones was an excellent preacher," said Hugh Roberts tremulously. "His figures were always homely and very striking. I remember him once preaching from the words, 'When he is tried, he shall receive the crown of life, which the Lord hath promised to them that love Him.' He began by saying, 'It is thus that God purposes to

"I WELL REMEMBER THAT SERMON," EXCLAIMED CALEB

reward the tried man. He promises him a crown. I do not understand that the new Testament contains any promise of a crown to an angel. The angel does not know what it is to be tried like man.' Then he proceeded to show how trials were among the necessary conditions of being blessed, and at last crowned. He added, 'There are some flowers which we call *"Winter flowers."* They are not to be found in the summer; but come in the winter. Is not the great Creator surpassingly kind in giving us a few of these in wintry days! How delighted we are to see their bright faces in November and December, and especially Christmas-time! Some of the graces of the Gospel are very much like these—they are "winter flowers." What are patience, endurance, meekness, and submission, but winter flowers, for which we should be profoundly thankful to God? These are with us in short dark days; yea, in long and dreary nights: in the winters of affliction and weakness, sorrow and pain. O my friends, make the most now of these graces. They foretell yet richer rewards which will crown your lives. The same Apostle exclaims, "Ye have heard of the patience of Job." Yes, we have heard a great deal about Job's patience; but we should not have heard of his patience were it not for his afflictions.'"

"That is exactly it, Hugh," responded John earnestly; "when the good Lord lets us suffer, it is always for our good. Probably you remember a sermon preached here by the Rev. John Jones, of Holywell, from the words, 'All things work together for good to them that love God,' especially the illustration which he gave about children sent to the boarding-school. He said, 'There they soon find many things withheld from them which they have been allowed to enjoy at home. There is an economy about everything there except tasks and manners. What with lessons and rules of etiquette, the little things are well-nigh bewildered at times, and begin to ask, "Why has father sent us to such a place as this, where there are so few comforts and so many rules and lessons?" At length they return home for their holiday, and one quiet afternoon they venture to ask their father the question they had so often repeated at school. He replies tenderly, yet firmly, "My children, I sent you there not for comforts; but for training. What you wanted was not indulgence, but instruction; and the school is the best place to get that. When you have learnt what you need to learn, I will have you home, not before." Brethren,' added the preacher, 'that is just what our Heavenly Father does with us. He keeps us in school, so that we may be trained; instead of taking us home, or giving us too many comforts; and then, when our education is complete, He'll take us home.'"

"Yes, there can be no doubt about that," replied. Hugh. "If there were any doubt about it, some of us would find it hard to bear some things. It is this that gives us patience to wait until God has accomplished His loving purpose in us. It is just as the Rev. Ffoulkes Jones, of Machynlleth, once said about Job—'Job, in the midst of all his trouble, said about God, "When He hath tried me, I shall come forth as gold." Job's friends had said hard things concerning him. Job replied, "Stop a little. Wait till my education is complete, and the final test comes!"'"

"That's it," added John. "The trials of the godly man not only do him good; but they also prove his worth and sincerity to others. They bring the true ring out of him. As I once heard Rev. Thomas Hughes, also of Machynlleth, say, 'When you go to the shop to purchase an article the shopkeeper does not always put your coin immediately into the drawer, or till; but often strikes it against the counter to see whether it will give the right ring or not. There may be a flaw in it, or, still worse, it may be counterfeit. So God does with men. He does not at once put them into His great treasury, but first tries them. He, by some trial, strikes them against the great counter of Providence to give them an opportunity of showing what they are made of, and whether there is a flaw in them or not. He struck Job against this old counter repeatedly until he cried, "The Lord gave, and the Lord hath taken away; Blessed be the name of the Lord"; and again, "Though He slay me, yet will I trust in Him"; and thus showed the genuineness of the metal that was in him. So with all the ancient saints. "The Lord does not afflict willingly the children of men." He only afflicts so that all true souls may send out the right ring, and false ones reveal their true characters. Trust the great counter of Providence my friends. It only enables you to give out a ringing sound that shows your genuineness if you are true.'"

"Mr. Hughes said many striking things about affliction," responded Hugh. "I remember him once comparing the lives of saints to days of mingled gloom and sunshine, which we so often have in this climate. Some days begin with clouds, but brighten as they proceed; others begin in brightness, but darken as they advance. 'So,' said he, 'it is often with God's children. Some begin life amid sorrow and affliction, but as life advances the clouds are lifted up and gradually disappear, leaving only bright sunshine behind them. Others begin their career amid brightness and song, but as they proceed the clouds lower, and storms gather, and the day closes amid the sighs and tears of misgiving and sorrow. But come what may, the Christian knows in his inmost heart that his Redeemer liveth, and that, though he walk through the valley of the shadow of death, he need fear no evil.'"

"Quite true," exclaimed Shadrach; "and yet, in spite of all, he does sometimes fear. Some men are a long time getting over their natural timidity. It often darkens their faith. I sometimes think my natural nervousness will stick to me to the very last. Besides, many of us need chastening even to the last hour of our life."

"It's something like what the Rev. John Jones, of Blaenannerch, once said," added Caleb Rhys. "He said that some good men were allowed to die very much in the dark. He then proceeded to compare it to a father in the neighbourhood of Blaenannerch who, one dark night, sent his boy, who had been disobedient during the day, to bed without a light. That seems to have been the most effective way of chastising the lad. The boy replied tearfully, 'It is dark, father.' The father answered, 'Yes, I know it is dark, but still you have to go; you have been a naughty boy to-day, and you must go to bed without a light to-night.' 'Ah, brethren,' added Mr. Jones, 'our Heavenly Father has to deal with some of us like that. He will have to send us to sleep without much light to cheer us; but still we are His children, and we shall yet sleep in His keeping until the day dawn and the shadows flee away.'"

"What a comfort it is," said Hugh, "to know that He attaches great value to us though He chastens us, and that He loves us dearly in spite of all our sins."

"As Mr. Williams, the noted Cardigan magistrate and Baptist minister, said long ago," interjected John Vaughan, "'God, in chastising us, does it for our highest good, and, as the result of all, He will reserve none of the chaff, and lose none of the wheat.'"

"One good thing," exclaimed Shadrach, "is that all the chastening is here, and none over yonder."

"Yes," continued John; "and yet some English preachers would have us believe that there is to be a great deal of scourging on the other side, and very effective scourging, too; for it is going to make saints of everybody without fail. Thus those who have rejected the Gospel here, and defied the Lord's loving chastenings in this life, are going to be whipped into saintship in the next world. In this way there is to be a wholesale salvation at last. What the story of Christ's

Cross, the appeals of mercy, and the loving chastening of a Father's hand have failed to do here, is to be done, so we are told, by a more drastic treatment in the next world."

"That is a sort of final reformatory, I suppose," murmured Jenkin.

"Ah, that's poor stuff to believe," exclaimed Shadrach impatiently, and shook his head.

"It *is* poor stuff to believe," responded John, "and a worse doctrine than even the purgatory of the Romish Church, for as I heard the aged Robert Jones, of Llanllyfni, once say: 'According to the teaching of the Church of Rome, it is not ungodly men that are sent to purgatory, but imperfect saints.' Now I would much rather believe that doctrine, than believe that God has in reserve a special method by which to manufacture saints wholesale out of daring blasphemers and others who, in this life, and in the day of grace, have ignored His love in Jesus Christ, have repudiated the Cross, have trodden under foot the Son of God, and done despite unto the Spirit of Grace. Yet the purgatory of the Romish Creed is bad teaching enough in all conscience. Very few papists seem to escape purgatory. The priests are very fond of putting people there, so that they may be well paid for taking them out again. Even Cardinals, and other high dignitaries of the Church—and I suppose even the

REV. ROBERT JONES, OF LLANLLYFNI

Pope himself—have to go there, and if *they* have to go, what can be expected in the case of smaller and less saintly folk? As old Mr. Jones further said, 'Paul evidently knew nothing. about purgatory. All the saints he spoke of were in God's family on earth, or in heaven. If there had been a purgatory, Paul would be sure to have heard of it; but as he knew nothing about it, we may rest assured that no such thing as purgatory exists.'"

"It is a pitiable thing," said Hugh Roberts, "to see men putting off for another world what they should see to in this; and if preachers will teach others such a doctrine as that to which you have referred, John, they will have a deal to answer for in the day of judgment for encouraging men to hope when there is no hope. Why leave present certainties for idle dreams of what yet may occur in another world. 'Behold, now is the accepted time; behold, now is the day of salvation.'"

"Yes," said John Vaughan "it is just as the Rev. Thomas John, of Cilgerran, once illustrated it. He said that in ancient days there was a king who was hostile to Rome. An ambassador was sent to him to discuss affairs with him. The king doggedly refused to give any decisive word either in favour of peace or war. At length the Roman drew with his staff a line on the ground around the king, and said, 'Before you step out of this circle you must decide whether it shall be peace or war with Rome.' 'Brethren,' he added, 'God has drawn a circle round us, which we call life, and before we step out of it we must decide whether it shall be war or peace with God.'"

"That is the preaching that will bring men face to face with their great privileges and responsibilities," exclaimed Caleb Rhys. "Men are ready enough to delay apart from preachers going out of their way to encourage them to do so, by assuring them that whatever they do, it will be all right in the long run."

"That is the preaching, too," responded John, "that has done everything for Wales; and God forbid that any weak sentimental nonsense, however pleasant it may be to the natural man, should take its place here!"

"Thomas John was a wonderful man!" interjected Hugh Roberts. "I shall never forget his preaching once upon the same subject, and speaking about men and women delaying their preparation till their deathbed. He said, 'Beware of such folly. The thoughts of the dying will be too fully occupied with the longing for life, and the fear of death, to admit of room for such an important matter as to prepare to meet their God. That is a business that cannot be pushed into such small compass as that; it must occupy all the thoughts and powers of our being, and not the distracted thoughts and exhausted energies of dying men.'"

"That was a theme upon which he often dwelt," responded John, "and his appearance and manner made him very impressive when he spoke on such subjects. I remember him once speaking about the madness of money-hunting, and of heaping up riches. 'Men go,' he said, 'to all lands, and have recourse to every means they can invent to amass gold. Have you ever thought,' he added, 'that all of it has to be left in heaps on the banks of the dark river of death? Why spend all the time and energy to carry it all so far, and no further? Friends, see that you seek and find that which you can take with you, and not what you must leave behind with the mass of fools' treasure which has been heaped on the banks of the Jordan throughout the ages by those who have had after all to cross without it.'"

The evening was now far spent, and the talk had reached a natural close. Thus with a nod of approval to John's last utterance, and a word or two in parting, the friends separated for the night, with the hope of meeting again at no distant period.

CHAPTER VI

John Vaughan and his friends at the Fellowship Meeting

EDNESDAY Evening was one of the two evenings of the week to which John Vaughan and Shadrach Morgan attached greatest importance, because of the Fellowship or Experience meeting then held. John used to say that next to the prayer meeting, that was the most important gathering of the Church. Prayer had, however, the precedence, and he used to repeat with much earnestness that according to the size of the vessel let down into the overflowing well would be the quantity of water brought up, and according to the size of the window would be the amount of light that entered the dwelling when God's heaven was bright above it.

But next to prayer, in which men unitedly communed with God, the most important Christian privilege, John held, was the fellowship which Christians had with each other. He therefore made a point of going on this Wednesday, as his custom was, to the Fellowship Meeting, although work had greatly accumulated during his absence at Llandrindod Wells. Shadrach stood on the corner of the cross-road, that intersected the turnpike road in the middle of the village, waiting for John. John soon came, and both friends went arm in arm towards "Horeb."

"What a blessing it is to have these meetings, John," exclaimed Shadrach. "Much as I enjoyed our holiday, I did not like to miss our services, especially the experience meetings. In religious matters as well as in family affairs, John, there's no place like home. No fire burns so brightly as that which shines on one' s own hearth. I soon catch cold in other people's houses, except when it is a very close friend's; and my religion would soon suffer if I could not attend our own meetings at Horeb, John."

"You are something like old Mr. William Griffith, of Blackwood, Monmouthshire, of whom Caleb Rhys speaks," replied John. "He went up to London as a witness in some Parliamentary inquiry, and stayed there about ten days. When he came back he thanked the Lord at the next prayer meeting for being brought home again; as, apart from very special divine grace, he was afraid he would soon lose in London the little religion he had."

"There's a great deal in that, John," exclaimed Shadrach; "only, of course, the good Lord does not forget His own even in London. In any case there can be no doubt that in all ages it has been a means of grace to God's children to be permitted to speak 'often one to another,' and the Lord has always 'hearkened and heard them.'"

"Yes," replied John, "yet none of us appreciate these blessings as we should; and some so-called Christians not at all. How much would the old saints in this neighbourhood, who used to go to Ffynon-henry in the times of persecution, have given for the opportunity of going, as we do, to our prayer and experience meetings and communion services, none daring to make them afraid! And yet those persecutions were the things which made heroes of them. Religion was more precious to them than all that the world could give. Even poor women and children were giants in faith in those days."

"Quite true," responded Shadrach. "You referred just now to what

Caleb Rhys once said about an old saint at Blackwood. What was
the story he once told us about a little girl who lived somewhere in
Glamorganshire in the times of persecution?"

"Oh, that was about a little maid who was on her way to the
Communion service at Whitecross, near Caerphilly, at the time of
the Five Mile Act. She suddenly met the clergyman of the parish at
a place where the road took a sharp turn. Instantly her heart beat
with fear. She said to herself, 'It is all over now. If I speak the truth
when he questions me, I shall be betraying my brethren and sisters;
but if I tell a lie I shall be false to my Lord and Master.' Just then
there flashed across her mind the words of Jesus to His disciples:
'When they shall lead you, and deliver you up, take no thought
beforehand what ye shall speak, neither do ye premeditate: but
whatsoever shall be given you in that hour, that speak ye.' The
clergyman, after saluting her, asked, 'Where are you going?' 'Oh,
sir,' replied she, 'my elder brother has died, and they read the will
to-day, and I want to hear it.' 'Was he rich, then?' asked the vicar.
'Yes, sir,' replied the maid, 'I expect he has left a good fortune for
us.' 'Very good,' was the reply; 'good morning.'"

"That's it," ejaculated Shadrach. "The Lord not only gave that
little maid courage, John; but He also made her wise as a serpent,
though harmless as a dove. I wish we had more like her to-day!"

"Ah, those were days when nothing could stand the test but pure
gold," replied John. "There was some sterling stuff in men's religion
then; and, thank God, much of it still exists. But there is no
persecution to prove it now like then."

"Those were the days to bring out some rugged characters, too,"
responded Shadrach.

"Yes," said John, "they had some rough work to do and men could
not do it with kid gloves on. They were very much like what we lately
heard the Rev. David Morgan,* of Cefn-coed-y-Cymmer, say about John
the Baptist, when he referred to the words of John concerning Christ—
'He that cometh after me *is mightier than I.*' He said that 'John caught
the strong side of religion. The *power and authority* of Christ was
what charmed him most. There was something very rugged about
John. He wore coarse clothing; he had "his raiment of camel's hair,

---

* Mr. Morgan, who was an able Calvinistic minister, died at an early age.

and a leathern girdle about his loins." In contrast to him our Lord said that those who wore soft clothing were in kings' houses. John lived, too, upon plain, and even coarse, food: "His meat was locusts and wild honey." His ministry was also rugged and outspoken, with a great deal more strength in it than politeness—"When he saw the Pharisees and Sadducees come to his baptism, he said unto them, O generation of vipers, who had warned you to flee from the wrath to come? Bring forth therefore fruits meet for repentance: and think not to say within yourselves, We have Abraham to our father: for I say unto you, that God is able of these stones to raise up children unto Abraham. And now also the axe is laid unto the root of the trees: therefore every tree which bringeth not forth good fruit is hewn down, and cast into the fire." He had rough work to do, namely, to prepare the way of the Lord, and he could not do that in any other garb or manner than that which he adopted.'"

"We haven't many like John now," exclaimed Shadrach.

"No," replied John Vaughan; "partly because men have not the same rough work to do in our country now as John, or, indeed, even some of our old preachers had. But we have one or two of the old style still among us. There is, for instance, the veteran Rev. Robert Jones,* of Llanllyfni. He says some terrible things still, and only such things as a man of his great age and well-known honesty and courage could speak to any purpose, or, indeed would be justified in saying. God does not give Elijah's message to any except Elijah. Robert Jones is our Elijah in North Wales. There is a member of the Baptist Church at Llanllyfni who was baptized by Mr. Jones, and who has since led a pure, moral life, but who has been very lukewarm in connection with the cause of Christ. Yet he is very fond of sitting prominently with the leaders in the 'big seat' or pulpit pew. One Sunday night Mr. Jones preached from the text 'Be zealous, therefore, and repent!' Having spoken like a prophet about zeal in the cause of the great Saviour, and of the worthlessness of an unfaithful and indolent professor, the old man stood beneath the weight of his message, shook his hoary head, and with tearful eyes pointed to the slothful professor in the big pew. Looking at him with piercing glance through his tears, and then at the people, he said, 'Now, here is our brother So-and-so.

---

* The reader will remember a preceding note referring to Mr. Jones's death.

He *must* feel to-night what a worthless man he is. He is of no good
to the devil, because he does next to nothing for him. And he cannot
be of any good to the Saviour, for he will do nothing for Him and His
cause. He knows all this as well as I do. Now, as He is of no service
to the devil, or to Christ, what can he be but lumber in God's
universe? Dear brother, "Be zealous, therefore, and repent."'"

"I say," interjected Jenkin, "that rebuke was a sort of spiritual
cat-o'-nine tails to that culprit."

"Yes—that was strong, John!" exclaimed Shadrach, evidently
desiring to endorse, and yet modify, the remark of his erratic son; "I
expect his tears gave great tenderness as well as force to those words.
It must have been touching to see such a strong man weep when
giving one of his people such a castigation."

"Yes," replied John; "and Robert Jones is, after all, one of the
most tender-hearted men in Wales, although you would scarcely think
so when he puts on his stern look. He fears no man. When quite a
young minister he walked fifteen miles to tell Christmas Evans face
to face what he considered to be his serious defects, when no one
else would have dreamt of doing so. He still believes that he was
right in that protest; but when he speaks of it his eyes moisten, and
his powerful countenance becomes relaxed, as he adores the grace
that prevented his youthful ardour from going to dangerous
extremes, adding, pathetically, 'Christmas and I will have an
opportunity of talking those matters over again.'

"It is this blending of the tender with the strong that gives a charm
to his character. They say that he is really as tender-hearted as a child,
and like a child is thoroughly lost in the narratives of the Bible. They
are all so very real to him, and occupy his whole mind at the time.
One day his successor suddenly entered his study. He found the aged
man with his hand placed under his head as the tears flowed down
his cheeks. He was startled, and asked him what was the matter. He
looked up with a dazed look, and then half recovering himself said, 'I
feel to the quick for the anxious and distracted mother, poor thing.'
'To whom do you refer?' asked his friend. Then suddenly wiping his
tears, and smiling, he replied, 'I was thinking about Mary and Joseph
losing the lad Jesus in Jerusalem when they took Him up for the first
time to the feast. It seemed to me as if I saw Mary quite bewildered
walking up and down the streets of Jerusalem, and the courts of the

Temple, and looking for her lad whom she loved so much. Oh, was it not something terrible to have lost *such* a son! I felt to the depths of my heart for her, and offered her my help. It was such a time, too, before she found Him! Yes, and I feel keenly for her still. But she found Him at last; and had she but thought of all she had been told concerning Him, she would have had no fear; for was not He the One that should redeem Israel? And yet we are far more foolish than Mary, for we often think we lose Him even now.'"

By this time the two friends had arrived at Horeb Chapel. Having greeted David Lewis, the village grocer, and a few others who stood near the door, they entered the sanctuary. There was a short pause before the meeting began, but soon the minister got up, and gave out a hymn—

> "Fy Mugail da! Mae'th lais o hyd
>   I'w glywed drwy holl leisiau'r byd,
> Yn galw'th braidd i'th gorlan glyd;
>   Fy Mogail da! rwyn dod."
> (Good Shepherd, mine! I hear Thy voice,
>   Mid earthly sounds, bid me rejoice
>   In that safe fold of Thine own choice;
>   Good Shepherd, mine! I come.)

Then followed the reading of the twenty-third Psalm—"The Lord is my Shepherd, I shall not want," &c. A prayer was offered by David Lewis, and another hymn was sung—

> "Y Bugail mwyn, o'r nef a ddaeth i lawr,
>   I geisio 'i braidd trwy'r erchyll anial mawr,
>   Ei fywyd roes yn aberth yn en lle.
>   A'u crwydriad hwy ddialwyd arno 'Fe."
> (The Shepherd kind from far off heaven came near,
>   To seek his flock in desert wide and drear,
>   His life He gave an offering in their stead.
>   And bore their sins on his devoted head.)

It was evident from the hymns sung and the Psalm read, as well as from the prayer offered by David Lewis, what the tone of the meeting was to be. The keynote had been struck, and already there was a glow of feeling which betokened a happy and profitable time. Indeed,

the minister usually gave a running comment on such occasions upon
the verses which he read at the commencement, by way of supplying
a leading theme for the conversation of the evening. Yet, as each
one spoke from his own experience, the conversations not
unfrequently diverged considerably from the lines laid down at the
outset. And it was often well that this should be so. On this occasion,
however, the theme seemed to have touched each heart, as had been
apparent from the earnest responses which the reading of the psalm
and the offering of the prayer called forth, as well as the great
heartiness with which the hymns were sung. Before the minister
got up, therefore, to speak a few introductory words, there was a
general expectation among those present of an inspiring message,
which made it an easy task for him to speak.

The minister stood up, and said: "I read at the commencement
of the meeting the twenty-third Psalm, or *The Sheep's Song.* It tells
us what the sheep has to say about its shepherd. David, I have no
doubt, as a shepherd lad often wondered what the sheep thought of
him, and what they would say about him if they could but speak.
They would, indeed, be poor, helpless creatures without him; he
wondered whether they knew it. He had on more than one occasion
endangered his life for a lamb of the flock. He wondered whether
the lamb took much note of that, and would out of sheer gratitude
grow up to be a good sheep, and never give any anxiety to the
shepherd for the rest of its life. It had by that deliverance become
doubly his. Would it rush again into danger, or would it keep close to
the shepherd's side? On the other hand there was an old sheep that
had cost him no end of anxiety; it was so fond of going on an exploring
expedition on its own account, and to lose its way in the attempt!
How often had he gone over hill and dale in pursuit of it! Some folk
had told him that he had worn out more clothes and spent more
vital energy in seeking that sheep and bringing it back again than it
was worth. Indeed, they had reminded him that it was getting
tougher and less woolly every time it wandered, and that there would
be but little left of it to bring back at last. But he felt that it was his
sheep still, and, foolish as it was, it was yet dear to him.

"Then he would think that there was a Divine Shepherd who felt
toward him just as he had felt toward his sheep. Indeed, the older
David got, and long after he ceased to be a shepherd, he felt the truth

of this more and more. All that he had been to his sheep, that, and much more, had the Divine Shepherd been to him. Yea, he had been a weak, helpless lamb, and how often had the great Shepherd snatched him from the very jaws of death! But he had since then sadly wandered; and it seemed to every one but the Good Shepherd that he was not worth all the trouble of bringing back again. Still that Shepherd had gone on seeking him until He found him. Indeed, at times when he had not gone astray, it was all through the special care of his Shepherd. His only joy as he reviewed the past, and his only confidence as he anticipated the future, was his Shepherd's ceaseless care of him.

"The first assurance that David had from the knowledge that God was his Shepherd was 'I shall not want.' He might have said, 'I am king, and have untold wealth, and am surrounded by a loyal army and a loving people, I shall not want.' But he did not say that. Kings, once as mighty as he was, had been known to suffer want. There was no certainty in being a king that he should not want. The only sufficient guarantee against want was that God was his Shepherd.

"Now he tells us first of all what his Shepherd did for him—'He maketh me to lie down in green pastures.' The sheep has a keen eye for the tender grass, but the Shepherd still keener. He well knows the best spots of pasture in the whole neighbourhood, and takes his sheep there. He also makes them 'lie down' even there where the grass is most tempting. You farmers and shepherds know that the sheep lies down when it has had enough. David's Shepherd made him lie down in *green pastures,* took him to the freshest herbage and satisfied him there. The Good Shepherd never stints His sheep.

"Again, 'He leadeth me beside the still waters,' or, according to the margin, 'waters of quietness'—that is, not stagnant waters, but waters that come and go gently and noiselessly. The sheep, as many of you know full well, are timid of noise. They are to be seen in a quiet nook, beneath the shadow of a tree or great rock, not by the bounding brook that skips noisily over its stony staircase, but near the quiet restful pool whose gentle waters mirror the serene heavens above, and the peaceful scene around. Besides, a shepherd once told me that sheep seldom, if ever, drink from the noisy brook. It terrifies them. They can only drink from the quiet, noiseless stream; and surely David refers to that here.

"But the sheep, too, often wanders; and David did. David refers to that experience when he next speaks about his Shepherd, 'He restoreth my soul.' It is notorious that there is no creature so apt to wander, and so helpless in its wanderings, as the sheep. It foolishly leaves the green pastures and the still waters. Yet the shepherd is mindful of his own, and, seeking it, brings it back again. 'That,' says David, 'is just what my Shepherd has done with me.'"

"Bless Him," interjected Blind Betty.

"Nor does the Shepherd's care end with simple restoration but, after the restoration, He grants special guidance. He is specially watchful over the sheep that is most apt to wander. 'He guideth* me,' exclaims David, 'in the paths of righteousness for His name s sake.' The *'leading'* of the second verse becomes *'guiding'* now after the wandering. There is need of closer attention, and the Good Shepherd does not begrudge it. He, who formerly 'led' the way, now 'guides in' it.

"Hearken again—'for His Name's sake.' He has a name to lose though the sheep has not. He will never have it said that, as a Shepherd, He has lost one of His flock. Did not the great Shepherd exclaim of old, 'Those that Thou gavest Me I have kept, and none of them is lost'? 'What wilt Thou do to Thy great Name?' asked Joshua of God. There was no other name at stake; but His was. The Rev. Dr. Owen Thomas, of Liverpool, once asked a dying saint whether she was perfectly restful and calm. She replied, 'Oh, yes, I believed Him at His word; and it will be worse for Him than it can be for me if He breaks His word, though it be but once. He has never done it yet, and He is not going to begin now.' Then, turning on her bed she smiled and said, '"I know whom I have believed, and am persuaded that he is able to keep that which I have committed unto Him against that day."'"

"Bendigedig," exclaimed Shadrach, and John nodded a vigorous assent.

"But I must proceed," continued the minister. "David adds, 'Yea, though I walk through the valley of the shadow of death, I will fear no evil. Most people believe that this refers to the last experiences of life, when the godly man is about to die. Bunyan, on the contrary,

---

* This is the Welsh rendering ("a'm harwain"), thus, as in many other instances, anticipating the English Revised Version.

SHEPHERD AND SHEEP

represented Christian as passing through it very early on his pilgrimage. There can be no doubt that it refers to some special season of trial and darkness.

"This comes to men at different times. But it is quite natural for most of us to look upon the last experiences through which we have to pass in dying as 'The Valley of the Shadow of Death,' although to many others that valley is lit up from end to end. Bunyan's 'Valley of the Shadow of Death' was reached by Christian very soon after he left the House called Beautiful. But, whatever dark experience we have to pass through, we need not fear if the Lord is our Shepherd. What is faith worth if it does not trust in the dark?"

"What, indeed!" responded Blind Betty.

"No doubt," continued the minister, "David well remembered some deep gorge among the hills of Judæa through which he had led his flock safely. To him that represented the trying passes, especially the last through which the great Shepherd led His sheep. He who had done so much already for His sheep would not fail them then.

"'I will fear no evil, for Thou art with me,' exclaims David. The sheep would be a poor creature without the Shepherd in such a place; but He who had been with His sheep in green pastures, and beside the still waters, would also enter the deep gorge, and go right through the dark ravine with it. Ah! my brethren, the old Valley of Death itself has never been so dark since the Good Shepherd Himself passed through it as it was before that."

"Very true," murmured John with a smile.

"How many a time," added the minister "since then has He accompanied others along that dark and lonely path! We are most of us afraid of death; but we have seen some timid ones enter the valley; and when they have all but passed through it, they have called back to us just as they were crossing the river at the other end, bidding us be of good cheer, since the valley was not dark at all with Jesus in it, and the River of Death neither cold nor deep with Him near. As in the case of Mr. Fearing, of whom grand John Bunyan speaks, when they came to cross it, 'The water was lower than it was ever seen before.' But, there, I must say no more—though I have said nothing about the 'rod' and 'staff' and much besides. There are many here, I doubt not, who will have much to say about them, and would like to tell us something about the Good Shepherd—how He found them in their wanderings, and how He has since then guided and protected them even unto this hour. Only let us not wait for each other, but each one tell out what is on his mind as opportunity offers."

As the minister had proceeded the responses had become more and more audible and frequent, especially as he spoke of the Good Shepherd's care of His sheep in the dark valley.

Blind Betty, who generally nodded her head when anything good was said, had repeatedly exclaimed, "Bless Him!" when the minister spoke of Jesus lighting up the darkest valley with His loving presence. Indeed, it would seem to anyone who looked at Betty then as if a light more radiant than even the light of the sun had lit up her blind eyes from within. There was a gleam of rapture, too, in the face which no outward circumstance could explain. Betty found her own dark valley very bright just then.

David William, of Ty-mawr, too, appeared in a wonderfully joyous mood for him. David was always very vigorous in utterance; but not always tender or even considerate. He was, however, intensely devout. He was always the first to walk steadily and resolutely through the village, neither turning to the right nor to the left, whenever there was a meeting to be held at Horeb. He saluted no one by the way beyond a vigorous nod of the head and a "Good morning" or "Good night." When people saw him pass they knew it would be time for them by-and-by to think of getting ready. He was looked upon by all as the forerunner of the service, announcing by his steady onward step that it was about to be held, and that it was time for them to prepare. He was the dread of the chapel-keeper, if he chanced to be late in opening the doors. He also entertained hard views of those who came late to the house of God. "The Psalmist," he used to say, "exclaimed, 'Praise *waiteth* for Thee, O God, in Zion.' David," he added, "was not one of those who came into the house of God puffing helplessly when the first hymn was being sung; much less did he arrive after it had been finished. He was there in good time tuning his harp—and his heart too—so that every string should be in tune, and ready for the first burst of praise that would go forth to God." Indeed, David William believed that "sometimes David would find all that he could do in keeping his fingers still after he had tuned his harp; and that at such times he would say, 'Praise *waiteth* for Thee, O God, in Zion:' in other words, 'Here it is ready

to leap out of every string, and my fingers tingle to let it free. It
waiteth for Thee; and longs to quiver on the harpstrings.'" Thus
David William had a grand opinion of his great Jewish namesake,
and a very poor opinion of those who, if they brought harps at all
with them to the house of God, brought them "with half the strings
gone, and the other half wretchedly out of tune."

It was not to be wondered, therefore, that David's tenderest and
sweetest psalm had touched even old David William on this occasion.
But even in his tenderest moods he was rigidly doctrinal. The great
thing that had charmed him about this Psalm was the assurance
which he found in it of the Final Perseverance of the Saints"—"He
restoreth my soul," and God's elective and protecting love—"Thy
rod and Thy staff, they comfort me."

Thus David William stood up suddenly in his accustomed place;
then stooping slightly, and closing his eyes as he leaned upon the
edge of the big pew, exclaimed, "Dear me, when we come to think of
it, what poor things sheep are! There's no one here who does not
know that. The only thing they are clever at is wandering. They have
never been known to find their way back—at least, I never heard of
a case, though I own a good number of sheep, and I do not suppose
they are more stupid than other people's. They can only bleat, and
go further astray. Their only hope is in the watchfulness of the
shepherd. It's just so with us. Our only hope is in the care of our
Shepherd. Once we are His there is no fear that we shall be lost.
Why, if the Great Shepherd only lost one of His sheep, He would
never hear the last of it. The devil would shout it exultantly through
all the caverns of hell, *'Jesus has lost one of His sheep!'* and all
perdition would resound with applause. But thanks be to God, our
Good Shepherd can still say what He said in the days of His flesh—
yea, and He will be able to say it to all eternity—'Those that Thou
gavest me I have kept.' When we wander He comes after us till He
finds us. He never gives up the search till we are safe in His grasp
again. This is my only hope; but that is enough—'He restoreth my
soul.' Once in His flock we always bear His mark. This, no doubt,
was what David meant by 'Thy rod . . . comforts me.' I could not
understand how the rod could comfort the sheep until I learnt that
David referred there to the counting rod, which reckoned each sheep,
as it passed under, as one of the flock. That is what Moses must have

meant by, 'Whatsoever (of the flock) passeth under the rod.' Ah! when we are permitted to pass under His rod, that is when He reckons us *as His own:* He never loses sight of us after that. Let us praise Him, and never trust to our own way, or have any confidence in the flesh, for, apart from His protection and guidance, we should rush every one of us through the first gap in the hedge which we could find."

All felt how much of truth old David William had spoken; and yet there might have been traced an unconscious smile on the face of John Vaughan and one or two others, who noted with what relish the good old hyper-Calvinist got foul, even in his most devout moments, of what he deemed to be Arminian tenets and tendencies.

John Vaughan—having been brought up in his earliest days among the Calvinistic Methodists, who, at that time, were very extreme Calvinists: but having early in life changed his views regarding baptism, and joined the Baptists—had undergone a reaction doctrinally. He thought hyper-Calvinism very extreme and mischievous; still he had great sympathies with moderate Calvinism, and as years passed by leaned more strongly towards it, so that what David William called "John's Arminianism," became more and more modified. John's growing experience, too, softened greatly the acerbity of his earlier style of combating hyper-Calvinism. Indeed, he had long since lost faith in doctrinal hair-splitting at the Fellowship Meeting, where men had met together to commune with the Saviour, and with each other. There was no temptation, therefore, for John to combat David William; nor had the latter ever dreamt that he had been talking doctrinally. Moreover, John felt that all that David said was very true, only, perhaps, they would not agree if they were to go too much into particulars. One thing John was very certain of, that David William was quite right when he said that the sheep owed all their safety to the Shepherd for he was only saying what David the Psalmist had said before him; and, for the matter of that, what John's own experience, and David William's, he felt sure, had proved to be true a thousand times.

David, therefore, had no sooner sat down than John got up, and continued—"I am sure that we all feel with David William that our only hope is in the watchfulness and protection of our Great Shepherd. We never learn that thoroughly, however, till we travel through some awful pass, which is to us The Valley of the Shadow of Death. It is then that we learn that He has a rod and staff. The rod, as David William said, which once numbered us, is carried by Him in the darkness, and if we go but a step out of the path we feel it placed gently against our sides, or its crook round our necks, to bring us back again. We soon learn that He is carrying His staff, too, in the gloom, by the heavy thud we now and then hear when He strikes our hidden foes—terrible beasts of prey—on the head, with such terrific force that their skulls cave in once for all. Ah, we little knew our spiritual enemies were so near, or so powerful, until we heard the terrific blow that was necessary to put them down. Yes; it is in the dark valley that His rod and staff comfort us. In times of sunshine, and out on the green meadows, or by the still waters, we are not so much in need of them; but in trial and sorrow and dark temptation they are of priceless value. And, dear brethren, there is no valley of shadows without His rod and staff. They are the Shepherd's grand compensations for the gloom and danger through which we have to pass.

"He never fails us in the darkest experiences of life. He is always better than His promise, and infinitely better than our hopes. Caleb Rhys told some of us a touching story the other night. He had heard it at Barmouth on one of his journeys selling flannel. He told us that at the foot of Cader Idris, on a small holding, there live—or at least there recently lived—an old man, his aged wife, and a devoted daughter. Not long since the old farmer and his wife promised £5 towards building a new chapel in connection with the church of which they were members. They made this promise expecting to realise that amount chiefly by the sale of a calf. But a short time before the opening of the chapel, when the money was to be paid, the calf died, and, although the old couple scraped together all they could, they only got £2 10s. The chapel was to be opened in a few weeks. The poor old farmer and his wife became very anxious, and often prayed together that the Lord would enable them to fulfil their promise. There was at length but a fortnight left, and on one afternoon a terrible thunderstorm burst upon the Cader, and the rain came down in torrents. The gloomy surroundings and the heavy atmosphere did much to depress the aged couple. It seemed to them as if the Lord had forgotten to be gracious, and as if there was no way of escape. They once more united in earnest prayer. They had barely got up from their knees when suddenly there was a knock at the door. When it was opened a Welsh guide, and an English gentleman and his family entered drenched to the skin. They sought shelter. They were sent to bed and wrapped in Welsh blankets while their clothes were dried. They were further supplied liberally with Welsh broth; and then when dressed were made to sit around the fire which burned brightly upon the old-fashioned hearth. At length when about to leave, the gentleman placed £2 10s. upon the table and explained to the guide that one sovereign was for the old man, the other for his aged wife, and the half sovereign to their devoted daughter who had vied with her parents in their kindness to strangers. The old farmer looked on; but not understanding English, he asked the guide, 'What does he say?' (Beth mae o'n ddeud?') The guide repeated in Welsh what the gentleman had said. But he no sooner uttered the words than the old man and his wife burst into tears and sobbed aloud. The gentleman was amazed and perplexed, and asked the guide what all that meant. The guide inquired in Welsh, and then the story was told by the old farmer, and the surprise expressed that they should have ever doubted their good Lord. When all was translated to the English visitor, he gently brushed aside the gold he had already given, and said that he had given that for their personal use, and taking £2 10s. more from his purse, he added, 'This is to enable you to fulfil your vows unto the Lord. I, also, have been poor, and now am rich; and I, too, love the Lord Jesus, and among the greatest joys of my life is this which you have placed within my reach'; and then he bade him and his be of good cheer for God would never fail to reward their trust."

"Gogoniant," exclaimed blind Betty; and there were murmuring echoes all over the chapel as strong men wept with joy.

John Vaughan added tremulously: "There is another thing about this Psalm that always strikes me, and our minister has to-night hinted at it. It is this—How wonderfully David was helped to understand God's kindness and patience towards him by his own experience as a shepherd-boy! David was a man who grew his own theology; and there is as much difference between home-grown theology and that learnt from books, as there is between vegetables grown in our own garden and those stale things which always appear to me as a compromise between leather and indiarubber, but are sold for vegetables in town shops. Or, to change the figure, David's theology in this Psalm is homespun, and homespun theology is like homespun cloth—there's no end of wear in it. The nap does not wear off like that on the 'superfine' cloth sold in Carmarthen to the gentry. The homespun cloth is made to 'wear,' the superfine to 'wear *out.*' David's theology here was homespun. For instance, he had done daring things for the sake of the lambs of his flock, and that had helped him better to realise what the Great Shepherd had done for him.

"Yes, and I have no doubt that there were some tiresome sheep that cost David endless trouble, like that 'one-horned sheep,' which Dr. William Rees in his later years used to say was the only trouble of his youthful days as a shepherd-boy on the hills of Hiraethog. How pathetically and quaintly he speaks in his 'Recollections of Childhood and Youth' about this! He tells us that in those early days he and his dog Tango were the happiest companions in all the country. They were both equally ignorant of the sorrows of life. Apart from that one-horned sheep, which he tells us was to them a perpetual care, they would have both been perfectly happy. Hence he loved to the last to visit the mountain slopes where he and Tango used to watch the sheep long ago.*

"He also tells us that, like David, he was taken from watching the sheep of his father's flock to be shepherd of the Lord's flock— His Holy Church—on Mount Zion. In later years, even in watching over the Great Shepherd's flock, he met now and then with a tiresome sheep that gave him great trouble, and reminded him painfully of the old 'one-horned sheep' of his early days. But it was by these experiences that he learnt, as he never could otherwise, the meaning of all the trouble he had experienced as a shepherd lad with that mischievous 'one-horned sheep.' He learnt, so he tells us, what he had little thought of amid his youthful worries—that Providence had a hand in sending that 'one-horned sheep' into his flock; that light crosses were placed upon his small, weak, and youthful shoulder, in

---

* "'Awn i rodio hyfryd fryniau
    Heu gynnefin praidd fy nhad,
  Lle bu Tango 'r ci a minnau,
    'R ddau ddedwyddaf yn y wlad;
  Mi ni wyddwn mwy na Thango,
    Am ofidiau bywyd gau,
  On' bai'r ddafad ungorn hono,
    Buasem berffaith ddedwydd ddau.'

order that he might be the better prepared to carry heavier crosses by-and-by as an under-shepherd of the Lord's own flock.*

"Now, just as the Lord had taught this and other lessons to Dr. Rees by his shepherd experiences when a lad, so, depend upon it, He taught David much that he tells us in this Psalm. David, as a boy, no doubt had an awkward sheep to deal with now and then—a sheep that at times required a great deal of patience on the part of the youthful shepherd. It would be always going astray and losing itself, and then would bleat stupidly among the thorns and bramble bushes, until the shepherd, after weary search, found it bleeding, and carried it back again. For a time—especially when it was brought back, and all the sheep would look at it in wonderment as it was placed once more among them, in a very different plight from that in which it left them—the old sheep would seem to be thoroughly ashamed of itself; yet, as the wounds began to heal and the wool again grew, hiding the ugly scars, it would again set to wandering, and the same story would soon be repeated. David would feel no doubt, as our pastor has told us, that really the old sheep got tougher and less woolly each time it wandered, and that for its real value it was not worth all the trouble it cost; yet he felt that it belonged to his flock, and as such was dear to him, and so he would go, time after time, in search of that silly sheep.

---

* "'Minnau ddygwyd, megys Dafydd,
    I fugeilio'r defaid mân,
  I fugeilio ar Sïon fynydd,
    Braidd yr Iôn—ei eglwys lân:
Mi gyfarfum. gallaf gwyno,
    Ambell ddiriad ddyn di 'ras,
Barai imi fynych gofio
    Am y ddafad ungorn gas.

"Ni feddyliwn fod bryd hyny
    Gan Ragluniaeth ddoeth y nen,
Law mewn amgylchiadau felly,
    A bwriadau iw dwyn i ben—
Gosod croesau ysgeifn, hynod,
    Ar fy ysgwydd fechan, wan,
Er fy mharotoi i gyfarfod
    Croesau trymach yn y man.'

"Ah, little did David the shepherd boy know that all the while he was learning by experience how the Lord, his Shepherd, would feel towards him when, later on in life, and when he ought to have known better, he would wander as he never did when he was a lamb. It surely could not be because of any special worth in him that the Great Shepherd would take such trouble over him, for he was one of the silliest of all the flock; but He restored him because of His own shepherdly tenderness towards even the worst of His sheep, and because His own honour was at stake if He lost even the most worthless that was entrusted to Him—'He guideth me in the paths of righteousness *for His name's sake.'* That's exactly it. If David had not been a shepherd himself, he would not have found out the secret of the Lord's patience towards him half so readily. What a blessing it is that we are not treated according to our deserts, any more than the wandering sheep is treated according to its merits!"

Shadrach Morgan—who had evidently been greatly interested in all that had been said, especially in what his friend John had stated about Dr. Rees, as a shepherd lad, and his dog Tango—got up as soon as John Vaughan had sat down, and said in tremulous and tearful, though joyous, tones: "Brethren it is good for us to be here. How pleasant it is for us, when thus safely folded from all harm, to have sweet converse about our Great Shepherd, and all that He is to us! I have been very pleased with what John Vaughan has just told us about Gwilym Hiraethog* and his dog Tango. I heard John once say that in the East shepherds have no dogs, as they go out before the sheep, and they follow. I fear a shepherd could not do much in this country without a sheep-dog. We seem to have a very different sort of sheep, or they have got into very different habits, from those in Palestine. I fear, too, that most of us are in this respect more like Welsh sheep than those we read of in the New Testament; for even the Great Shepherd has to use sheep-dogs with us. That I know. I know, too, that He has to send His sheep-dog often after me."

"And after me, blind as I am!" ejaculated blind Betty.

"Yes, and there are others like us if they would only speak out," responded Shadrach. Here responses of approval were loud and frequent from all parts of the chapel. "I thought so," added Shadrach.

---

* Dr. William Rees's *nom de plume.*

BLIND BETTY

"I expect we all know something about the bite of the sheep-dog. So that, whatever may be said of the Eastern shepherd in this respect, it is very evident that our Great Shepherd has sheep-dogs, aye, and a good number, too, for us. For instance, there's the sheep-dog of poverty, and the sheep-dog of disappointment, and that other sheep-dog of sickness, and that other sheep-dog of bereavement." Here nods of approval were given, as each trial was mentioned, from those who had evidently felt, the bite of that particular sheep-dog. "Yes," said Shadrach, "and a good many more."

"Blindness," responded blind Betty, as her dim eye became luminous with tears.

"And lameness," exclaimed William John, Ty-isaf, who generally took an hour to walk the mile between his house and Horeb.

This was too much for Shadrach. Tears filled his eyes, and a great lump in his throat choked utterance. With supreme effort, and in tremulous tones, however, he added, "Yes, thank the Lord for them, I do not know what would have become of us if these sheep-dogs had not sometimes tripped us up and driven us hack to the Great Shepherd."

Shadrach had evidently touched a chord that vibrated readily in the hearts of all present. All who had some special trial or sorrow seemed to be more reconciled to them for what Shadrach in his warm enthusiastic fashion had said. How easy it was for them to bear the bite of poverty, pain, disappointment, bereavement, and of many other trials, once they were convinced that these were but sheep-dogs sent by the Great Shepherd to bring them back from their wanderings, and to keep them nearer to Himself. There are some sheep, doubtless, who scarcely need these severe measures; but those who were present at the Fellowship Meeting seemed to feel that they were not among that number.

Even Evan Richard, the old mountain shepherd, who seldom spoke, got up. He was much moved by all that had been said that night, and now exclaimed, "Dear brethren, there's more Gospel teaching in keeping sheep than I had ever thought, although I had always felt there was a great deal. Every shepherd knows the value of a sheep-dog, although I have no doubt the sheep would be glad to be rid of it, and go on wandering to their heart's content. Ah, as David William said, sheep are poor silly creatures. It only requires a sheep to rush through a bit of a gap in the hedge, and thus tear off half its wool, to induce all the others to follow, and so make the gap wider and wider each time. They have no better reason to give than that some silly sheep has set them the example. Indeed, if one sheep happens to jump over some real or imaginary stone or stump, every other sheep jumps precisely at the same place, and to the same height, even though there should be no longer anything to jump over. I often think how much like them we are. It only requires that some self-made leader should give the example in going astray, for all the rest to do precisely the same, for no better reason than that the first did it. Our only safety is to keep near the Shepherd, and pay little heed to what others do."

The time for closing the Fellowship meeting had now come. The minister, therefore, at the conclusion of Evan Richard's short address, got up and said: "Dear brethren, every shepherd is a poet; yet every poet is not literally a shepherd, although I think there must be a great deal of the shepherdly nature in him. David was a shepherd and a poet. There is a wonderful amount of poetry, and as Evan Richard has just said, a great deal of Gospel teaching, connected with keeping sheep. In this Psalm we find both. Here we have the godly life set to music. Of course, it is the story of restoration, and of the Divine Shepherd's protection and care after the restoration of the wandering sheep, that we find here. But in view of this restoration David could have even set the wandering to music had he so wished, just as Handel in his 'Messiah' has so harmonised those words, 'All we like sheep have gone astray; we have turned every one to his own way,' that as we hear the music we seem to see them scattering, and one sheep after another wandering away along its own path. This is so striking and vivid that I am quite sure Evan Richard, if he heard the music, would immediately call for his sheep-dog, and be impatient to bring the silly sheep back at once."

This remark was received with a smile by all present. Evan's smile, however, appeared somewhat sceptical, as if he thought that he was far too experienced a shepherd to be so taken in by a mere trick of music by a man whose name he had never heard before. Even the Welsh bards, with their grand inspiring songs to the accompaniment of the harp, could not have made him so self-forgetful as that; and if they couldn't it was not likely that any singer who wasn't a Welsh musician could—so Evan evidently thought.

The minister proceeded—"We have heard a great deal about the wandering sheep. How true it is that the more we wander from the Shepherd's flock the more prone we are to do it again! I verily think that the more we wander the tougher our hides and feet become, and therefore we feel less the sharp touch of the thorn and bramble, and of the many stones along the rough paths we tread when we go astray from God. It is not at once that we go far astray. At first when we wander we feel, as the Rev. Joseph Evans used to say, like the child who has to walk a rough path barefooted for the first time. He feels keenly every little stone upon which he treads; but by long practice his feet may become so hard that he can dance upon the roughest path without the slightest inconvenience. Or we are like the young thief who after the first theft feels the compunctions of conscience, and complains to an old, hardened thief that his conscience troubles him because he has stolen another man's goods. The old practised thief smiles at the sensitiveness of the younger one, and tells him to steal again, and yet again, as soon as he can, so that he may lose that feeling. That is the course he must take if he would be hardened to indifference. That, brethren, was also the way in which we once hardened ourselves in our wanderings, so that we ceased to feel as we formerly did. But, thank God, we were at length brought to a terrible pass, in which even we were terrified and subdued, and then, when we were hopeless and undone, the Great Shepherd Himself appeared, and delivered us from death, and carried us back to His fold. Since then the devil has often reminded us of our wanderings, and will do so, probably, to the last; but if God be for us, who can be against us?

"Ah, brethren, our hope is in the Great Shepherd who has laid down His life for the sheep, and who, having risen from the dead, watches over us with loving and ceaseless solicitude. If we were ever left to ourselves, it would be a sad affair. Adam, sinless as he was, had the opportunity once of taking care of himself, and a poor job he made of it. Thank God that our salvation is in our Good Shepherd's hands; and 'He is able to save to the uttermost them that draw near unto God through Him, seeing He ever liveth to make intercession for them.'"

A short prayer, and then a hymn sung, brought the Fellowship Meeting to a close. The closing hymn, like those which were sung at the commencement, dwelt appropriately upon the theme which had engaged all thoughts that evening—

"Fy Mugail, fy niwallu wna,
    Fy rhan, Jehofah yw;
Mewn porfa fras ymborthi ca'
    Wrth ffrydiau dyfroedd byw."
        &c., &c.
("My Shepherd will my need supply,
    My lot Jehovah is;
In pastures green He makes me lie
    By peaceful streams of bliss.")

This hymn, which throughout is an excellent rendering in Welsh of the Twenty-third Psalm, was sung vigorously to the old tune "French."

The little company, having exchanged greetings and farewells, and thus having so blended and interwoven with each other in ever-varying groups as to supply an interesting lesson on the surprising possibilities of "permutations and combinations," gradually separated. But still along the road there were groups of twos and threes of fellow-pilgrims on their way homeward. Evan Richard, the old shepherd, who spent almost all his time with his sheep among the mountains, and was seldom seen in the village, save for the services held at Horeb—who also generally, at the close of the meetings, was in a hurry to return to his lonely home in a distant glen—seemed to be in less haste that night than at other times. The theme of the meeting, being so familiar and sacred to him, had greatly charmed him, and, drawing near to John Vaughan and Shadrach Morgan as they reached the road that passed by Horeb, he gave expression to the joy of his heart as he said: "John, this meeting is worth walking many a mile for. I shall often think of it among my sheep."

"I have no doubt you will," interjected Shadrach. "It would have been a pity, Evan, if you had missed this."

"Ah, your work after all, Evan, must often remind you of the Good Shepherd and His sheep," exclaimed John. "I suppose when a wayward sheep has gone astray, you don't say, 'There, let it go for all I care, it is a greater bother than it's worth.'"

"Bless you, no," exclaimed Evan. "It's a strange thing that the more you have risked of danger for the sake of a lamb or sheep, or the more trouble it has cost you, the greater the value you seem to put upon it. A

"MY LAD WENT BAREFOOTED ALONG THE NARROW LEDGE OF A ROCK, AND TORE HIS CLOTHES TO TATTERS IN ORDER TO SAVE A LAMB THAT HAD GOT FIXED IN A THICKET"

few weeks ago my lad went barefooted along the narrow ledge of a rock, and tore his clothes to tatters in order to save a lamb that had got fixed in a thicket which overhung a precipice; and bless you that lamb has been everything to the boy ever since. I have often thought that David must have set a big price upon the lamb that he delivered from the paw of the lion or bear. Yes, and even if some old wanderer had often got into dangerous places among the rocks and precipices, and thus cost him great trouble and anxiety he would always have a sneaking tendency to think that that old sheep was worth more than anyone else who knew its tricks would think it was. I know I have often felt so, and I expect David did. I am sure that the Great Shepherd thinks much of the wandering sheep He has saved, and watches over it with all the greater care because He has done and suffered so much for it. The more I learn about what the Great Shepherd of the sheep has done for me, the more confident I am that He will never lose His shepherdly interest in me. Ah, and once we have been carried back on His shoulders—*shoulders,* notice, not on *one shoulder,* but on both, and not with our heads hanging down, as some think—once we have known what that means by personal experience, we shall never lose confidence in His care of us, or in the strength of His shoulders to carry us."

"Ah, that's it," responded John enthusiastically. "That is very much like what I heard the Rev. David Jones, of Treborth, once say. He described the Great Shepherd in all ages seeking His lost sheep; for instance, in Egypt and Babylon, and indeed wherever they had gone astray, adding that His shepherdly cry in all ages has been, even when His under-shepherds have forgotten their duty, 'Behold, I Myself, even I, will search for My sheep, and will seek them out. As a shepherd seeketh out his flock in the day that he is among his sheep that is scattered abroad, so will I seek out My sheep; and I will deliver them out of all places whither they have been scattered in the cloudy and dark day . . . and I will feed them on the mountains of Israel, by the water-courses, and in all the inhabited places of the country. I will feed them with good pasture, and upon the mountains of the height of Israel shall their fold be; there shall they lie down in a good fold, and on fat pasture shall they feed on the mountains of Israel. I, Myself, will feed My sheep, and I will cause them to lie down, saith the Lord.' Then Mr. Jones proceeded to say that the Good Shepherd not only went in search of *the flock* when it went astray, but also of *every sheep* that wandered in the loneliness and hopelessness of its wanderings, and brought it back upon 'His own shoulders.' As you say, Evan, how gracious and kind it is of the Great Shepherd to lay us gently on both His shoulders, where we can perfectly rest on His Almightiness! Well, the preacher went on to say that He who measured the waters in *the hollow of His hand,* and gathered the wind in *His fists,* and held the deep places of the earth in *His hand,* places the poor wandering sheep on *His shoulders.* He then added, in tones which I shall never forget: 'O, thou poor wounded and helpless sheep, now that the Great Shepherd has found thee, thou art resting on the strongest place that even God Himself owns—*His very shoulders.* Thou canst never sink there; for they can never give way beneath thee.'"

"Thank the Lord!" exclaimed Evan Richard. "That is enough. We can hear nothing better than that to-night, John. Good-night, my dear fellow; you have given me something to think about on my journey home to-night."

The crossways in the middle of the village where Shadrach's smithy stood had now been reached; and, as Shadrach and John were as little disposed as Evan to say any more just then, the three parted for the night.

CHAPTER VII

John Vaughan and his friends Hay-making

T an early day in the month of July, as the hay-harvest was fast approaching, Hugh Roberts of Pentre-mawr, sent a message to John, Shadrach, and other villagers to ask them to oblige him by giving him a day's hay-making. John owed a few days for some oats supplied him, and Shadrach owed a few for hay which he had bought of Hugh Roberts for his cow, back in the winter. There were others in the village who owed a day or more in return for butter and other commodities received from Pentre-mawr. Even Llewelyn Pugh, the schoolmaster now that it was holiday-time, had responded readily to Hugh Roberts' appeal for help. Thus, on the morning specified, quite a company of men and women, and not a few boys and girls of tender age, who were thrown into the bargain as being worth just the food they consumed (although this throwing in was a questionable boon to the farmer), went along the familiar lane that passed the smithy toward the hayfield. Shadrach and Mary Morgan and their son Jenkin were the last to join the company.

When they had reached Pentre-mawr, and joined Hugh Roberts and his servants, as well as others who had come from the neighbourhood, a bright and merry-looking procession, carrying rakes as soldiers carry bayonets, advanced toward the hayfield, sometimes in solid file, at other

ON THE WAY TO THE HAYFIELD

times, when the whim took the children, in two companies—one consisting of the boys and girls, who rushed on in hot pursuit, in anticipation of the joys of the hayfield, while the other consisted of the parents, who still proceeded with steady step, deeming it prudent to reserve their strength for the later and somewhat unfamiliar tasks of the day; for this was the first time that most of them had been hay-making since the preceding summer. To all, however, hay-making was a

pleasant and welcome, although a tiring occupation, and when they
had entered the hayfield they set to work with a heart.

There are few sights in summer to compare with that of a harvest-
field—a hayfield none the less than a cornfield. Indeed, in some
respects, the hayfield, before machines had come into fashion, took
the palm, for it supplied scope for the endless activities and
inexhaustible energies of the children, who, without learning much
of the art of hay-making, could toss the hay to their hearts' content,
and thus performed a useful service—not to emphasise the occasional
tumble in the hay, which was an amusement of which they never
grew weary. Of course there was a limit to the erratic movements of
the children, even in the hayfield; but there was at least sufficient
scope there for the exercise of their surplus energies to add greatly
to the liveliness and variety of movement which usually characterised
hay-making. Thus the whole scene in former times presented a very
bright and festive aspect.

Next to the joy of tossing the hay and tumbling in it, perhaps the
part which boys and girls liked most was to tread it down on the
waggon or in the hay-rick; but here again they had to be checked
somewhat in their youthful enthusiasm, and made to remain in the
centre, because of the danger, especially on the loaded waggons, of
falling over. This, however, they were generally glad to do, for the
pleasure of treading the hay under, and the delight of being carried
on the top of the load to the farmyard. The writer has vivid memories
of those delights of boyhood, and can even now feel something of the
thrill of joy he often experienced on the loaded waggon, or the proud
and swelling hay-rick, that needed a great deal of treading down to
keep it in its place, and much trimming to prevent its becoming top-
heavy. These delights are largely now only the delights of memory,
except in out-of-the-way spots among the hills of Wales; for machinery
has taken away the poetry of the hayfield, and where there is no
poetry children have no wish to be.

Mercifully, when John Vaughan, Shadrach Morgan, and their wives
and children were wont to go forth to the harvest-fields, rattling
machinery had not monopolised the scene. Then there was scope for a
little humanity, and grateful and festive mirth, in gathering in the
fruit of the field; now there is only room for a horse, and a machine of
startling appearance and of inexplicable movement, at the summit of

which is a seat for a solitary man who, with a whip in his hand and a
pipe in his mouth, drives hither and thither, all the while inverting a
time-honoured custom—for he, instead of carrying his scythe or rake,
is forsooth carried by them. The only creature who works now right
earnestly in many a harvest-field is the horse, who patiently trundles
a machine; while the man, sitting in royal state, looks on and cracks
his whip for a diversion. The rich and varied humanity which added a
charm to former harvest-fields has in many instances, disappeared
from them for ever. The ringing voices of children, and the melodious
undertone of men and women's voices, at the time when the joy of
harvest possessed them, have given way to the crack of the whip, the
clank of chains, and the rattle of cogs—sounds which neither heaven
nor earth can accept as in the least expressive of the joys of harvest.
This may be necessary; so presumably are the smoke and poisonous
fumes which have blighted the rich luxuriance, and silenced the songs
of merry birds, in some of the loveliest valleys in Wales.

It is well, therefore, that the story of former days should be
sometimes repeated, and that the experience of John Vaughan and
his compeers should be fondly told.

That morning the field immediately beneath Pentre-mawr Farm
presented a pretty sight. Young and old, male and female, in quaint
garbs of varied hue and shape, vied with each other in the activities
of the hayfield. They all seemed to be mindful of the old Welsh proverb,
"Woe to the idler during harvest" ("Gwae oferwr yn nghynhauaf"),
and no one seemed disposed to win for himself that reputation or
retribution. Thus, in spite of the increasing heat as the day advanced,
operations were at their full swing until old Hugh Roberts, generous
and kind-hearted soul, bade them halt about twelve o'clock for
refreshments and a few minutes' rest in a corner of the field.

This was a welcome pause to all, and the drink, which consisted
of either oatmeal-water or milk and water—for Hugh Roberts was a
rigid, old-fashioned teetotaller—was extremely welcome to the thirsty
harvesters. The wheaten cakes were consumed voraciously by the
children and all that the elder ones had left of drink in the jugs was
also speedily appropriated by that youthful tribe, whose hunger could
only be equalled by their thirst. The sight of their activity in this
direction would have suggested to a less generous soul than Hugh
Roberts the question whether it was economical to have children of

varying ages in the harvest field on any terms. There were, however, many mothers present who could not have come had not the children been freely admitted. Thus the restless, hungry, and thirsty youngsters had to be taken "for better, for worse;" and they were evidently more than satisfied with the arrangement.

Soon again the field was full of activity; men, women and children went to and fro vigorously tossing the hay with their rakes as they went, each one, meanwhile, snatching a brief conversation with his neighbour as best he could. An occasional cross-firing of words also, as the more jocular of the company passed each other, helped to impart vivacity and brightness to their operations. It would have been an interesting study to a keen observer to note the triumph of the law of affinity all over the field. By its mysterious and subtle workings, Jenkin found himself always near Margaret, the miller's daughter, and other honest and innocent swains, by the operation of the same beneficent law, found themselves next to the blushing damsels whom they loved best.

That law was equally unerring in its application to John Vaughan, Shadrach Morgan, and Llewelyn Pugh, for this redoubtable trio were ever found together ; and not unfrequently did the aged Hugh Roberts await their arrival at the end of the field, to walk a little way with them on their return, meanwhile tossing a little hay by way of diversion, but all the while listening intently to what the three friends had to say, and occasionally interjecting a few words, which were generally to the point, and always appreciated.

It was during one of these conferences that Hugh Roberts exclaimed: "I like the harvest-field, if it were for no other reason than that all drop their distinctions and differences here. Now who could tell that you, Mr. Pugh, were a schoolmaster, or that you, John, were a shoemaker, or you, Shadrach, a blacksmith, by the way you toss the hay to-day? You all look like honest farmers at their familiar work. I suppose when the spiritual harvest of the world will come that we shall lose our denominational distinctions and differences as you have to-day lost your distinctions of trade or calling."

"I notice, Hugh," said John quietly, "that you say we have lost our distinctions to-day, and have become farmers like yourself; do you also suggest that by-and-bye we shall lose our denominational differences and become Calvinistic Methodists like you?"

There was a little playfulness about John's eye which the old farmer caught. "Now, my son," said Hugh smilingly, "don't be quite so sharp on an old man. I have no doubt that what I said applies to all denominations alike—Calvinistic Methodists as well as Baptists."

"Quite right," responded John heartily; "and yet I expect to all eternity we shall be better for what we receive of truth here, each in his own denomination. 'There shall be *one flock* and one Shepherd.' Mr. Pugh told us the other day that the right translation is, *'one flock,'* and not *'one fold.'* I am not, therefore, sure that when the millennium comes denominations will be done away with. There will probably be many folds still; only that then the sheep will no doubt realise more fully than they do now, that they belong to the same Shepherd and the same flock. I do not see, if the millennium came to-morrow, why I should be ashamed to say that I am a Baptist, or you that you are a Methodist. I do not think the Master would have us to be ashamed of our old convictions which we have held dearer than life unless they have been erroneous. That which is distinctively true in every denomination will be among the things 'which cannot be moved.' If we as Baptists have existed to uphold a truth which the other denominations have ignored, then to all eternity I shall in that respect be a stronger man for having upheld that truth in life. So with regard to other denominations, so far as they uphold any despised, but true, principle. I do not think, therefore, that denominational distinctions are necessary evils. Every denomination that teaches a neglected truth has a right to exist ; and the world and heaven would be poorer if that denomination had never existed. At the same time, I have no doubt, as you say, Hugh, that in the great harvest of the world all denominations will have dropped a great many prejudices and bigotries which they once cherished dearly. But what are prejudices and bigotries, and what is the truth? That is the question."

Hugh Roberts smiled and said, "We will have another chat about that," as he retired to another part of the field, where the harvesters were at work, and among them Jenkin, and Margaret, the miller's daughter. Margaret blushed, and slackened her pace, thus allowing Jenkin to increase the distance between them; and Jenkin, acting upon the same impulse to conceal the fact that he and Margaret had been exceptionally near to each other all the morning, vigorously proceeded to toss the hay as if he had no thought for anyone or anything except his work. Old Hugh Roberts, although aged, was quick to detect such devices, for he remembered that when he himself was young, there were very similar ones in vogue. He, therefore, gently walked up to the young couple, and repeated the old Welsh proverb "Nid ymgêl cariad lle bô" ("Where love is, it will not be hidden"). Margaret made a feeble pretence of not having quite caught what the old farmer had said, while he, by way of making his allusion more pointed, and mindful of the fact that Jenkin and Margaret lived in neighbouring hamlets, added, "Ni châr morwyn mab o'i thrêf" ("A maid will not love a youth from her own hamlet"). Margaret was slightly confused, but Jenkin came to the rescue by expressing his surprise that Mr. Hugh Roberts, old as he was, had not forgotten the old proverbs with which, sixty years, he used to charm the damsels of that day.

Hugh smiled and added that no doubt he remembered enough to see what Jenkin and Margaret were bent upon, and, in leaving them, he expressed the hope that they would not forget to invite him to their wedding. Jenkin assured him there would be an honourable place for him there, an assurance to which Margaret gave her ready and hearty assent.

The two were then allowed to proceed on the even tenor of their way, and gradually to re-assume their former proximity to each other, while Hugh proceeded to exchange a few playful words with other lovers, and hearty words with all the harvesters.

Nor were the children forgotten, for, old as Hugh was, he ever had a youthful heart, and enjoyed few things more than a chat with the little ones, which generally ended in a lively but not too exciting or exhausting game. On this occasion he chatted freely with the children who gathered round him, eagerly listening to the tales he had to tell them about the time long ago, when as a boy in those very fields, which his father then farmed, he played in the hay with his youthful comrades, all of whom had now passed away. He then initiated them into a game or two which were played when he was a lad; but which had now long since passed out of fashion.

The time at length arrived for the mid-day meal, and the servants, laden with baskets, were crossing the field to place the repast in the shadow of the oak under which Hugh Roberts and the children were. That was a signal for a general exodus on the part of the children, who were desirous of helping the servants to carry some of their burdens—a help joyfully rendered and as gratefully accepted.

It was not long before the meal was arranged, and the harvesters were summoned to partake of it. There was a noisy, tumultuous talk at first; but suddenly all subsided so that Hugh Roberts might ask the blessing. Then the meal was proceeded with, amid a general hum of genial conversation, and an occasional burst of merriment which convulsed the younger people chiefly, who were again found conveniently grouped together. John Vaughan, Shadrach Morgan, and Llewelyn Pugh were also once more found together, and it was not long before Hugh Roberts joined them.

"I have been thinking a little, off and on," said Hugh Roberts, "about what you said this morning, John. There is no doubt that you are right in the main; but you are a very rigid Baptist, John, and think, I fear, that the Kingdom of God cannot get on without your denomination."

"Well, Hugh," replied John, "I think that God and His Kingdom could get on very well without the whole lot of us; but it does not appear to be God's will to do so; and as long as you Pædo-Baptists will go on ignoring the Lord's first ordinance, and go on sprinkling infants instead of immersing believers, as He would have us do, I don't think that the Kingdom of Heaven would get on as well without Baptists, as it does with them; and any union that is brought about at the cost of despising, or even treating with indifference, that leading ordinance, to which He gives a prominent place in His Commission, is not going to be very helpful to the Kingdom of the Redeemer, depend upon it. There are, of course, other great principles which must not be sacrificed to any so-called union, but I am speaking now of Christian baptism."

"Ah, John," answered Hugh, "you could not live without a little discussion; but there, it agrees with you and seems to hurt no one else. Yet I fear you forget the glorious prophecy of Isaiah, 'The wolf shall dwell with the lamb, and the leopard shall lie down with the kid; and the calf and the young lion and the fatling together; and a little child shall lead them.'"

"I confess," responded John, "that I never thought those words applied to denominational reunion; and I even now think, if that were so, that it would be very hard to fit the creatures on. We should all be wishful to avoid the wolf, for instance. But even supposing that Isaiah referred to this, it is worth noticing that the wolf does not lose his identity though he dwells with the lamb; and so with the other creatures. The ferocious creatures only lose their ferocity, and not their special differences. They are not all put into a reunion machine, and all turned out lacking all their former distinctive features, out of respect to each other. God's creation would be reduced to a pitiable dead level if that were the case. No, Hugh, the Master never intended that the different denominations of Christians should pass through such a machine as that, and out of sheer regard for each other, but, I fear, less for His Truth, have every prominent line and feature removed, or so squeezed down as to be no longer recognisable."

"He is an incorrigible Baptist, isn't he?" ejaculated Hugh, partly in earnest and partly as a by-play, as he looked at Llewelyn Pugh, who, having received a university education with a view to holy orders, but having subsequently from conviction left the church, had become the village schoolmaster, and was looked upon as an authority in most things.

"Yes," replied Llewelyn Pugh; "and yet, although I am not a Baptist, I agree with John in the view he takes of the talk there is just now about all denominations sinking their differences, and throwing themselves into a bundle of love, in which nothing shall be found that will clash with anything else. The question is—supposing such a thing were possible—what would be left after such a process of elimination? The course generally adopted evidently is to extend the greatest consideration to those who believe least and hold nothing very sacred. It is not intended that those who believe next to nothing of God's Word shall be braced up in their belief of the great truths of our religion, so as to be in harmony with those who do believe; but that the latter should so far drop their convictions as at least to say nothing about them, and act as if they did not exist. The process to be adopted evidently is to take the backbone and distinguishing limbs out of those who have any, and thus make them as much as possible like those who are not in possession of these commodities. The only type of creature that will lose nothing by such a compromise is the jelly-fish, who has no backbone to lose, and no manner of limbs to eliminate save those that will readily collapse and fit into any mould into which that interesting creature is put. Scientists tell us that all varieties of creatures have been evolved out of sea jelly, and, by a process called 'differentiation' (here John and Shadrach opened their eyes in wonderment), have in course of time become what they are now, in their infinite variety of shapes and colours. I pity the people who have sufficient credulity to believe such nonsense. But this Christian reunion which is now suggested is evidently based upon some such supposition in the spiritual realm as that is in the physical, and is an attempt to go back to this beginning of things by retracing the supposed process by which a bit of sea jelly has developed into all varieties of intelligent existences, and reduce them, in the interests of so-called union, into the soft, pulpy object, which has no body to be kicked and no soul to be lost. This kind of thing, forsooth, is to bring about the millennial glory for which we are asked to yearn, and which, by ridding ourselves of every conviction that gives strength to character and individuality to devotion, we are required to do our part to hasten. No, Hugh; if we cannot become united without ceasing to be true to our distinctive principles and convictions it is better that we should agree to differ, and let each denomination work on its own lines."

"But couldn't we unite all denominations in a grand federation," responded Hugh, "so that while each shall be faithful to its principles, all shall work together in things in which they are agreed?"

"By all means, Hugh," replied Llewelyn Pugh, "there are common objects which we can further unitedly; but no such federation should rob any denomination of its separate existence, and its own freedom of action. In other words, we ought to be separate denominations still—that is, as long as we have different convictions. It will never do for us to hold our principles with a loose hand, and sacrifice them for the sake of any union. All that sort of thing would be an unnatural union, hampering each denomination in its activities, until all would end in bondage and activity. Depend upon it, Hugh, the union that is secured by every one being, in any sense, untrue to himself is not a union worth having. There have been many attempts to confound uniformity with unity in the past but most of those were sustained by the arm of the law, and even the gibbet and the stake, and all failed. Now the attempt is sustained by false sentiment and personal unfaithfulness to convictions which should be sacred to every man, and this must fail in the same way. Union there can be, and doubtless much more than there has been hitherto; but it must be a union in points of agreement between those who otherwise differ, and who do not ignore the importance of their differences when in certain points they are united. There can also and should be a greater readiness on the part of each denomination to give the credit of sincerity to others but in so doing it is no part of its duty to sacrifice its own creed and practice upon the altar of so-called union. I have my misgivings, I must confess, about nondescripts in politics and religion."

"Mr. Pugh, you are worse than even John," exclaimed Hugh Roberts. "When you get old, like myself, I have no doubt both of you will long, as I do, for greater union among Christians."

"No doubt," replied Llewelyn Pugh; "and even now there is not a man of us here present who would not rejoice to see more of it among Christians of all denominations; but what we protest against is sacrificing great principles for the sake of so-called union. The prescription for union to-day is to hold rigidly to no conviction but to be ever ready to let it go, if, by so doing, we can make ourselves agreeable to those who differ from us. What a blessing it is to us that our fathers did not deal with principles in that slipshod fashion. They thought their convictions were worth suffering for, and, if necessary, worth dying for. Depend upon it, Hugh, the union that can only exist by everyone being untrue to himself for the sake of being on agreeable terms with those who can only be induced to be affectionate at such a cost, is not worth a second thought. It is a miserable hybrid that will die in the birth."

"That's right," ejaculated John earnestly. "That kind of union will never come to anything. Those who take part in union conferences talk very sweetly on such occasions, and seem to be ready to give up everything for the sake of general agreement with the community at large. You would think that, on their return home, they would have forgotten to what church they belonged; but, bless you, it is by no means so. When they come home they are just as they were before. They leave all this supernatural charity behind them. Why, there's Mr. B——, the parson at C——, he talked so sweetly at the conference, that I fully expected him on his return to embrace us all when he met us. Poor innocent as I was, I made quite a mistake, for, on his return he told his people that the days of Nonconformity were numbered, for already the leading dissenting ministers were at heart seeking reunion with the Church, and yearning for the privilege of partaking of its holy communion. This, he said, was proved at the conference which he had just attended, in which all had partaken of holy communion as administered by the Church of England; and since then he has been a greater proselytiser than ever."

"Now, John," replied Hugh, "it is scarcely fair to give Parson B——'s view of reunion as the one adopted by the majority of those who are in favour of it."

"But, Hugh," responded Shadrach, "how is it that bishops and clergymen do not express their readiness to accept the communion from some leading Nonconformist by way of brotherly exchange, if they mean anything else by this union than absorption into their Church?"

"Besides," added John, "when it comes to the point, if ever it will come even to that, that is just what all Nonconformists as well as Churchmen will want. Now, supposing this reunion will take place, Hugh, what will you do? Will you be willing to give up your Calvinistic Methodism, and to renounce, or at least to ignore, all the opinions that you have held so dearly all your life, and still hold to be true? Are you willing that all your distinctive Methodist tenets should be let slip, on the condition that I let go my distinctive Baptist views, and Mr. Llewelyn Pugh his Independent views, and Parson B—— his Church views?

"Oh, no," said Hugh Roberts warmly. "I could not be other than a Methodist, with my present and my life-long convictions."

"So it comes to this," interposed John hurriedly "the reunion you long for is that which will make Calvinistic Methodists of us all."

"No, no; not quite that," exclaimed Hugh. "I believe in every man sticking to his own honest opinions, but yet ready to join as far as possible with other Christians in the common cause."

"Exactly; and that is what I felt sure *you* meant," replied John; "but that is not the reunion that is being talked about. No doubt we should look for opportunities to work as far as possible with all who love the Lord in sincerity and in truth, and do so more than we ever have in the past. There we are all thoroughly at one with you. But what is pleaded for to-day is that every denomination should give up insisting upon anything that other denominations cannot adopt; in other words, that they should be everything in general, and nothing in particular. The question is, when that process of emptying out has been sufficiently accomplished by all denominations to meet the necessities of this universal union, what will be left? Nothing as Mr. Llewelyn Pugh has said, but a jelly-fish Christianity that will fit any mould into which you care to put it."

"I agree with you, John," replied Hugh, "when you say that no denomination ought to give up any truth that it considers sacred for the sake of union; and that no denomination that exists to enforce a truth which otherwise would be overlooked ought to cease to be; but the question is whether every denomination has such a reason to give for its existence. Again some denominations may have so succeeded in impressing others with the distinctive truth they have taught as to lead them to adopt it; so that the reason which those denominations had for existing in the first place has almost, if not quite, vanished. In such cases they ought to unite with those from whom they do not differ in any vital question; and if only that were done a great point would be gained, which might lead up to a still greater union."

"Quite right, Hugh," replied John. "If denominations have no reason for remaining separate from others, they ought not to exist; but then, who is to decide that, but each denomination for itself? I expect you are not prepared to say that Methodism has no longer a right to exist; and I am sure that I am not prepared to admit that the Baptist denomination has no right to exist. I have a strong suspicion, too, that Mr. Pugh would cling tenaciously to Independency, and so with all who have strong convictions. So that the day has not come when the differences between the various denominations of Christians are so slight and unimportant as to be ignored with advantage. In many respects there are vital differences; and while they exist we must remain as we are, although no doubt there are some minor differences which are not in themselves a sufficient reason for our remaining separate."

"Well," interjected Hugh, "I suppose we must leave the matter there now. I hope you have all had enough to eat, and that you are ready at least for another attempt at reunion in bringing in the hay."

While John Vaughan, Hugh Roberts, and others were thus engaged in the discussion of the weighty and abstruse subject of Christian union, the younger portion of the company were engaged in a livelier talk about the probabilities of other unions. Thus, when Hugh and his companions closed their conference, the younger people had come to a kind of tacit agreement that whatever might be said about denominational reunion, matrimonial union was a divine ordinance, which should be observed implicity and joyfully as opportunity offered.

There were some present who hoped soon to consummate that happy event; there were others who had no immediate prospect, but on the principle that "Hope springs eternal in the human breast," they had distant glimpses of better days, and thus possessed their soul in patience.

Lunch being over, the company, which presented such happy combinations of youth and age, and their various characteristics, as only a harvest field can supply, resumed their work beneath as bright and clear a sky as ever arched over earth's harvest fields. As the afternoon advanced, the sun cast slanting shadows across the field. At length it only glanced through wood and coppice, and through thickly set hedgerows, abounding with hazel trees richly laden with nuts, and profusely adorned by honeysuckles, from which a sweet perfume, mingled with that of the new-mown hay in such exquisite proportions as no perfumer could imitate, and was wafted by the gentle evening breeze to the merry harvesters.

Now and then, too, as the haymakers drew near the hedges, they were greeted by the hedge-sparrow and robin-redbreast, which hopped from bough to bough; and were rewarded with the song of the blackbird and thrush, which poured forth their melody into the perfumed air and the mellowing light. Gradually thin fleecy clouds were borne across the blue sky by a gentle breeze, and congregated in the distant west as if to bid the setting sun "God-speed" until it should rise again on the morrow over the eastern hills. The sun in setting returned to them a warm "Adieu" in hues of glowing red, gorgeous gold, and delicate purple, thus transfiguring the fringes of the changeful clouds, which appeared in ever-varying shapes and subtle groupings. At times a shaft of golden light was shot across the landscape, as a parting blessing to the harvesters by the sun, ere it sank below the horizon, and touched with an unearthly beauty the broken and abrupt banks that overhanged shaded dingles and shallow brooks, and at length tipped with gold the summits of the opposite hills. It finally disappeared, no longer visible save by the upward slanting light, that was still reflected in prismatic hues by the friendly clouds which seemed to take a last glimpse over the brink of the western horizon after their departing friend. It was a scene which cannot be described, but only remembered; yet upon memory it remains photographed as "a thing of beauty and a joy for ever." Life is richer and mellower for all time for such a sight; and such, indeed, are frequently to be witnessed on the harvest fields of Wales—the land of rugged mountains and wild ravines, of wooded hills and fertile valleys, and the dear old home of religion, poetry and song.

As the company left the harvest-field for the night they bore traces of a hard day's work beneath a burning sun. Even the children, who had liberally blended playful mirth with labour, were far less inclined to run, or climb up hedges, than they were in the morning. The long day had produced a subduing effect upon them. Hunger, too—for they had not had a substantial meal since the mid-day lunch, although they had received light refreshments during the afternoon—had considerably modified the exuberance of their youthful spirits. Thus there was an air of sobriety even about the youngest in that motley group as they left the harvest field and approached the farm-house for their evening meal.

In passing, however, through the farm-yard where the haystack was being constructed, the younger portion of the company, with Jenkin at their head, amused themselves in quietly criticising the movements and general demeanour of Samson Lloyd, the village tailor, who was making frantic efforts to arrange, in time for supper, the last load of hay, which had been just brought from the field, and was now being vigorously pitch-forked to the top of the rick. Jenkin, as was his wont, found no little pleasure in satirising the little conceited tailor, who seemed, to himself at least, to reign supreme at the top of the rick. The only two things which were not diminutive about the tailor were his name and his conceit. He never was so pleased as when, on those occasions, he was exalted above his fellows and enjoyed a prominence denied him at other times. Jenkin knew this, and suggested to his companions ironically that it was an immense gain to have a man of Samson's proportions and weight upon the top of the rick, so that the hay might be well pressed. He observed, moreover, that Samson kept well in the centre of the rick, while others had to arrange the hay near the edge; because if he budged from the centre, the rick would instantly lose its equilibrium and topple over. He added that Samson always acted in life upon that principle, and kept as near the centre as possible, well knowing that if he but stood at one end of the world it would be sure to tip up at the other. These and similar witticisms were indulged in by Jenkin among his friends as they watched Samson fussily engaged in treading

MAKING THE HAY-RICK

down the hay in the centre of the rick. On account of his lameness, and the necessity for using the crutch in walking, that was the only service which he could render at harvest time; and this was well ordained, for it was by far the most congenial task to a man of Samson's ambition and pretensions.

When the work was at length completed for the day, the tailor very cautiously approached the ladder to descend, the others giving him the precedence, partly because he liked it, and partly because he was lame and needed a little help, or at least extra caution, in planting his foot upon the highest rung of the ladder. Samson, too, keenly conscious of the value of his life, and the importance of his own personal safety, always emphasised on such occasions the necessity for the ladder to be held firmly at the top, as well as the bottom, when he planted his feet upon its rungs.

Soon all the harvesters had entered the large kitchen of the old farmhouse, and were seated around the tables. Small wooden bowls filled with broth, and accompanied by wooden spoons, were served out to the elder portion of the company, who preferred what they had been accustomed to from their childhood to the earthenware basins and metallic spoons, which had now been largely adopted in Wales, even far inland. The older folks held that nothing could compare with a wooden basin and spoon for broth, for they so soon cooled it; whereas earthenware and metal retained the heat for an unconscionable length of time. On the other hand, the younger portion, who believed in moving on with the times, and had what they considered superior notions of refinement as compared with their seniors, preferred the metallic spoon and the earthenware basin. Broth, however, was supplied alike to all. The table was further laden with wheaten bread and oaten cakes: the old barley loaves of earlier days being only partially sought for even by the most aged veteran present.

Hugh Roberts called upon John Vaughan to ask the blessing; and when this had been done, the meal was proceeded with. Following the Welshman's favourite broth were meat and potatoes, served on wooden or earthenware plates, which, like the basins, were distributed according to the preference of the guests. The younger portion and a few of the older ones were further served with rice pudding, boiled in milk which had never caught a glimpse of the pump-handle or scented the water cans afar off.

The meal being over, all assembled together for family worship, which Hugh Roberts himself conducted. His venerable and beautiful face, and his long hoary locks, presented a charming picture in the light of the candle on the table, and the brighter blaze of the wooden fire that burned upon the large hearth beneath the open chimney, as he sat upon the old oak settle. Having adjusted his spectacles, he opened the Family Bible that had descended to him as an heirloom from his father. The old clock ticked solemnly, as it had done thousands of times before, while Hugh read the Scriptures, and now and then, with a tick louder than usual, seemed to emphasise an exceptionally important word as it was read. Thus the old clock, with its solemn and dull thud, presented an impressive contrast to the tremulous, musical and tender voice of the aged farmer, who looked and spoke as if he had been John at Ephesus, surrounded by the children whom he so greatly loved. Both the clock and its owner represented a bygone age; and each in its own way spoke to the younger generation present in solemn tones that sounded weirdly amid the hush and gloom of that peaceful eventide.

There was a general movement on the part of the company when prayer was over. Mothers were anxious to take their elder children home, and in some instances, to return to the younger ones who had been left to the care of a sister or neighbour during the day. Many had also to start again early the following morning either for Hugh Roberts', or some other farmer's hayfields. Thus there was a general exodus as soon as family worship was over. The narrow road leading

THE HARVESTERS AT SUPPER

to the village was well filled by the returning company. The moon had just risen, and now cast its silvery light over the whole landscape. The dew, too, was rapidly descending, and a slight mist covered the meadows. Now and then a snatch of a Welsh melody, sung by other harvesters, returning home from their day's toil, was heard, and was readily caught up by the younger portion of this happy, though weary band; while the lowing cattle and bleating sheep on the surrounding slopes came in quaintly, at irregular intervals, as amateur accompanists.

On the hedges and roadside, too, there were evident signs of life. The birds had retired to rest; but there was a stir still in the bushes, and an occasional partridge or pheasant, and here and there a rabbit, were surprised by the children as they rushed up and down the hedgerows.

As the company drew near the smithy, one of Shadrach Morgan's hens—a wretched wanderer, who laid the few eggs she had the decency to produce in the hedges of the neighbourhood—had just laid an egg, and was evidently desirous that all creation should be made acquainted with the fact. Shadrach took note of the spot, with a view of finding the nest in the morning. At the smithy itself were two men-servants from Ty-mawr Farm, who had hastened on to sharpen their old scythes on the smithy grindstone.

On the smithy corner, just where the by-road crosses the highway that runs through the village, were a few jovial drovers who had paused to quench their thirst at the Inn, and Billy Thomas, the old village fisherman, who, bearing the weapons of his craft, had returned from a day's fishing, and had just settled a small score with the landlord by selling him a salmon, which had in reality been caught by an otter that had the misfortune of being surprised by the wily fisherman as the first dainty morsel was being taken off the upper part of the salmon's back just below the head. The fisherman too, had a good basket of trout, some of which he had sold to the drovers, who were bent upon having them cooked for supper that night at the "Stag and Pheasant," the next inn on their journey. Thus old Billy Thomas, now in possession of the remaining trophies of his day's pursuit, and the drovers bent upon reaching the "Stag and Pheasant" with as little delay as possible, were about to separate when the harvesters reached the popular village corner.

Their advent did not delay the departure of the drovers, who felt but little interest in hay-making, but Billy Thomas—although harvesting was by no means his *forte,* as it was far too monotonous for a man of his temperament—waited to exchange greetings with his neighbours. Billy, in spite of the fact that he was over sixty years of age, had an eye as sharp and merry as a trout's. In the pale light of the moon, therefore, he hailed John Vaughan, Llewelyn Pugh, and Shadrach Morgan at a distance, and expressed the hope that they had had a good day. They heartily reciprocated the good wish; but only to draw forth from him at first the usual word "tolerable," and then the further intimation that an old friend, a master fisherman, had helped him that day. His eye twinkled in the moonlight as he related with high glee how he had relieved the otter, just at the nick of time, of the responsibility of the fine salmon he had caught.

Llewelyn Pugh suggested that this was a striking instance of a man entering into the labours of others; to which old Billy replied that he had too often to enter into his old friend, the otter's, labours in an unwelcome fashion, by finding that a favourite fish he had sighted was before the morrow removed to the otter's den; and that it was about time that the otter did something handsome by way of return. With that brief comment the merry fisherman bade them good night.

Llewelyn Pugh, John, and Shadrach, remained together for a few minutes and talked about Billy Thomas as one of the last of his race— namely, of the old fishermen who gave their whole time to their congenial task, and made their own tackle, including flies of all varieties, without any adventitious aid. To such fishing was a calling in life, and not a pastime. As the competitions and pressure of life's duties had increased, fishing in streams and rivers, save in close proximity to the sea, was fast vanishing as a calling. This the three friends regretted, as it deprived country life of another quaint and primitive phase of rustic character which added greatly to its charm.

The moon now shone very brightly over the meadows, and brought into vivid relief the surrounding hills in the evening air, which was exceptionally clear, save where the dew was condensing in the lowlands.

"It is a charming night," said Shadrach, "and the air is so clear that the moon appears at its best. I am not surprised that poor old Molly Prys, when she went to see her son at Landore, and saw the moon through the mirky smoke of that place, told him what a miserable moon they had: that it wouldn't stand comparison with the bright and pretty little moon she had at home in Carmarthenshire; and added that there was no moon in the world to compare with that."

"Although Molly's knowledge of astronomy was evidently a little defective," said Llewelyn Pugh, "I profoundly sympathise with her remarks. I have seen the moon through the smoke which almost always hangs over such places as Landore, and I confess that, apart from knowing that it has been the same moon as ours, I should not have thought so. It looked like a very poor counterfeit which could deceive no one."

"Yes, that is one of the penalties which men pay for money-making," responded John. "They darken God's heaven, and conceal its glories from their eyes while they breathe fumes and smoke of the most obnoxious kind. If we but have God's light and fresh air, unpolluted by all the smuts and smells which man can invent; that will go a long way toward maintaining our love for purity and brightness in higher things. It must be specially difficult to live a life of holiness amid the smuts and pollutions of ironworks; although even that, of course, by the grace of God, is possible."

The friends nodded assent, and having shaken hands, bade each other good-night.

CHAPTER VIII

Caleb Rhys' Return from "The Hills"

S the hay harvest was drawing to a close, and the corn was ripening for the sickle, Caleb Rhys, who had been on one of his periodical journeys selling flannel in Glamorganshire and Monmouthshire returned, and had a great deal to say about his experiences "in the hills." He therefore called upon John Vaughan the first night after his return. In the workshop he found David Lewis, the village grocer, besides John and his apprentice.

Caleb had during the journey heard of a very quaint old character among the Calvinistic Methodists, very similar to the well-known Sami Shon* among the Baptists. Like Sami, he was very interested in preaching and preachers. He used to follow, and often accompany, well-known ministers on their preaching tours, and in doing so had failed to attend to his duties as a farmer, so that he had to sell his farm, Esgair Eithin, near Traeth-saith, Cardiganshire, and remove to Pen-y-cae, Monmouthshire, there to begin life anew. He still persisted, however, in going far and wide with the great preachers on their journeys, and not infrequently used to take the devotional part of the service for them; which he did with great effect, although he seemed to have no gift or desire to preach.

He soon became a noted character in Monmouthshire, as he had already been in Cardiganshire. As a leader of the Calvinistic Methodist Church at Pen-y-cae, it fell to his lot to select preachers for the pulpit. It should be noted in passing that at that time even more than now, the ministers among the Calvinistic Methodists were itinerant preachers, and not stated pastors; so that all churches had to arrange as best they could for pulpit supplies.

Among those who had gone to supply the pulpit at Pen-y-cae for a Sunday was a young minister of promise, who afterwards was known throughout Wales as the Rev. William Prydderch. At that time the preacher had an extremely youthful appearance. Owen Enos was very sceptical about his qualifications as a preacher when he first saw him, and subjected him to a severe cross-examination. At the close of the Sunday, however—and, indeed, long before that—the old leader was convinced that the young man was destined to become one of the greatest preachers in Wales, and taking out his diary asked him to fix upon a date not far distant for Pen-y-cae. Mr. Prydderch said: "Oh, no, it is folly for me to come all the way from Carmarthenshire when you have so many excellent preachers nearer home, and even in your immediate neighbourhood." "Excellent preachers in our immediate neighbourhood, indeed!" responded Owen Enos "there are only two in the whole of this valley, and the devil knows nothing about the existence of either of them."

---

* A Welsh colloquial name for Samuel Jones.

Caleb Rhys had heard much of this old worthy, who was now no
longer living, but whose name was still a household word at Pen-y-
cae, and whose quaint sayings and eccentric deeds were often recited
around the hearth, or in social gatherings, throughout the country.
Sufficient has been said already to show that Owen Enos was
intolerant of poor preachers. He would only follow those who came
up to his standard and he was exceedingly anxious not to fix any but
good preachers for the pulpit at Pen-y-cae. Whenever there chanced
to be a Session,* or even a monthly meeting in the neighbourhood,
Owen Enos was sure to be on the look out for the best ministers, so
as to secure their services, if not for the Sunday, at least for a week-
night service on their return journey.

On one occasion—so Caleb Rhys learnt, and now that he had come
to John Vaughan's workshop he soon repeated it—the Methodist
Session was held at Brynmawr. Owen Enos was very busily engaged
in looking out for leading preachers but was not very successful.
Meanwhile he became very impatient and restless. He elbowed his
way hither and thither. At length a minister from the neighbourhood,
who did not occupy a very high position in Owen Enos' opinion, but
who was not aware of that fact, accosted him, and jocularly said:
"You are very proud to-day, Owen Enos, you don't see us little
preachers." "Indeed, I do," replied the old man, "that's the worst of
it, that I am eternally seeing you little ones, and no one else."

John Vaughan was greatly charmed with Caleb Rhys' account of
Owen Enos for he had heard much of him from ministers and others
who hailed from the neighbourhood of Traeth-saith and Aberporth.
He therefore responded: "Ah, yes, he was a wonderful character and
as famous in Cardiganshire in his early years as he was, I should
think, in Monmouthshire in his later days. There are many stories
told of him when he lived at Esgair Eithin. On one occasion he entered
Blaen-annerch chapel when a minister, who was a stranger to the
neighbourhood, was engaged in prayer. Owen fell down on his knees
at the door, and gradually made his way to the table-pew that was
near. The minister was very demonstrative and rather boisterous.
He was also as energetic in his sermon as he was in prayer. Owen
Enos could not quite decide what to think of him, and in one of the

* "Sassiwn" is the Welsh word for a Calvinistic Methodist Association.

brief pauses whispered to his neighbour, 'Who is the preacher?' His neighbour replied, 'So-and-so.' 'He churns tremendously,' said the old farmer; evidently referring by this homely figure to the preacher's vigorous style. But as the preacher proceeded Owen Enos became very interested, and added in a whisper to his neighbour, 'And, what is better, he is getting some butter too.'"

"He must have been an extraordinary character," interjected the apprentice, "we should be glad of more of his sort."

"Indeed, we should," added John. "Well, Caleb, tell us some more of your experiences on the journey."

"Yes, I will tell you one thing—I heard Rev. Thomas Edwards, an old apprentice of yours, John. He is a wonderfully original preacher, and quite an honour to the lapstone."

John's face instantly lit up, and his eyes gleamed with delight. "What, Thomas Edwards!" he exclaimed. "He was one of the most brilliant, and, I must add, one of the most mischievous boys I ever knew. Remember, his mischief was always the mischief of a good-natured, happy-go-lucky, and boisterous boy; but he *was* mischievous, and full of exuberant joy and fun. On that account you never could be angry with him: his excuses were so clever, and his remarks so quaint and comic. Tell us what he said," added John, in a tone that was expressive of honest pride in his former apprentice, as well as intense interest in his welfare.

"Well," replied Caleb, "I heard him say a good number of quaint things. He was preaching from the text, 'The law of the Lord is perfect, converting the soul.' He began his sermon in a most striking fashion. He said: 'The law of the Lord is perfect, and therein, as in many other respects, it differs from human laws. You are acquainted with the saying that you can drive a carriage and pair through any Act of Parliament, and we are all convinced of the truth of it—at least, all of us who have ever had a lawsuit. There, are, indeed, great gaps in English law, *and in these gaps the lawyers live.*' The last remark came so suddenly and forcibly as to convulse the audience, and it was with great difficulty that they suppressed their amusement. But, when the irrepressible smile had passed, the saying remained, for it stuck like a burr in the memories of those who heard it. On the way out I heard one, who I found was a lawyer, say to a friend: 'Well, I must confess that is one of the best things I have ever heard about us

lawyers. There's nothing course or abusive about it, and yet it hits
us off mercilessly. Yes, it is very true that there are great gaps in
English law, and that we lawyers live in them.'"

"That's just like him," exclaimed John, "and I can imagine hearing
him say it. He always had something original and quaint to say when
he was an apprentice here, and I'll undertake he will be the same to
the end. It's certainly a surprise to me to hear that you heard him
preach, and I shall be glad to learn more about him when we have
leisure. How is he looking?"

"Right noble," said Caleb.

"Well, as you are going to tell John again at leisure more about
Rev. Thomas Edwards, tell us something else about Owen Enos. He
was evidently a fine old fellow."

"There are no end of stories told at Pen-y-cae about him," responded
Caleb, "most of which I fear I have forgotten; but there's one I just
remember. I should say that Owen Enos was very impatient of elaborate
sermons not 'understanded of the people.' On one occasion a well-known
minister, who was not given to lucidity, but prided himself in making
the cloud his chariot in his public utterances, occupied the pulpit at
Pen-y-cae. Poor Owen Enos, and many besides, vainly attempted to catch
the preacher's message, if, indeed, he had one. The profound look and
the high sounding words of the minister were very tantalising to the old
man, as they conveyed no meaning except that of mystery to him. He
became impatient; but managed to curb his impatience as he hit upon a
plan for the evening service. When the evening came, he went as usual
early to chapel; but instead of going to the big pew as he was accustomed
to do, he seated himself on the top seat at the end of the gallery and
directly in front of the preacher. The old man was the wonder of saints
and sinners in that exalted position. 'Why,' they asked, 'is Owen Enos
seated there instead of in his usual place?' The preacher, too, was
perplexed by his change of attitude and altitude. At the close of the
service the preacher asked the old man why he had so suddenly deserted
the big pew and gone to the gallery. Owen replied: 'Well, to tell you the
truth, everything you said in the morning went clean over my head. I
hadn't a morsel; and I made up my mind to go as high as I could to-night
to catch anything that did not go straight out through the ceiling.'"

"I say," ejaculated the apprentice, "that shot didn't fail: it must
have hit the bull's eye."

"Yes," replied Caleb, "and they say that particular preacher never preached above people's heads after that."

"Owen Enos seems to have been rather sharp upon preachers. They must have wished him further," said David Lewis.

"By no means," responded John. "He was a great friend of ministers, if he thought that they had been called to preach; and he thought it a great honour to commence the service for such. Indeed, his attachment to Ebenezer Morris and other great preachers was what led to his having to give up farming. He followed them frequently during their journeys, and was very useful in taking the devotional part of the services for them, and thus too often neglected his farm."

"Yes," said David Lewis, "but that is a very different thing from treating kindly less distinguished men."

"Their distinction or otherwise weighed very little with Owen Enos," answered John. "The question with him was whether they preached the Gospel with simplicity and power to men. For instance, the very man whom he rebuked for preaching above people's heads at Pen-y-cae was well known and highly respected. On the other hand, Owen Enos would often encourage an obscure preacher when he believed that he had a message to his fellows."

"That reminds me," responded Caleb, "of another story I heard which illustrates that. There was a little local preacher at Pen-y-cae who had gone from Merthyr Tydvil to live there. He was not greatly gifted, yet he could preach a very useful and acceptable sermon. He was a man, too, of retiring disposition and nervous temperament, who was given to under-estimate his gifts. Some time after his settlement at Pen-y-cae the leaders of the church of which he had been formerly a member at Merthyr, and which at that time was considered to be a very important one, asked him to supply their pulpit for a Sunday. He was filled with consternation, and consulted Owen Enos about going. Owen Enos replied: 'Go, by all means; and I will come and commence the service for you.' That was the highest compliment he could pay Thomas Evans, for had he not commenced services for the greatest preachers of that age! The time arrived when Thomas Evans and Owen Enos made for Merthyr Tydvil. Thomas Evans was exceptionally nervous in prospect of preaching at Merthyr, and his friend vainly tried to encourage him. The old man, however, bethought himself, and adopted a plan in introducing the service which he thought might

prove helpful in overcoming his friend's timidity. Thomas Evans was
an adept at pitching a tune, and there was an old one sung at Pen-y-
cae to a very peculiar metre, which was quite unknown at Merthyr.
After reading and prayer, Owen gave out that peculiar metre. No one
had a tune for it. At last the old man gave a sign to Thomas Evans,
who immediately pitched the tune, which, although new, was sung
with great vigour by the congregation. 'There,' said Owen Enos quietly
to his nervous companion, 'preach to them now and don't be afraid,
for you have already had the best of them.'"

"Our talking about some men being a terror to poor preachers
reminds me," said John Vaughan, "of old Mr. David Beynon, of
Pencader. He was the dread of weak men who occupied Pencader
pulpit as supplies. He had his own notions about preaching. He was
always suspicious of men who attached importance to fluency and
the *hwyl*. He cared little how slow or hesitant a man was in utterance
if he talked sense; nor did fluency or eloquence have any effect upon
him save that of annoyance if the matter of the discourse was not up
to the requisite standard. He was very impatient, too, of men who
took great themes to which they could not do justice. It was easy to
see when David Beynon was not edified. He was a man of very peculiar
appearance, who had heavy and shaggy eyebrows. Beneath them were
deep caverns, from which piercing eyes looked out intently. When
the sermon was poor, David Beynon would gradually contract his
eyebrows, close his eyes, and, resting upon his elbows on the
bookboard in front, he would bend his head pensively. On one occasion
a young minister of considerable self-assertion occupied the pulpit,
and took for his theme a subject which greatly overweighted him. I
think his subject was the Godhead. He struggled persistently, but
hopelessly, with it. Yet he himself was not conscious of any lack. At
the close of the service the young preacher boldly asked David Beynon
why it was that he closed his eyes and hung his head during the
greater portion of the time the sermon was being delivered? The old
man looked intently at him and said: 'I am a man of very tender
feelings, and could not look at a man drowning.'"

"That young man did not undertake to discuss the subject of the
Godhead very soon after that, I should say," said David Lewis.

"No, I should think not," replied John. "Old Mr. Beynon taught
him a very useful lesson, for which the young preacher would no doubt

thank him in later days. But it was your story, Caleb, about Owen Enos that reminded me of that. We should be glad to hear more about him, for he was a fine old character. He had plenty of backbone."

"There's no doubt about that," responded Caleb. "He was very conscientious and straightforward. There's a very good story told of him as a workman at the works at Pen-y-cae. He was requested, like many others, to work on Sundays occasionally. He strongly protested; but his employers insisted upon it. He was advanced in life, and naturally disliked the thought of being thrown out of work; he, therefore, after making a final protest, consented. In due time came pay-day, when Owen Enos in common with others, received his wages. When paid the old man objected, because he had received more than his due. A discussion ensued between him and the clerk. At length one of the proprietors, overhearing the discussion, immediately stepped forward and asked what was the matter. Owen Enos replied that he was paid too much, whereas the clerk asserted it was all right. The time-sheet was referred to, and the clerk said: 'There is so much due to you for one Sunday when you worked.' 'Ah,' replied the old man, 'I have nothing to do with that; you must settle that matter with my Master, for that is His day, and not mine.' As he uttered these words he left the Sunday wages on the counter, and would have none of it. It was not long after this that the employer met his manager and told him to see that old Owen Enos was not sent to work on Sunday again."

"Ah! that reminds me of another story I once heard of Owen Enos," responded John Vaughan, "in connection with his having to work sometimes on Sunday. It was evidently a very sore point with the good old man that he had to go to 'the works' on the Lord's Day. It seems that on one Sunday the horse that was employed in taking away the hot cinders on a tram from the furnaces to the tips fell over into the glowing fire where the hot cinders were usually hurled, and was instantly consumed. The manager came to the spot and bitterly lamented the accident. Owen Enos lamented it with him. 'But there,' he added suddenly, 'this is not much of a fire, depend upon it, compared with that which awaits those folks who make men and horses work in such a place as this on Sunday.'"

"I say, that was straight," exclaimed the apprentice.

"And hot," added David Lewis.

"Yes," replied John, "and one can scarcely realise how that

manager could have needed any further hint after that from the proprietor not to send old Owen Enos to work again on Sundays. But there, some sinners' skins are as tough as this bit of leather I am now hammering on the lapstone. It takes a long time to pierce them."

"Just now," said David Lewis, "you, Caleb, gave a bit of Thomas Edwards' sermon about lawyers hiding in the chinks which imperfect laws provide for them. I suppose that there is no class of sinners more thick-skinned than lawyers. I heard two abuse each other mercilessly in Carmarthen Assizes a few weeks ago, and they seemed to enjoy it immensely, for ten minutes later they were going up Lammas Street, arm in arm, laughing heartily, and evidently amused with what they had been saying to each other."

"Yes, no doubt," exclaimed John, "and yet you can sting a lawyer sometimes, and make him wince. Old Rev. David Davies, Rhydgymmerau, was a rare hand for getting the better of lawyers. One day he was walking along the road and met two lawyers arm in arm. Before they met him, one said to the other, 'I'll take a rise out of old Mr. Davies now.' He had no sooner said so than Mr. Davies came up, and the lawyer said to him, 'Mr. Davies, if we had been on earth when devils used to enter men, which of us three do you think they would try to enter?' 'They would try me to be sure,' replied old Mr. Davies in his slow, deliberate fashion. 'Why?' asked the lawyer. 'Because they would know very well,' was the answer, 'that there were far too many of them already in you both, and that there would be no room for more. They would rather go back to their own perdition than be squeezed up with so many in so small a compass as a lawyer's heart.'"

"Ah, that's exactly like him," said Caleb Rhys. "He could say uncommonly hard things when he liked, and he was fearfully hard on lawyers."

"Lawyers sometimes get very much the worse of it," added David Lewis. "You, John, remember the story of 'Stammering Jim' at the Assizes in Carmarthen. Jim was a witness, and knew something of the barrister who cross-examined him. For some reason or other his memory on that occasion seemed to be conveniently defective. In answer to every other question which the counsel on the other side asked him, he would put on a pleasant smile and stammer out, 'I d-d-d-on-'t know; I-I f-f-for-g-get.' The barrister who questioned him was a big and bumptious man and was naturally impatient of all this, for it appeared evident to him that Jim was evading all awkward questions. Besides, his pride was wounded at the thought of a country clown like him foiling his cross-examination. Gathering his robes, therefore, together, and pulling himself up to his full height, he put on a judicial frown, and called out at the top of his voice, and in his most pompous style, 'Now, sir, will you tell us what you *do* know, and what you *don't* forget?' Jim's opportunity had come. He put on a most winsome and innocent-looking smile, and in a clear and sonorous voice said, 'I'll t-t-try to ob-b-blige you, sir. I *do* know that when your f-f-father was living in our p-p-lace he *failed in b-business, and left a-all of a sudden;* b-b-but whe-e-ther he p-paid his c-c-cre-ditors ever after—I *d-don't* know, I *forget.'* The wig and gown suddenly collapsed, and Jim was triumphant."

"I remember that well," replied John Vaughan. "Jim was just the man to take a bumptious lawyer by surprise, because he looked so innocent, and his stammering made him appear so helpless; and yet there wasn't a keener man in all the county than he, as many stories which we have already told about him abundantly show. And after all it is well that a man like Jim occasionally takes down the barristers, or there would be no living with them. They are so imposing in wig and gown, and they put on such bounce as they cross-examine, that it is a good thing to let them see sometimes that they are taken at their value; and that a wig and gown are not impregnable against wit and repartee."

"But come, Caleb," added John, "tell us something else of what you heard or saw during your journeys. Who would not be a weaver, who can take up his pack and be off on a journey through our beautiful country, and see some of the loveliest landscapes that are to be seen on earth!"

"There's a great deal in what you say, John," replied Caleb, with a smile, "but I would not have you think that all the districts through which I go are of that description. Those who go to Glamorganshire and Monmouthshire may no doubt see some charming sights, and be delighted with towering hills lifting their bare heads towards the heavens, while their slopes are covered with verdure and skirted with forests. They would also be delighted in many places with deep glens through which noisy brooks prattle on their way to the sea or broad valleys along which sluggish rivers meander heedlessly along, reflecting the heavens on their smooth surface, and caring little whether they ever reach their destination or linger amid their charming surroundings but for every such glimpse of nature you have in those two counties, you will have many of mountains and valleys blighted by the smoke of furnaces and kilns, and smothered into barrenness by the dust that ascends incessantly from coal pits and coal trucks. It is a sad sight to see how utterly man can spoil God's work with the smoke and dust which ever accompany his own! There are regions upon which the eyes of our preachers and bards once rested with delight, which have now scarcely a blade of grass to cover their nakedness, and even the trees, which have survived man's devastations, are in many instances as unclad in summer as in winter, and hold up their naked arms in utter despair amid the destruction which has befallen vegetation on every hand.

"It is wonderful how in other places the foliage protests, and fights a persistent though unequal fight. Sooner or later, however, man's sulphurous fumes and thick clouds of coal dust either wither blade and leaf and flower, or, failing that, cover it with a film of black and unwholesome dirt. Then, again, the rivers which once sparkled brightly, and abounded with fish, are in many instances as black as ink, and have no fish to stir their waters, except an occasional eel—which, like a cat, has nine lives, and manages to exist in the slimy deposit at the bottom. Otherwise they are as dead as the Dead Sea, and I should say a great deal blacker. No, John, it is not all joy for a man born and bred in Carmarthenshire, and who has for forty years journeyed at different times through almost every county in Wales, to see glories of landscape spoiled through what men call 'the necessities of the times;' but what I call in many instances the greed of gain."

"I have no doubt you are right about that, from all I can hear and see," exclaimed John. "I am afraid that the smoke and coal dust they have in those districts blight not only trees, and flowers, and grass, but also many a healthy young fellow, who leaves farm-service for the ironworks and coal-pit, for the sake of higher wages. They look a sickly lot when they come back here. All the colour is gone, and all the freshness, for the matter of that. They all seem to look very dingy and badly washed out; and what wonder when we remember what they have to do."

"You may well say that, John, even about the young men who once left this district with fresh and bright complexions, but who come back here with hollow cheeks and pallid faces," exclaimed Caleb; "but I do not know what you would say if you saw some of the young fellows who have been brought up from childhood among the coal-pits, and who were sent to work underground when they were but very little boys. During the early years of growth, they have been bent up in all positions, digging coal in very small headings. The result has been that in many instances their growth has been stunted, and their bodies have been often deformed: and when they walk along the road they look as if they had been astride casks all their life. It is not pleasant to see fine fellows disfigured for life in that way.

"Again, those who do not work in collieries are generally engaged at blast furnaces, or iron or tin works. 'Puddlers,' 'ballers,' 'rollers,' have a hard time of it. They wear as few clothes as possible when at work, for the heat of the livid white, and sometimes molten, iron with which they have to deal is intense, and many of them, after a 'turn,' or, a day's work, look as if they have been roasted alive. All their strength is thus sapped out of them before they are middle-aged. Those men, whether they work in collieries or ironworks, shorten their lives by years, and they richly deserve all they can get in the form of wages.

"I'll tell you of other depressing things, especially in Glamorgan-shire: they are the canals. There's nothing natural or beautiful about them. They are dug out and filled with water by man. There is practically no flow of water in them. They are like trenches filled with more or less stagnant water. And then the horses that are employed in drawing the barges are sights to behold. I have seen many a lean horse in the country, but nothing to compare with these. They look really as if they must be screwed up every other mile to be saved from falling to pieces. And then the thinner the horse the stouter the whip, and the more vigorous the application of it to the animal. Altogether, I detest the sight of a canal, and never walk along its banks if I can help it."

"You are almost as bad as Mr. Morgan Howell," said John laughingly. "Old Mr. Howell believed that the angels took care of men only along lawful paths. He was once going to Ystrad-gynlais Chapel, and he was asked by a brother of the same cloth to come to his house along the canal bank, as that was a near cut. 'No,' said Mr. Howell, 'I will not come that way—it is neither safe nor pleasant.'

The brother rebuked him for his want of faith in God's protecting care and in angelic ministries. Mr. Howell immediately took out his Testament, and read, 'He shall give His angels charge over thee, to keep thee in all thy ways.' 'You see,' he added, 'the angels confine their ministries to recognized "ways"; I have yet to learn that they frequent the *banks of canals,* even to serve the saints who are foolish enough to go to such places.'"

"Mr. Howell had evidently as little liking for canals as old Mr. Evans, of Llwynfortun, had for a well that was supposed to be haunted," interjected Shadrach. Mr. Evans was really superstitious, but would not acknowledge it. As he passed near a well with some companions one dark night he took a circuitous path. His friends observing his timidity, said, 'Why, you have no faith, Mr. Evans.' 'Faith, indeed,' responded Mr. Evans. 'I have faith in God; but not in that old well!'"

"Well, I should not like to bind myself to Mr. Howell's exposition, John, or even Mr. Evans' defence of his faith," replied Caleb: "but I confess that, like old Mr. Howell, I have found it rather hard to believe that angels would have any liking for canal banks. If I believed that, it might reconcile me a little more to them."

"Notwithstanding all you have stated, Caleb," said David Lewis, "you evidently like to go on your journey. I suppose it is because there's a good market for flannel in those districts, and that makes up for the lack of angels."

"Ah!" replied Caleb; "I fear there is too much truth in your suggestion, David. Prosperity too often reconciles us all to earth, even when there are but few traces of heaven about it. I confess that the busy centres of commerce in Glamorganshire have a charm for a man who has something to sell. There, too, we come into contact with a phase of life we do not find here. When things are prosperous and in full swing, the colliers and ironworkers earn good money as compared with workmen in agricultural districts; and they spend money freely on flannels, for, like all the Welsh people, they have strong faith in woollen clothing. But, beyond all that, they are, after all, a wonderful people, 'in the hills.' They have splendid enthusiasm in whatever they undertake. You asked me just now, John, to tell you a little more of what I saw and heard. I should like to tell you something about the National Eisteddfod that was held about a month ago. I was there for a couple of days, and it certainly was a marvellous gathering; but as Llewelyn Pugh was there, and he is a great 'eisteddfodwr,' we had better wait till he is here before we have that subject on board. The only thing I should like to say is that I never heard such choir-singing in my life as I heard there; and all the choirs consisted almost entirely of colliers, iron and tin-plate workers, and quarry-men, and their conductors belonged to the same class."

"It is a wonder," said John, "that Llewelyn Pugh is away so long. But we must have an account of the Eisteddfod soon, Caleb; and Shadrach, too, must be here on that occasion."

CHAPTER IX

John Vaughan and his friends in the Corn-field

ORE than a fortnight had passed after the hay harvest at Pentre-mawr before the corn harvest began, and no place had a greater charm for the villagers at that season than Ty-mawr, old David William's Farm. The attraction, however, was not David William, as much as his wife and charming daughter, especially the latter, who, when the harvesters arrived was the first to greet them with a radiant face and ringing voice.

John and Shadrach had promised a day each to Mr. David William,

"THE FIRST TO GREET THEM WITH A RADIANT FACE AND RINGING VOICE"

of Ty-mawr; and they had, as usual, arranged to be there on the same day. Shadrach, according to promise, called upon John; and both friends went together along the old turnpike road to Ty-mawr, which was at the extreme end of the village.

Ty-mawr had many interesting associations to John and Shadrach, for as boys they had indulged in many an adventure on old David William's farm. They were specially reminded of one incident which had been indelibly impressed upon their memories. When they were boys, bent upon mischief, they had on one occasion climbed the hill above Ty-mawr Farm and entered another farmyard on the summit of the hill. There they saw an old grindstone, which had been well worn, and had been replaced by a new one. It was a beautiful day in summer, and it occurred to the vivid imagination of these lively youths that very few things could compare with the sight of that old grindstone rushing down the hill-side. John suggested it, and Shadrach vigorously endorsed his cousin's suggestion. Immediately the lads were busily employed in trundling the stone along the sloping ground to a favourable starting-point, opposite the thickest part of the hedge at the bottom of the field, where they judged the stone would be easily arrested. The start was made, and gloriously did the grindstone proceed on its downward course, now and then leaping many feet as it increased in velocity, until at last, to the intense surprise and terror of the boys, it dashed through the hedge as if it had only been tissue paper, and disappeared out of sight.

They began to realise the possible mischief it might accomplish when they remembered that immediately below the second field, and through a deep cutting in the rock, the old turnpike road ran. They shuddered with the thought of what might happen, and ran in another direction homeward. Happily for them they escaped notice, and reached home unobserved. It transpired that just at that time David William was seated near his front door in the farmyard, when the grindstone coming into contact with the hedge above the turnpike road bounded clean over the road, and from the bank on the lower side and leaped within a few inches of David William's feet, and rushing on its headlong career smashed into atoms a milking pail, and, dashing through the fence opposite, disappeared in the field below.

Such an incident as this soon became known in the village; but John and Shadrach were home before the news had spread, and they looked, and really were, as surprised at the news as any who heard it. That secret had been kept by the two friends for many years, and even now was only known to a few in their own families; for they had never lost the sensation of the horror which long ago possessed them at the thought of what might have been the tragic end of that boyish freak, apart from the fact that another Hand than those which had set the stone in motion had guided it in its wild career.

As the two friends entered the farmyard on this occasion, although more than thirty years had passed since then, they instinctively looked up at the spot whence the stone had taken that final leap, and exchanged a few words about the well-remembered incident.

As they turned towards the front door, old David William was talking to a number of harvesters who had assembled, and who were about to go to the harvest field. They exchanged greetings with the old farmer, and then joined the company as they proceeded to their day's toil.

John had a special liking for the corn harvest. He used to say that while the hay harvest was for the sustenance of those creatures which serve man so faithfully, and therefore one in which men should engage with a will, the corn harvest was for the direct sustenance of man himself; and that God had wisely arranged that man should till the soil, sow the seed, and reap the harvest before he could be supplied with his daily bread. Sowing, like spinning, was a task specially human. Indeed, some other creatures could spin, but none sowed. This, John held, was one of the glories of man, and no place testified to the dignity of human labour more than the harvest field. The corn would die rather than grow wild: in other words, it could only exist as God's reward upon human toil. How gloriously, therefore, was man in the harvest field a worker together with God! It made him feel his responsibility and true dignity to put in the sickle and bind the sheaves, as perhaps he did nowhere else in nature; for as there could be no harvest without God's blessing, so God ordained that there should be none without man's cultivation of the soil and sowing of the seed. What a promise that was, that seed time and harvest should not cease! Harvest would soon cease if seed time were overlooked; but if man did his duty in seed time, God would see that the harvest should not fail him—at least so far as to deprive him of the staff of life. John added that it did a man good to go hand in hand with God in the harvest field.

Shadrach was struck with John's remarks, and added: "I suppose, John, that is why Christ spoke so much about sowing and reaping, wheat and tares, good ground and bad ground. He could not take any figure more familiar to the farmers who listened to him; and

certainly there was nothing they did in their daily work in which
there was greater responsibility than sowing or reaping."

"And I suppose, too," interjected David William, as he looked
anxiously at a cloud that hung heavily overhead, "that they were
not troubled with wet harvests in the East. What with the low prices
wheat sells at now, and the difficulty we have had of late years to
gather it in good condition, the farmer has a hard time of it now-a-
days. There's that cloud just above us: it looks as if it is going to
drench us by-and-bye, and spoil the day's work."

"What a strange thing it is, David William," responded John
Vaughan, "that you, who are a Hyper-Calvinist, have so little faith in
God. You evidently don't think with the Rev. John Jones, of Talsarn,
that the good Lord does not allow every threatening cloud to pour its
contents upon us, but often—and how often few of us take note—ties
up the cloud at the bottom, so that it shall not pour a drop until he
sees fit. Now, do you think that the gracious Lord is going to allow
that cloud to do you more harm than good if you commit all your ways
to Him—you, too, who are one of His elect? Do you really think that
God has elected you and after all make you the victim of every passing
cloud? Whoever ought to worry himself, a Hyper-Calvinist ought not;
and any worry on your part won't mend matters."

"You forget, John," replied the farmer "that whom He loves He
chastens——"

"No, I don't!" interjected John; "but you seem to forget it, when
you get so despondent at every trouble that threatens you."

"Ah, it's not only the weather," responded David William, shifting
his ground slightly; "but there's this foreign competition. It's
something terrible."

"I have no doubt it is, and I know this makes farming increasingly
trying; but then, you know, God allows all this to take place in His
Providence, and the grand thing about His Providence is that no
particular class is served by it to the injury of others, but in the long
run it furthers the interests of the many, even at the cost of the few
having to suffer. There have been times when the few have fought
against the aims and purposes of God's Providence, but the more
they do of this the more sure is Providence of having its revenge by-
and-bye. Now, many years ago, when there was no foreign
competition, how often had the poor to suffer, because the farmers

in many instances used to lock up their corn until they could get exorbitant prices for it! Meanwhile the poor man and his family, in thousands of instances, were brought to the verge of starvation."

"That's quite true," exclaimed Shadrach; "and it was that that made the poor old weaver in Anglesea thank the Lord for the rats. He said, 'O Lord, we thank Thee for the rich harvest Thou hast given us this year, and the glorious weather Thou didst grant us for bringing in the sheaves. But we thank Thee, too, Lord, for the rats, for our miserly old farmers would have kept the wheat in the ricks unthreshed until the markets had risen sufficiently, so that the poor could not afford to buy half as much as they and their children needed. But we thank Thee, Lord, that Thou hast plenty of rats to go into the farmers' ricks to consume all the wheat for them unless they thresh it.'"

"If that weaver," said David William, "had himself been visited by rats, which had spoiled his yarn, he wouldn't have been quite so grateful, I suspect. It seems to me that people can only be grateful for rats when they don't visit them; but only spoil other people's goods: and that is gratitude of a very questionable kind. I don't think the Lord is much moved by it."

"That's rather beside the mark," replied John, as he and Shadrach laughed at the old farmer's repartee; "but I don't think we can do better than leave the matter there, now that we have reached the harvest-field. Besides, we are told to honour an elder; and are taught that 'days should speak, and multitude of years should teach wisdom,' although that is not always the case in life."

The harvesters had reached the field some minutes before the arrival of these three friends; and were now waiting for David William, and getting ready for the day's work. The cloud that had hung above the harvest-field, and had threatened to pour its contents upon it, had meanwhile been gently borne on the breeze, and was passing quietly over the eastern hills, covering the sun for the time being and casting a heavy gloom over the landscape. Meanwhile the sun cast its burning rays through every chink in the cloud, and as soon as the cloud passed by, the sun's rays shone brightly on the slopes of the opposite hills, and speedily descended into the valley as they chased the fleeting shadow across the landscape. Thus, amid a flood of light, and without a cloud in sight, the harvesters stood ready for their work, while David William's gloomy fears had vanished in the sunshine.

The way to the harvest-field was very sinuous, and through a narrow dell covered with low growths of birch and hazel, thorns and briars, the roughest part of Ty-mawr Farm. Some of the harvesters commented freely upon the roughness and tediousness of the path, remarking that the ancient "Wandering through the Wilderness" must have been something like that, only on a larger scale. Indeed, most of the women, from sheer regard for their garments, had taken a still more devious, but less thorny path on their way to the field.

"It reminds me," said Shadrach, "of what I once heard about the Rev. Henry Rees, of Liverpool. One good minister, who thought that, wonderful as Mr. Rees' sermons were, they wanted a great deal of patient following before folks could get at the wealth that was in them, said about him, 'Mr. Rees' mind and sermons are very much like the land of Canaan, full of milk and honey; but you must journey through a great and terrible wilderness before you can ever enter them.' I think this field is very much the same. It is covered with a rich golden harvest, but it is little short of a miracle if all of us will arrive safely."

A smile stole over the countenances of the harvesters, as they enjoyed this good-natured home-thrust at David William. But the old farmer was more than equal to the occasion.

"You omitted to say, Shadrach," replied he, "that when Dr. Edwards, a mutual friend, repeated this criticism to Mr. Rees, he answered, 'Yes; but our friend has forgotten that the reason why he and some others cannot enter, is precisely the same as the reason why so many of the Jews did not enter—because of their unbelief.' Besides," added the old farmer, "I fear this field is not quite so rich in corn as it looks. The ears have not filled well this year, for want of rain a little while back, and of sun more recently."

"I am afraid the Lord's weather never is right with you farmers," replied Shadrach, mischievously, by way of the best repartee he could give; "I suppose when the Millennium comes, every farmer will have the management of his own weather. At least, I notice that now Hyper-Calvinists, in spite of their creed, seem of all men to be the least satisfied with the Divine decrees; and while that continues there can be no Millennium for them."

David William was keen enough to trace the mischief in

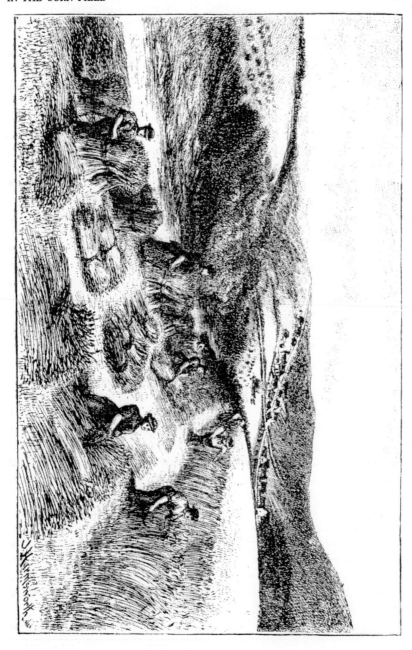

Shadrach's eye, as well as the tremulousness in his voice which betrayed an effort on his part to appear in earnest, and merely replied smilingly: "If ever we do get the management of our own weather, I hope we shall make it fit in better than you fitted the shoes last week in shoeing my horses."

"What hope is there," replied Shadrach merrily, "of pleasing those people whom even Providence can never please?"

John Vaughan quietly suggested that the best way out of the argument, as well as the best way to please David William just then, was to join hands and begin to work in right earnest. Indeed, he added that was the best way generally out of arguments. When people worked well together they postponed discussions; and such postponements were like Parliamentary postponements—very few subjects survived that operation.

The harvesters soon adopted John's suggestion, and put in the sickle with a will amid the bending corn. The wheat was here and there very ripe, and rapidly loosening itself from the husk. John and Shadrach, as usual, kept close together. Shadrach referred to the ripeness of the corn, and the relaxed hold which the husk in some instances had upon it.

"It reminds me," said John, "of a sermon I heard Rev. Daniel Jones, of Llanllechid, preach once. His text was, 'What is the chaff to the wheat? saith the Lord.' It was a wonderful sermon."

"Indeed!" replied Shadrach; "what did he say, John?"

I remember much of it, though I fear I have forgotten more, but now that we are hard at it I will only give his leading points. I remember his eyes glistening through his spectacles as he described the chaff growing with the wheat, and rendering it service in protecting it, yet forming no part of the grain itself, but only its clothing. Thus, as the wheat ripened, it loosed itself from it gradually but certainly. Then he described the flail on the threshing floor furthering the separation; and then he described—oh, how powerfully—the winnowing process, by which they would be finally and for ever separated from each other. The effect was terrible, Shadrach. We all seemed to feel the breath of that terrible winnowing fan!"

"No doubt, John," replied Shadrach, earnestly, "and that is what we need think of seriously, all of us."

"Yes," answered John, "and yet when we do think of it we soon gather confidence if we are Christ's. Old David Evans, of Ffynon-henry, was quite right when during his monthly visits to Horeb, he once preached from the Lord's words to Peter—'Simon, Simon, behold Satan hath desired to have you that he may sift you like wheat,' &c. You, too, remember it well. Who could forget it?"

"Yes," replied Shadrach; but anxious to hear John repeat what he felt only John could repeat properly, he added, "but I am not quite sure of the part you refer to."

John answered, "Why, that part where he said that when the good Lord allowed Satan to hold the wheat sieve, He Himself used the fan, and when the devil had the winnowing fan the good Lord Himself took very good care to hold the sieve. I am not sure that that was exactly what Jesus meant in the words He spoke to Peter; and yet I know it's all very true to life. The gracious Master will not suffer us to be tried above that we are able to bear."

"There are few places which teach man such solemn lessons, John, as the harvest-field and the threshing floor," responded Shadrach solemnly. "There's that lesson of the chaff, for instance, growing with the wheat, and even rendering valuable service to it; and yet at last separated from it, and either scattered by the four winds of heaven or burnt up."

"Yes," said John, "they no doubt teach us that there are many things in life, not in themselves evil, or altogether useless—although that, no doubt, was what the prophet meant when he applied the figure to the teaching of the false prophets—which yet are only useful for a time and for a certain purpose, and beyond that are of no good. There are many things in life like that. For instance, all temporal blessings. All these are gifts of God, and, like the husks, they are intended to be helpful to something far more valuable than themselves; even the spiritual grain which God, the Great Husbandman, would gather at last into His garner. But all these temporal blessings have no further mission. The sad part is, that men pay more importance to the growth of the husks than that of the wheat, little realising that at last all they have held dear will be utterly useless, and, like chaff, will be driven away with the wind. How often has the rich man who has lived only for this world lived just long enough to see the heap of chaff which he has grown, and gathered, scattered as useless refuse by the winds of God!"

"Very true, John," replied Shadrach. "And then there is that other class, who not only spend all their energies in gathering those things which are only useful for a brief time, and thus forgetting the true end of living, but also sow even bad seed, to reap all too certainly a wretched harvest. They 'sow to the flesh, and of the flesh reap corruption.' What instances we have known of that, have we not, John?"

"Yes, Shadrach," responded John, "and they reap the bitter harvest, not only in eternity, but very often in this life. You remember, for instance, the story which your father and mine used to tell about the murder of that traveller at the Old J——y T—r, in C——, many years ago, and how the murderers, after more than twenty years of delay, reaped the awful harvest of their iniquity."

"I have a glimmering of it, John," replied Shadrach; "but I have forgotten most of it, I fear. You have such a memory, John, that you seem to forget nothing. Just tell the story again."

"Oh, simply this," answered John. "A traveller whose name is not known, put up at the Old J——y T—r many, many years ago, when your father and mine were quite young. He was evidently wealthy, and had a good deal of money in his possession. The gentleman died suddenly; and in those days there were no inquests, or at least they were not conducted with the care they are now. He was in due course buried in the parish church, and the incident was soon forgotten. Nearly twenty-one years later the gravedigger opened an old grave for a fresh burial, and in so doing threw up a skull and other human bones with the soil. A gentleman chanced to pass through the churchyard, and turning over the skull with his walking-stick noticed that a long thin nail had been driven into it near the temple. He immediately asked the old gravedigger—who had been at that work for a generation—who it was that had been buried there. The gravedigger replied that it was a stranger who long since had died suddenly at the Old T—r. Further inquiries were made. The landlord and landlady still lived. They were taken into custody, tried, and hanged for murder after a lapse of twenty years. What an illustration of the words, 'Be sure your sins will find you out,' and 'Whatsoever a man soweth that shall he also reap'!"

Just then David William, the old farmer, came up and said, "Well, what subject is uppermost now, friends?"

"John was just telling me the story of the sudden death of the gentleman at the Old J———y T—r, in C———, many years ago, and the way in which his murderers were found out more than twenty years later. You, no doubt, remember something about it, David William."

"Well, I was not born when the murder took place," replied the old farmer; "and I was only a little boy at the time of the trial and execution; but I remember it as if it had been only yesterday. Both husband and wife had thrived for twenty-one years largely on the proceeds of the deed of blood, and had kept the terrible secret and had passed muster in the town as respectable citizens all the while; but only at last to reap the terrible harvest for which they had long since sown."

"That's it," exclaimed Shadrach, "that is just what John was saying; and we could not help remarking what a wonderful teacher the harvest-field may become to us."

"Yes, very true," responded David William; and our Lord, and indeed the Apostle Paul, as John reminded us the other Sunday in class, taught us some of the most glorious truths from the harvest-field."

"Ah, yes; that was when we had the subject of the resurrection from the dead," said John meditatively.

"And a very mysterious subject, too, John, is it not?" added Shadrach.

"Yes," replied John, "and everything that pertains to life and death has mystery about it. This life would not be half the thing it is if there were no mystery to arrest thought and to awaken faith."

The time had now come for the mid-day meal, and from all parts of the field the harvesters assembled in a shady nook where the provisions had been laid.

Jenkin, who had just come to the harvest-field, having been engaged in the smithy, had seen Rev. Benjamin Thomas (Myfyr Emlyn) in the village, and was intensely interested in the lecture on "David Evans, of Ffynon-henry," which Mr. Thomas was to deliver that evening at Horeb Chapel. The lecturer was a great favourite with Jenkin, and he predicted, in his usual dogmatic fashion, that a lecture by Mr. Thomas on such a quaint character would be brimful of interest and amusement.

John Vaughan agreed that the theme would be a very congenial one to the lecturer, and would no doubt afford abundant opportunities for racy talk and quaint humour. Indeed, John Vaughan, as well as Shadrach and the old farmer, had heard the lecturer on a previous occasion speak on *The Celebrities of the Welsh Pulpit,* and he prophesied that they would have a lively time that night. "We shall almost think that old David Evans is with us once more," said he, "as some of us imagined other old preachers were alive again when we heard him describe them in Carmarthen, at the Tabernacle where the Rev. Hugh Jones preached for so many years. The dear old people were crying on all sides when they heard the tones of their dear old pastor; and one aged woman, who came rather late to the lecture, vowed that when she was in the lobby, and heard those familiar notes, so musical, amid the pauses of Hugh Jones's well-known asthmatic cough, she concluded that he must have risen from the dead. 'Dear old Mr. Jones,' she exclaimed, with tears in her eyes, 'was as natural as ever.' It was amusing, too, to hear the lecturer reproduce Rev. Edward Williams, of Aberystwyth. But there, I must give up, or I shall never know where to end. It was capital."

"Tell us, John," exclaimed Jenkin eagerly, "as we have at least twenty minutes to listen; besides," added Jenkin, with a mischievous twinkle in his eye, "David William will, no doubt, give us a few minutes extra, if there is need."

"Yes, perhaps, *if there is need,"* said old David William reluctantly, as two laws warred in his members; for, on the one hand, the old farmer, although he was an extreme Hyper-Calvinist, was a great believer in works whenever the villagers came to help him at harvest time; while, on the other hand, he was intensely anxious to hear John (whose memory was proverbial) repeat things which he himself had heard, but, alas, had largely forgotten.

"Come, John," urged Shadrach, "repeat some of the things we heard then."

"Well," said John, with an evident relish, "Mr. Thomas having referred briefly to Wales and its early preachers, and the fondness with which their memories are cherished in the cottages of our land, high on the mountain slopes and down in the valleys and deep ravines, suddenly stopped, and imagined some one present addressing him, 'Thou art not yet fifty years old, and hast thou seen Abraham?' and in his own quaint way replied, 'Well, no, I have never seen Abraham, neither has Abraham to my knowledge seen me.' Indeed, long before I opened my eyes on this world, many of the eminent patriarchs of the Welsh pulpit had gone to sleep. I have sometimes wished they had kept awake a little longer, that I might see them. I never heard the melodious voice of the brilliant and philosophical Williams, of Wern; the thrilling oratory of John Elias never fell on my ears; and the wild romantic eloquence of Christmas Evans; the powerful messages of John Herring, and the burning appeals of Ebenezer Morris, were bygone wonders when I was a child. I have only heard the echoes amid the rocks and streams and sanctuaries of our land; but if the echoes be so inspiring, what must the clarion sound have been in the day of battle!"

"That's good, and exactly as he said it," exclaimed Shadrach enthusiastically. "Tell us now what he said about old Mr. Williams, of Aberystwyth."

"Oh, yes," exclaimed Jenkin, "he used to tell a very good story about his courting, did he not?"

"Stories about courting seem to have a special charm for you, Jenkin," replied John significantly. "Well, I'll oblige you, Jenkin. Mr. Thomas told us that it was delightful to hear him relate the story of his courtship with the lady that afterwards became his wife. But it was not to everyone that he would tell that story. The company had to be select, and the social surroundings congenial. The presence of some would make him dumb, just as a peevish and bad-tempered maid will cause a cow to withhold her milk."

"Ah, I remember that well," said old David William, to whom anything that referred to cattle was specially interesting. "Tell us how he described the cow and the servant maids."

"Well, he said," replied John, "that the cow will not give her milk to every maid that demands it. When milked by an impatient, cross-grained servant girl, who is rough and domineering in dealing with her, the cow will first of all move her leg by way of gentle complaint. The impatient maid at once fires up and shouts sharply, "What is the matter with the old cow; behave, will you?' The cow again protests, and now a little more decidedly, and the girl shouts louder than ever as she gives her a push, 'What is the matter with the old cow? I'll make you behave yourself!' 'Oh, no,' replies the cow, 'if it comes to that, not a drop of my milk will you have, you saucy little thing,' and with that she gives her a kick that sends her, and her pail after her, towards the other end of the field. But, added the lecturer, "the sensible, good-tempered milkmaid touches the cow gently, and she responds by a movement of her hind leg and tail, as if to say:—

> "'Be tender, be gentle, my lassie, to-day'
> The milkmaid replies, 'I will be as you say;
> My touch shall be softer than velvet or silk,'
> 'Very well,' says the cow. 'I'll give all my milk.'

Just so, Mr. Williams would not tell his love story to everyone, but only to a sympathetic few. To such he told it much like this: 'I first met Mary in Manchester, and soon loved her. I thought that Mary also loved me. But Mr. J——, a wealthy timber merchant, loved Mary, too. I was in a terrible fix, and I suppose she was in a fix as well. To decide the question I went to see her one day, and said, 'I love you, Mary, very much, but Mr. J——, the merchant, appears to love you, too. He is a rich merchant, and I am but a poor minister. You do not know what may befall me. I may lose my voice; and what would become of you then, my dear? Perhaps you had better accept Mr. J—— for I love you so much that I would rather see you happy, even with him, than unhappy with me. You had better go with him, dear Mary.' 'What are you talking about, Edward?' replied Mary. 'I would rather come with you, if you had no coat to your back, than go with him, though he carried a wardrobe on his shoulders.' 'Very well, come then, Mary dear!' immediately exclaimed the cunning Edward."

"Good man as he was, there was a great deal of the wag about him," remarked Shadrach smilingly. "Tell them the story, John, about Mr. Williams and Rev. Morgan Davies, of Aberdare."

"Yes, that certainly shews his waggishness," replied John. "Mr. Williams and Mr. Morgan Davies were on a journey together. I ought to have said that Mr. Thomas spoke of Mr. Morgan Davies as being exceedingly innocent. He was a man of great ability, but also childish in some things, and often very absent-minded. When his thoughts were required at Aberdare they were in America. He had a habit of raising his hand and smacking his forehead in a dazed fashion, to make sure, I suppose, that his head was there, and had not gone on a pilgrimage. He used to make some amusing blunders. When baptizing a woman, for instance, he would probably say, 'I baptize thee, my brother'; and in baptizing a man he would be likely to make up for his first mistake by saying, 'I baptize thee, my sister!' Well, Mr. Williams and Mr.

Morgan Davies were walking one day on the banks of the river Rheidiol, on their way to a certain place. Mr. Williams suddenly asked, "Are you a good jumper, Mr. Davies?" 'Well, I used to be, years ago,' replied Mr. Davies, 'and I don't feel much the worse for age yet.' 'Well, if we could jump over the river just here at the narrowest place,' responded Mr. Williams, 'we should save a mile and a half. Will you try first?' 'Very well, Mr. Williams; but what shall I do with my carpet bag?' 'Oh, you had better throw that over first,' replied Mr. Williams with a twinkle in his eye, which escaped Mr. Morgan Davies' notice. Over the carpet bag went. 'Well now,' said Mr. Williams, 'jump across just where you have thrown the carpet bag.' Mr. Davies took a leap and landed about midstream. 'Dear me,' exclaimed Mr. Williams, 'you ought to have jumped further than that. How can I jump it if you have failed?' 'Can I carry you, Mr. Williams?' replied the innocent Mr. Davies. 'Well, as you are wet, and cannot get much more so, I really think that would be the best plan,' replied Mr. Williams naively and the patriarch of Aberystwyth crossed the river Rheidiol as on dry land."

"Really, that was too bad," exclaimed the old farmer.

"I think it was a splendid joke," ejaculated Jenkin, in high glee.

"Well, I don't suppose you would have liked the trick played upon you, Jenkin," replied Shadrach, half reprovingly, and yet evidently enjoying the story.

"I hope I should not be so dull as not to see through it," responded Jenkin. "Besides, father, you seem to enjoy the joke, for it was you that asked John Vaughan to tell the story."

John Vaughan, thinking it about time that he should come to the rescue, said, "Well, it is difficult to estimate the merits of the joke without knowing what a character Mr. Morgan Davies was. He was enough to tempt a saint of a far less humorous sort than Mr. Williams to play practical jokes on him. As I have already said, he was so provokingly absent-minded and even childish that it would require very special restraining grace not to have a joke at his expense sometimes."

"That's right," exclaimed Jenkin. "Besides, I think the best people are generally those who have a bit of fun in them. Only those who laugh can weep in true human style. Old Sobersides who never smile and never indulge in a joke, only manage to snivel when they try to cry. I never expect to find much sympathy or grace in people who do not enjoy a joke now and then."

"That's very extreme," exclaimed David William, the farmer, who was horrified at these remarks, which so shockingly contrasted with his Hyper-Calvinistic notions of saintliness. "I don't think that laughing or practical joking has anything to do with piety: they are of the earth, earthy."

"No doubt, David William," responded John Vaughan, "that merriment, or, for the matter of that, wit and humour, can lay no claim to piety; but it is another thing to say that they are not compatible with it. It is a very strange thing that the greatest servants of Jesus Christ, whose ministries have been most productive of good, often, indeed most frequently, have been those who have had a rich vein of humour in them, and who would not have so readily condemned Mr. Williams for that joke as you have; although I have no doubt, on the other hand, they would not have commended him so warmly for it as Jenkin has. Indeed, some of our greatest preachers to-day are brimful of wit and humour, and are men who cannot check this entirely, even in their sermons. The fact is, they cannot help themselves. Besides, you may depend upon it, if God has given men these gifts, it is in order that they may use them aright, and not condemn them as infirmities, much less sins."

"Well," said Shadrach, "whatever we may think of these things in the abstract, there can be no doubt that Mr. Williams was one of the excellent of the earth. He could often indulge in a quiet joke, but he could also be very earnest, most pathetic, and could subdue into solemnity and melt into tenderness all who listened to him. But tell us, John, what Mr. Thomas said about Rev. Daniel Jones, of Tongwynlas. That was excellent."

"He spoke about two or three well-known preachers, before he came to Rev. Daniel Jones," replied John Vaughan. "Having done so he proceeded—'The voice came to me again, saying, "What seest thou, son of man?"' and then he went on to say: 'I see an old man of patriarchal appearance; his hair white as snow waving gracefully down over his coat collar. He has a decent black suit of clothes on, a white neckerchief around his neck, but no collar. His dress and person are peculiarly clean and neat, his countenance very beautiful, and much humour and good temper play upon his brow. As he walks through the fields, the grass bends softly under his feet, the flowers smile upon him, the bees hum, and the birds sing at his coming, and the cow and steer raise their heads to see him pass, and as he approaches the house, the children, and the cat and dog, run to be the first to meet and welcome him; he has some choice relish for the cat and dog, and some "sweets" for the children, and in a soft and dulcet voice addresses and blesses them all. Who is he, think you? Who, but Daniel Jones, of Cwmsarnddu, Liverpool, Felinfoel, Tongwynlas, and now of the heavenly Paradise. In one sense he was neither a great man, nor a great preacher, still he was very natural, humorous, and eloquent. The nightingale is not great, but she is the chief songstress of the wood; the streamlet is not great, but it is full of enchantment; so Daniel Jones was not great, but very popular and effective. There was but one Daniel Jones.

"'If you ask what sort of a man he was, I answer—he was a fine man: *particularly fine,* fine in body and fine in soul. His hair was fine as silk his skin: as smooth as velvet: his eyes as bright as two stars, and his nose as imposing as the "tower of Lebanon which looketh towards Damascus." His teeth were like "a flock of sheep that are even shorn, which come up from the washing." His speech was comely, and his voice like the sweetest strain of the harp. He was called "The golden harp of Ton." He could not speak but in song could not talk but in music—not in mechanical tones, but the tones of nature; not in a borrowed accent but his own. Daniel Jones was also the son of peace. His sweet voice would tame the lion, and his placid face would charm the serpent.'"

"That's it exactly," exclaimed Shadrach, rapturously; "tell us the story Mr. Thomas gave of him as Chairman of an Association Conference."

"Yes, that is amusing," replied John. "Mr. Thomas said that Daniel Jones was a very able and suitable chairman in conferences, especially if a ticklish case had to be tried. On one occasion a good old man, a local preacher, whose name was John Rollins, was very anxious to be ordained; but being not over bright as a preacher, and advanced at that time in years, there were many who objected to this. The case was brought forward at the conference of a quarterly meeting, and Daniel Jones was in the chair.

"He introduced the subject by saying, 'Well, my dear friends, the long-expected Conference has arrived at last, and we have met under auspicious circumstances. The weather is fine, the sun is bright, the fields are verdant, the trees are blooming, the birds are singing, and we are all happy together. The first thing which is to come before the Conference is the ordination of our dear brother, John Rollins. Well, my dear brother, you will probably have some to speak against you, but I will venture to say a word in your favour, so that you have the chair on your side. My friends, you know that many young men rush to the pulpit very thoughtlessly and unprepared, with but little experience, and without knowing whether they like the work, and whether the work likes them. But this charge cannot be brought against our dear brother. John Rollins has been on probation long enough, for he is over sixty years of age. Speak honestly, but kindly, my friends, what you think of the matter.'

"One got up and said—

"'Mr. Chairman, I respect our brother very much; but as he has been so long without being ordained, and cannot expect to live many years, I think it very unwise to ordain him now.'

"'Mr. Chairman, I think the same,' said another, and yet another and then there was a pause.

"'Well, my dear brother Rollins,' said Mr. Jones, 'the brethren appear to be agreed against your ordination. What do you think of it now?'

"'Mr. Chairman,' was the prompt reply, 'I will not be ordained if you do not all wish it.'

"'Well, my dear brethren,' added Mr. Jones, 'great is the power of Divine grace. Godliness teaches man to be content in whatsoever circumstances he may be, and its influence is wonderfully manifested in the conduct of our dear brother John Rollins; because ten minutes ago he was willing to be ordained, and now he is willing *not* to be ordained. God be praised for His abundant grace.'"

"That's precisely as Mr. Thomas said it," responded Shadrach. "What a memory!"

"Old Mr. Jones must have been a fine old character," replied Jenkin.

"Yes," said old David William pensively; "I knew him well; he was wise as a serpent, and harmless as a dove. I never knew a man who was much wiser, and certainly never knew a man more harmless than Daniel Jones."

All nodded hearty approval of the words of the old farmer.

The dinner hour being now over, there was but little more said during the afternoon, save an occasional reference to old preachers by John and Shadrach as they harvested together. Each one went with a will to work in order that all that had to be done might be finished soon. Even the evening meal in which the harvesters joined at Ty-mawr was uneventful, because of the evident desire of most present to hasten to the lecture.

CHAPTER X

A Lecture at Horeb Chapel

REV. BENJAMIN THOMAS (MYFYR EMLYN)

WHEN the hour arrived for which the lecture on David Evans, Ffynon-henry, by the Rev. Benjamin Thomas (Myfyr Emlyn) had been announced, Horeb Chapel was well filled. The name of the lecturer, and the subject selected, combined to make the lecture attractive.

There was a brief introduction, during which a hymn was sung, a prayer offered, and a few words spoken by the minister of the church and chairman for the evening. Then the lecturer stood on his feet, and at once began to speak of the gifted sons of Wales in the past generation, who had devoted their great talents to the proclamation of the Gospel, especially Caleb Morris, of Fetter Lane, London, whose heart, however, was always in Wales, and who at length died at Gwbert, near Cardigan, at the mouth of the lovely Teivy—Gwbert as rocky as Patmos, and with a sea as blue as ever beat upon the jagged coasts of that lonely island. The lecturer had known Caleb Morris and loved him. There were tears in his voice as he paid him a passing tribute, and laid a wreath upon his grave.

REV. CALEB MORRIS

"There was Caleb Morris," he continued, in subdued tones; "he was one of the greatest men I ever knew: a man in whose company one would derive in half an hour more benefit than in half an eternity at the feet of many who occupy theological chairs in our colleges." Then, in a playful reference to the slight turn in one of Mr. Morris's eyes, the lecturer added, "There was more theology in the squint of his eye than there is to-day in all the dry, long-winded, and formal lectures of many an old dry-as-dust 'Domini.' He shook London with his message, and created a new era in the history of preaching by his burning eloquence and brilliant thoughts. Yet there is barely a word said about him in Welsh or English that will give succeeding ages even a feeble conception of what he was. Having served faithfully his age and generation with his great powers, he fell asleep, and now lies peacefully at the foot of Voeldrigarn mountain, in Pembrokeshire, the slopes of which he climbed a thousand times when he was a lad."

Just here John's eyes began to moisten, and forgetting it was a lecture, began to respond as if it had been a sermon. Shadrach, too, felt a lump in his throat that kept him silent.

The lecturer proceeded: "Why is it that publishing the biographies of such men involves an expenditure which is seldom met by the sales; and that, in vending wares for the public, it is far safer to speculate in shrimps, cockles, or periwinkles, than in a good book? It is only fair, however," added the lecturer significantly, after a brief pause, "to say that it is seriously affirmed by the public that the chief difficulty is not in the purchase of a book, for after having given half-a-crown for a biography, it is often honestly worth an additional half-a-sovereign to read it: it is so intolerably dry. But, whatever may be said on both sides, it is a poor sign when, in any country or among any people, the memory of the just, the brave, and the good is ignored and forgotten."

This and much more was said by the lecturer by way of introduction to the subject of his lecture. At length he said: "David Evans, of Ffynon-henry, has passed away for the last five years, and there is no sign of anyone placing on record anything about the quaint old patriarch. The two old sisters, *Tradition* and *Folklore,* are the only ones who seem to cling tenaciously to the memory of his savings and doings. It would, indeed, be a thousand pities if David Evans, one of the most original characters of the present century, were ever forgotten. He stood by himself. It is a waste of labour and of money to write the biography of any man who has no distinctive attributes, which may with advantage be studied, even if not always imitated. David Evans has not left his like behind. Naturalists enthusiastically collect fossils of certain types of life which have become obsolete. It is with some such feeling that I recall the memory of David Evans to-night. He belonged to an age which has now passed away, and can never be reproduced in Wales. Forty years ago there was a glorious fraternity of this type to be found in the Welsh pulpit; for instance, David Rolant, of Bala, Robert Thomas, of Llidiardau, Rees Powell, of Cardiff, and David Evans, of Ffynon-henry."

Having spoken of the birth of David Evans in the year 1778, and the circumstances connected with his early life, the lecturer proceeded to speak of his striking personality. He said that a special charm attached to the persons of great and good men. The house in which each lived, the clothes he wore, the paths he trod, the staff upon which he leaned, and, above all, the body in which he tabernacled, became objects of intense interest to the hero-worshipper.

"There was something very striking," added the lecturer, "about the appearance of David Evans, although there was nothing very exceptional about his stature or bulk. It was easy to see, at once, that he was not intended to excel as a muscular Christian, like some of the old fathers—to wit, Christmas Evans; Timothy Thomas, of Aberduar; John Jones, of Edeyrn; and many others who were Samsons in physical strength. David Evans, on the contrary, was of a somewhat slender build; but his body was the home of a bright and vivacious spirit.

"He possessed two wonderful eyes. They were not large, but they were full of light, and at once suggested that there was a soul possessing a keen and piercing vision behind those windows. That soul was never at rest, and those two small but brilliant eyes, which soon attracted attention, were as keen and restless as the soul that looked out through them."

David Evans was indeed an exceptional man, and very difficult of classification. Men were, as a rule, sooner struck by his peculiarities than by his greatness. People did not know whether to put him down for a genius, or for an innocent who was not in complete possession of all his faculties. They generally leaned to the latter conclusion. This is not to be wondered at, as it requires men other than of the ordinary type to see such a man as David Evans. People as a rule see only what they look for. A cooper only sees in the thicket the wood from which he can make hoops for his casks, while the hare hides among them all the while unobserved by him. He has not gone forth to see hares. So the men of Conwil and Ffynon-henry did not go out prepared to see a genius, but only men of their own type. Such men as David Evans found no place in their philosophy of the universe, until at last he made a place for himself.

"Although David Evans' body was in no sense imposing, yet it was a very serviceable instrument for his great spirit. It responded readily to all the movements of his soul. When humorous thoughts bubbled up, his eyes and lips, hands and feet, and every part of his nature were full of mirth and laughter. Every movement of his body gave quaint and eloquent expression to the thoughts and feelings which at such times were exuberant and charmingly youthful. So, too, when on rare occasions his soul was subdued by a great sorrow, every movement and look were charged with solemn significance. There was a close and very sympathetic connection between soul and body in David Evans."

This description of a man whom most present had known intimately for many years was greatly appreciated by the audience. John Vaughan and Shadrach Morgan were specially demonstrative. A family relationship that existed between David Evans and John Vaughan added naturally to the interest with which he listened. Besides, had not the Church at Ffynon-henry been affiliated to that at Horeb for many years? The numerous services which David Evans had conducted in the latter place would be remembered by the people at Horeb, and above all by John Vaughan, as long as memory would last.

The lecturer proceeded, "David Evans was not specially trained for the ministry. But little help could be got in those days by way of preparation for the Nonconformist pulpit; yet God more than made up for that defect. He put very special quality into the preachers of that age.

"If we would see David Evans in college, we must follow him along the banks of familiar rivers and brooks, into ravines and hollows, and up wild hill sides and mountain slopes; we must follow him into Nature's great university, where he caught from the heavens above and the earth beneath, from storm and tempest, sunshine and shower, the rich imagery with which his sermons abounded.

"Mr. Evans was no doubt peculiar," said the lecturer, after one of his characteristic digressions, which we need not follow here, "but he was peculiar because he was intensely original, and ever true to his

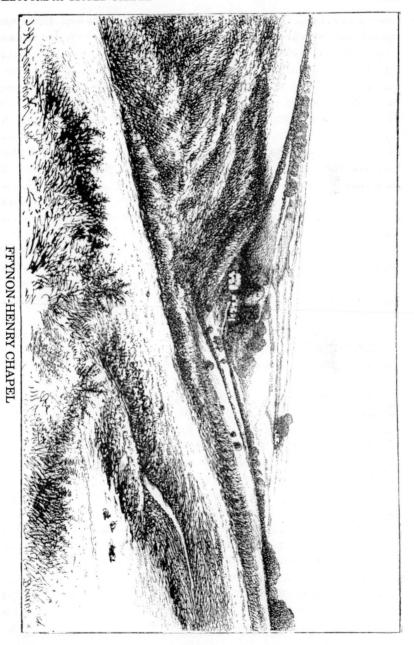

FFYNON-HENRY CHAPEL

own nature. God had made David Evans the man he was. He never copied any one: and it would not have been well if anybody had copied him. Such men, above all, are not to be imitated. As our English friends say, God breaks the mould after he has produced an exceptional man. Yet it is the supreme ambition of a host of men to imitate the inimitable. There is a tradition in Bristol College that the great John Foster used to wander in the fields in the neighbourhood of Stapleton, and gaze by the hour at a daisy. One of my fellow students heard of this, and forsooth, when he ought to be at his tasks he used to wander over the same fields and stare inanely at every daisy he passed, flattering himself all the while that he, too, was a John Foster. He never mastered the fact that there is a difference between the look of a genius and the stare of a fool. John Foster could not be imitated. He was a man apart from men. So was David Evans, in his way. His originality was of a different type from John Foster's; but it was every bit as genuine. He spoke out of the abundance of the heart, and with never-failing freshness. He told his own message, and not another's. He was not an imitator. The parrot can say 'Pretty Polly,' but someone has said 'Pretty Polly' before it.

"David Evans never repeated what Christmas Evans, or John Elias, or any of the old preachers had said before him. You know the old Welsh proverb—'It is difficult to steal a man from his uncle.'* The meaning evidently is that men bear a strong family likeness, so that they can seldom be dissociated from their relatives. They are often as much like each other as so many marbles. But David Evans was stolen by nature from uncle and aunt alike. No other man among all his contemporaries was like him. No doubt God made many equal, and even superior to him; but not like him. He was perhaps not as original as the spider, of which he used to say that he got all the silk thread he used out of his own shop. It is possible that he had some of his material from other sources; but he spun his own yarn, and weaved his own cloth. It is not always so, even with preachers. It is often the hand of Esau, but the voice of Jacob; and it is a good thing for the borrower that the congregation, like the old patriarch, is as blind as a gate post, or it would soon detect the imposture."

There was considerable amusement at this suggestion throughout

---

* "Anhawdd ydyw dwyn dyn oddiar ei ewythr."

the congregation, and a wholesome blush on the faces of two or three ministerial brethren present, who, nevertheless, seemed to enjoy the home-thrust. Meanwhile, mischief lurked in the lecturer's eye. He soon, however, proceeded—"The never-failing naturalness of David Evans was the secret of his freshness as a teacher. In imagination he was far behind Christmas Evans; but in naturalness he was far ahead of him. The grand old one-eyed seraph excelled all as he ascended in his great chariot amid principalities and powers in the heavenly places; but the patriarch of Ffynon-henry far surpassed him amid the humble walks of life, and in the company of birds and flowers.

"They 'train' preachers in our day," added the lecturer significantly, "in many instances, as they do horses. They are taught how to run and how to gallop, and how to trot and how to walk, and a host of other things. David Evans was never quite 'broken in,' and was certainly never 'trained.' No theological jockey was ever on his back. The result was that he could never be reined or stirruped.

"Of course," continued the lecturer, "the strait-laced folk found fault with what they were pleased to call David Evans's trifling. They shook their weak, narrow, bigoted heads till the little that was in them became very confused. They had little sympathy with his exquisite naturalness and rich humour. He hated all shams, and exposed unsparingly such humbug, as that of the old shopkeeper in Cardigan, who used to indulge freely in giving too little weight in tea and sugar on Saturday nights; but on Sunday used to look very pious, and on Monday morning, on one occasion, hanged his cat for catching a mouse on Sunday! David Evans exposed such folk with scathing irony and crushing ridicule. Thus was he true to himself and faithful to his Master and his mission."

Among the secrets of his popularity were his charming naturalness and sincerity. He stirred up the gift that was in him, and not the gift that was in anyone else. He walked on his own feet, and not on crutches. He drew water out of his own well instead of taking his pitcher to strange streams, which are so apt to dry up. No man can well deprive himself, his God, and the community at large of their due more effectively than by becoming the slavish imitator of another. It is a far greater honour to be a genuine and original man, than it is to ape, even with a measure of success, a seraph. Indeed, it is better to be an ape than to be like one. Apes of men are a curse to every circle, whereas a man of original resource is a blessing. The blacksmith who makes his own tools upon his own anvil is in that respect far in advance of the smith who gets all his tools from Sheffield or Birmingham."

Here Shadrach gave an emphatic nod, and smiled as he looked round approvingly at John.

"The man who utters even ordinary truths out of his own head and heart," continued the lecturer, "is higher from his shoulders upward than the man who repeats the most glorious things after Christmas Evans, John Elias, or Williams of Wern. No one has a right to tell a dream unless he dreams, or to say, 'Let us see, in the *second* place,' unless he has already seen something in the *first* place.

"Here David Evans was a king among men. He thought for himself, and in his own fashion, and expressed his thoughts as they had never been expressed before in Welsh, or probably in any other tongue. He was largely uncultured and unlearned; but mentally he was an *independent gentleman* in God's creation. He had found the key that opened the door to his own grounds, and not into other people's gardens. Let the fop, the philosopher, and the scholar say what they may about that natural genius, who was consecrated to the service of his Master, he lives to-day in the grateful memories of the Welsh people: his name is a household word, and his sayings are proverbial from Holyhead to Cardiff.

"Every little river has its own bed," exclaimed the lecturer, as he warmed up to his subject, "and every man should carve out his own course. David Evans undoubtedly did that; and did all to the glory of his God and the praise of his Redeemer."

This but briefly and very imperfectly expresses even the outline of the lecture since much is left unrecorded, and what is given necessarily lacks the force which the speaker's personality and voice gave to his utterances.

The audience had been charmed by the faithful description given of one whose life-work was so familiar to them, as well as the affectionate tribute which had been paid to the memory of one so dear to those who had known him.

John and Shadrach were specially pleased. They had known David Evans, and had admired him for many years. Yea, many had been the tales told in the shoemaker's workshop and the smithy about that quaint old preacher. For the last hour they had once more been brought back to the company of that departed saint, and that had given them unspeakable satisfaction.

"There, John," exclaimed Shadrach Morgan, as he and his cousin left the chapel, and walked along the familiar road, that led through the village to their homes, "we have seen good old David Evans alive

THE SPIDER AND HIS WEB

once more. We shall never see his like again but, really, it is a sort of resurrection to hear Mr. Thomas lecture about him."

"Ah," replied John, with a smile, "he had a congenial task tonight. There's a great deal in common between old Mr. Evans and the lecturer. You could see his eyes twinkle exactly like the old man's when he repeated some of his jokes and humorous sayings. Bless you, in preaching I would almost as soon trust old Mr. Evans, that he would not say anything which would upset very proper and long-faced people, as I would the lecturer. Both would be equally dangerous; and neither could help himself. And, though that sort of thing is in danger of being carried too far, I have long since come to the conclusion that it is much preferable to dulness for quaint humour is after all a gift of God, to be wisely used; while I have yet to learn that dulness is, or that there is any use for it. Besides, those who make us laugh generally manage to make us weep, too, before they finish with us."

"When Mr. Thomas repeated old Mr. Evans' saying about the spider and his web, that he got all his silk thread out of his own shop," said Shadrach, "I wish he had given us a bit of David Evans' lecture on Nature's colleges for teaching diligence."

"Yes," said John, "and he very often does it in his lecture; but, there, we heard old Mr. Evans give that himself."

"Quite true," replied Shadrach, "but it would be like hearing him over again; besides all of us haven't your gigantic memory, John."

"And some of us have never heard it," interjected Jenkin, who had just overtaken them; "I should immensely like to hear some of it, John. Do repeat a little to us."

"Well I can repeat some things," replied John, "for they were so easy to remember. He said that we can go to three or four colleges near at hand to learn diligence. 'The education will cost us nothing,' added Mr. Evans; 'but now that it is winter'—for it was winter when he lectured—'they have a recess, and all are out for their holidays. They will not resume studies till next spring. These colleges are: (1) The Ant's; (2) The Bee's; (3) The Wren's; and (4) The Spider's.

"'1.—The Ant's College.—"Go to the ant, thou sluggard, consider his ways and be wise." They have ways—old ways, wise ways, and busy ways. The ant always makes his little mound in the face of the sun, and never in the shade; and yet the ant never learnt this from a book. He builds his house also in the summer. He is not like the farmer who limes his fields in the winter, and makes hedges in the summer, nor like many a sinner who lives an ungodly life in bright summer days, and only becomes religious during the winter of old age. Would that such people went to the ant to learn life's first lesson. How much happier they would be in the end! "The harvest is past," says the man, "and the summer is ended; and yet I have no house, no food, and no raiment for winter. What shall I do? What shall I do?" The ant hears him complain, and says, "I haven't a spark of pity for you; you had the same chance as I had. You ought to see to your interests better in the summer, instead of lying idly in the sunshine. You lay once on my mound and fell asleep there in the bright sunshine, and I was obliged to stir you up, and make you promise never again to sleep on the roof of my house. But you soon forgot it. Sleep now, if you can, in the snow and frost of winter."

"'The ant does not spare his body, although he is small and slight-waisted. You may often see him carry his heavy loads, especially when a shower comes on and when he cannot carry it, he calls his companions, and, by dint of pushing, pulling and uplifting, gets it into his house, and often goes down to the lower storeys. Sometimes the rain soaks his goods before they can be stored in the dry; but as soon as the sun shines brightly on the front of the ant's house, you will see some of the inmates turning the wet parcels over, very near the door, to dry in the sunshine. But before evening all is covered over. Thus the ant goes on from day to day, and makes the best of the weather and his opportunities while he is able, and so when the winter comes he is safely sheltered amid plenty in a house of his own, and free from all anxiety.' That's about all I can remember," added John.

"That's first class," ejaculated Jenkin.

"Tell us what old Mr. Evans said about the wren," said Shadrach.

"Oh, let me see—he said that the wren has an important college," responded John, "adding, 'The wren is a small grey bird, known to all in Wales as being very industrious and thrifty in bringing up his family. He builds his house in some safe dry place under a bank on the roadside, in as quiet and secret a spot as possible. The nest is splendidly upholstered with moss, and lined with the finest feathers that his wife, Mrs. Jenny Wren, can find. This is the home of a numerous family. It is no joke to have to feed the little ones. The father has to go over the river to one parish, while the mother explores the country in the immediate neighbourhood of the nest. They work early and late to bring up their family in a respectable manner without becoming dependent on the parish, or borrowing of their neighbours without any hope of ever paying them back. Very often fourteen children are brought up at once in this way.

"'Now many a man thinks he has done wonders if he has brought up a family of seven or eight children once in a lifetime; but what is that to compare with the feat of Mr. Wren and his good wife? When

we bring up a family, the eldest help to nurse the youngest; Tom will
carry Jack, and Mary will rock the cradle when baby cries. But, in

THE WREN

the wren's family, there are
fourteen children of the
same age. One cannot help
the other. They all cry for
food at the same time, and
it requires great nerve, tact,
and resource to satisfy them
all. Not one can go out to
service, and not one is old
enough to be apprenticed to
any trade. No one helps Mr.
and Mrs. Wren except God.
They are both so busily
engaged that the father has
no time for repeating stories
at every street corner, or the
mother to hunt gossip from
house to house.

"'One thing more, he added, 'Mr. Wren's house has no window, and only one door; and when he or his wife feeds the little ones the doorway is quite filled. How they manage to feed such a host of children in the dark without wronging any one of them is a mystery which I have never solved.'"

"That's good," exclaimed Jenkin.

"And exactly as old David Evans said it," added Shadrach admiringly, to whom John's memory was a source of ever-recurring wonder. "Now John, tell Jenkin what he said about the spider."

"Oh, he, had no end of things to tell us about him," replied John. "He said the spider taught the arts and sciences at his college. He also said the spider himself was not a very comely-looking creature; but was exceedingly clever at making a very fine net. It was then that he added: 'The spider gets his silken thread with which he makes his net all out of his own shop. He has a patent for it, and lets no one use it but himself and his family. He will not sell it to anyone. And it is so fine that no one would know how to use it except the spider himself. The wonderful skill with which he works his net in various patterns, according to his need, is beyond imitation. The net exactly answers the purpose, and woe betide the gnat or fly that gets near enough to fasten its wings or feet in it. He makes two kinds of nets—big and small. When he put the large ones out it is a sign of fine weather; while the small ones are signs of wet and stormy weather. Thus the spider's web is a capital weather-glass. But he sometimes meets with misfortune. He occasionally makes a mistake in his calculations. And then his net like many a fisherman's net, catches bigger prey than it was intended to catch. The result is a sad havoc. An occasional bumble bee carries everything away with it, and thus many gnats and flies already caught, but not killed, escape. But he catches well at other times, and makes up for losses. He and his family, however, consume all the sport. The result is that they have rich times of it sometimes; but at other times the larder is very bare, and they have to live largely on past memories and future prospects. The spider sells none of his game, nor does he send a single brace he catches for a present to his neighbours.'"

"That's capital," responded Jenkin, with a smile.

"Give that bit about the spider and the toad, John," said Shadrach.

"You see, you remember it better than I; I had forgotten that," answered John.

Shadrach vigorously shook his head, and laughed incredulously.

"Well," said John, "if I remember rightly, he gave that before what I have already repeated. But there, it doesn't matter. He repeated a story told him by a man who had witnessed it all. 'One beautiful Sunday morning in summer, when he and others were sitting in the porch of Llangadog Church, waiting for the clergyman to arrive for service, they heard a dolorous sound. They searched for the place whence it came, and at last found under the decayed flooring a toad crying piteously, as his eyes gleamed wildly. Just then a spider descended like lightning along his thread, and gave the toad a knock on the head, and then another, until at last the toad turned helplessly on his back, apparently to die. But why, you ask, did not the toad get away? I cannot tell. He was evidently too charmed, or too frightened. The snake, too, is overpowered in that way. The snake will not cry, but it hisses and blows furiously. The spider, however, cares very little about that, and periodically comes down and gives the snake a sharp tap on the head. Thus you see the spider is a clever calculator, and a cunning worker; but I'm afraid he hasn't much conscience, or if he has it is a very peculiar one.' That is about all that I can remember," added John.

"But can that be true?" asked Jenkin.

"True enough that someone told old Mr. Evans so," replied John; "but I am not sufficiently well up in the habits of spiders, toads, and snakes to know whether the man's story was strictly accurate or not. No doubt the man thought so; and indeed such things are often told and generally believed all through the country."

"I should not believe it unless I saw it," answered Jenkin; "but anyhow it's interesting enough to be true."

"Speaking about toads," interjected Shadrach, "tell Jenkin what he once said about the frogs sent to Pharaoh in one of the plagues."

"He must have already heard that," replied John.

"No, indeed," answered Jenkin.

"Oh," added John. "He was speaking about the ten plagues, and was just then describing the plague of frogs. He described God telling Moses to strike the rivers with his rod, and thus summon the frogs to cover the land, and especially to visit Pharaoh's palace. 'They came,' he said, 'like a great regiment. They travelled all night, and when Pharaoh awoke the following morning, lo, a huge frog was seated on his chest, looking intently into his eyes, while the rest exercised themselves like gymnasts over the coverlet. "Dear me," said Pharaoh, who looked as white as a sheet, "these are terrible creatures," and he and his family hastened to dress forthwith. After much delay, while the servants were endeavouring to clear the breakfast room of the invaders, Pharaoh and his family were seated at the table; but just as the breakfast had been served, a frog jumped up into Pharaoh's plate, and looked steadfastly at him. "Stick the fork through his eye father," said the children. But Pharaoh shook his head and became unnerved, and calling the butler, bade him take the plate away. "What am I to do with the frog?" replied the butler, as he hesitated. "Am I to kill it, your Majesty?" "Nay," exclaimed Pharaoh, as he trembled like an aspen leaf, "do not touch the frog: the God of Israel has sent it, and I *see the fierceness of His anger in those eyes.*" I shall never forget," added John, "the effect produced when, after the humorous description, David Evans uttered those solemn words."

"That's splendid!" exclaimed Jenkin. "Anyone must listen to preaching like that. I should think David Evans was like the spider of which he spoke. He evidently got his sermons, as the spider did his thread, 'out of his own shop.' They were all homespun."

"Yes," replied John, "he had his own way of saying everything. Things appeared to him in a light which they seldom, if ever, appeared to other people. I remember, for instance, his talking in a cottage meeting about Methuselah, what a long life he lived. He immediately looked at the old-fashioned 'grandfather's' eight-day clock that ticked vigorously in the room, and then adapting himself to the occasion, he said, 'Clock-cases in those ancient days must have been very long, so long that it took an immense time before the weights touched the ground. God wound up Methuselah, and he was nearly a thousand years before the weights ran down. Hezekiah's clock well-nigh stopped at one time; but God repaired and cleaned it, and then wound it up anew, and it went after that for fifteen years, and kept time much better after the cleaning than it did before.'

"On another occasion—you no doubt will remember it, Shadrach—he was speaking from the text, 'He that hath ears to hear, let him hear.' He began in a most original style. He asked, 'Why does God pay such attention, I wonder, to man's ears? It is not because of their size. Many creatures have much bigger ears than he has. The ass has the distinction of having much larger and longer ears than man. Nor is it because he can hear much quicker than other creatures. The mole, for instance, excels in that direction. If we walk as quietly as we like it will hear us, in spite of our efforts. Well, then, what can the reason be that God pays such attention to man's ears? It is because of that which is priceless and immortal beyond his ear—namely, his soul. God has something to tell a man's soul which He has to tell no other living thing on earth.'"

REV. DAVID EVANS PREACHING ABOUT METHUSELAH

"I remember that well, John," exclaimed Shadrach. "But his prayers were as striking as his sermons, were they not?"

"Yes," said John. "He did not repeat phrases which other people were accustomed to use: but spoke to God reverently, and yet in his own natural style."

"Do repeat one or two of them," ejaculated Jenkin, earnestly.

"Well, one scarcely knows where to begin," responded John. "I remember him praying on one occasion, 'We thank Thee, Lord, because axes are used in our day to hew trees instead of beheading Thy servants for fidelity to Thy cause. We would remember that far better people than we have lost their heads for doing what we have now the opportunity of doing without fear. We thank Thee for liberty, our gracious Lord.' On another occasion he said in prayer: 'O Lord, we have come to Thee with our needs. We have much to ask for, but we thank Thee because we can come to One who can give all. We thank Thee because Thou givest feathers to the birds every year, and restorest to them their song in spring, yea, and givest a new beak to the eagle in his time. O Thou who dost replenish the need of all Thy creatures, give new hearts to those who need them, and renew the strength of others who have long served Thee, and who need refreshing from Thy presence, and Thou shalt have the praise for ever.'"

"He never prayed long, did he John?" asked Shadrach.

"Never," replied John, "and he had no patience with those who did. He used to say that the Publican, and Peter on the sea, when he was about to sink, offered model prayers, and that the nearer we got to them the better. Often, too, he would add: 'If you are ever troubled by those who offer long prayers, if you could only take them and hold them up to their chins in water, like poor Peter on the sea, they would soon learn to pray briefly, "Lord, save us."'"

"Yes," said Jenkin, "and if we could only have prayers of that kind we should have better prayer meetings and more to attend them."

The two older friends nodded concurrence; but as they came to the parting of the ways at the corner of the smithy, they parted for the night.

CHAPTER XI

A Service at Carmarthen

THE following day was wet, and thus afforded an opportunity for John and Shadrach to work at their respective trades, and finish some jobs which had hitherto been neglected, owing to the pressing claims of the harvest. In the afternoon the rain abated sufficiently for Shadrach to call on John to urge him to accompany him to Carmarthen to hear a young preacher that evening, who had already created a considerable stir, the Rev. Aaron Morgan.

It required but little persuasion to convince John that the weather would clear up, at least sufficiently to enable them to walk to Carmarthen and back—a distance in all of about eight miles. Indeed, John had already made up his mind to go at any cost, if only Shadrach would go with him.

The two friends decided to start immediately after tea, which was done. About half-way they had to seek shelter from a storm that lasted half an hour or longer. This made them late for the service. As they entered the chapel the congregation was singing the last verse of the hymn before the sermon.

The preacher, at the close of the hymn, got up to announce his text. There was a homeliness about the preacher's demeanour and movement which charmed John. College evidently had not spoiled him—so John thought. He preached from Matt. xxvi. 51-54, the theme being—*Peter cutting off the ear of the servant of the high priest; and his Lord's prohibition.* It was soon evident that the two friends had not walked in vain to Carmarthen. John was struck with the thoughtfulness, and Shadrach with the quaintness, of the preacher. He commenced by entering fully into the circumstances which led up to this incident, beginning with the exit of Judas from the upper room. He said:

"Judas left before the meeting had been brought to a close. The service is generally considered too long by those who have no sympathy with what is going on. Judas left because he was anxious to complete the contract of the betrayal. The disclosure of his motives, too, hastened his departure. There are many still who are ill at ease at the service, because there is some contract outside which they are anxious to complete."

Proceeding a step further, the preacher said: "Jesus, as He entered Gethsemane, said to eight of His disciples, 'Sit ye here, while I go and pray yonder.' Three followed Him a little further: but even they had to pause about a stone's-throw from the place where He struggled. Jesus has a path to walk, and a distance to cover in which no one can follow Him. He was supremely alone in the great struggle for our redemption."

The preacher, having spoken of the multitude with their lanterns insulting the moon, referred, in the first place, to *"Peter's failings, or shortcomings.* He 'struck a servant of the high priest's, and smote off his ear.' Man misses the mark when he has recourse at once to the last weapon that should be used. To strike is God's last resort. The ancient world had one hundred and twenty years of grace before God began to strike. Jerusalem, had, for centuries, God's prophets to warn it, and His priests to offer sacrifice on its behalf, before the Roman eagle was finally permitted to plant its destructive beak into it. Peter misrepresented his Master by striking. The enemy has two blows to give before Christ's disciple can give one. 'Whosoever shall smite thee on thy right cheek, turn to him the other also,' is the Master's injunction. The Christian has to endure two blows, and even then he is not to strike back. 'If thine enemy hunger, feed him; if he thirst, give him drink, for by so doing thou shalt heap coals of fire upon his head.' He is to bless even his enemy, and by thus laying his hands upon his head, will he 'heap coals of fire' upon it. According to the inspired Time-table, the train of revenge is not due until the Day of Judgment. 'I will repay,' saith the Lord. Peter must await his Lord's own time."

Then the preacher proceeded to speak of *the Lord's intervention*— "'Put up again thy sword into his place: for all they that take the sword shall perish with the sword.' When the disciples had *two* swords *in their sheaths,* Jesus said, 'It is enough'; but *one* became too many *when it was unsheathed.* There is no danger in a sword while it is in the sheath. It is when men take it out that the danger comes. The sword at such times is not in its proper place. To those who, like Peter, take it out of its place, Jesus says, 'Put up again thy sword into its place.'"

The preacher next proceeded to dwell upon *The greatness of Christ's resources:*—"More than twelve legions of angels." He said: "Heaven's reserve is always greater than what is in sight. The angels are heaven's artillery—the Highlanders who, in their onward march, stride over the everlasting hills. One of the greatnesses of Jesus Christ was His power to check the onward rush of these celestial forces. Armies are generally called out in extremity; but Christ kept them back at such times. He could have instantly had this immortal army to His help by merely sending a telegram to His Father. Peter forgot this. Jesus exclaimed, 'Thinkest thou that I cannot now pray to My Father, and He shall presently give Me more than twelve legions of angels?'"

The next point the preacher dwelt upon was *Christ's mercy and tenderness.*—"He healed the ear of Malchus, and thus showed tenderness and sympathy when everyone else seemed to cherish in the spirit of revenge. In the midst of the battle He restored an ear to a foe bereft of it by one of His own soldiers. On Calvary all appeared revengeful, but even then Jesus sheltered a thief beneath His forgiving wing, and uttered a tender petition on behalf of his bitterest foes—'Father, forgive them, for they know not what they do.' The tongues of the friends of Christ were dumb in the court on the day of trial; but the ear of Malchus spoke eloquently for Him there. What a testimony was this! 'Let not the sun go down on your wrath.' The sun should witness the funeral of all wrath and bitterness."

The preacher concluded with an earnest appeal to his hearers to accept Christ as their Saviour, and to drink deep of His Spirit. The service then concluded in true Welsh fashion—namely, with a prayer, and finally the singing of a hymn.

The meeting had no sooner ended than friends from the surrounding districts greeted each other with characteristic Welsh heartiness, and then gradually divided off into groups according to the directions they were to take on their homeward journey.

John and Shadrach joined the group that passed along Priory Street, for this was the only exit from the town to their native village. John's father-in-law was also among the number. He lived at Maes-y-gaer, in the neighbourhood of Allt-y-walis, about two miles and a half further than John's home. He had only a short way to walk in John's company, as he and his friends would diverge at Francis Well by the new turnpike road, which had been opened many years before, and which had done so much to divert the traffic from the old turnpike road running through the once busy, but now lethargic, hamlet, in which John and Shadrach still prided themselves.

John Vaughan's father-in-law was a striking character. He had lost one eye when playing hockey in his youthful days; but by a gracious law of compensation, the eye that remained was an orb of no ordinary brilliancy. Like Christmas Evans' eye, as described by Robert Hall, his was "bright enough to light an army through a wilderness on a dark night." He was a weaver by trade; and it was an interesting sight to watch his piercing eye follow the shuttle in its lightning flight all through the live-long day. At the age of sixty he began to learn Greek, and now that he was about sixty-five years of age he could read his Greek Testament almost as fluently as he could read his Welsh Bible. He was, moreover, a frequent contributor to the Welsh religious press, especially *Seren Cymru,* and was never as happy as when engaged in a theological discussion. He was a keen critic, and yet a jovial man bubbling over with good nature. He was, moreover, related to David Evans, Ffynon-henry, and had inherited, in common with him, much of the quaint humour for which the whole family was noted.

His besetting sin was a quick temper, and an occasional intolerance of those who differed from him in doctrine. The Rev. Aaron Morgan on this occasion had in the main pleased him. The preacher had not given as much theology as he could wish: there was no great question discussed; the sermon was more poetical than doctrinal; yet it *was* true poetry, and withal the preacher had the gentle, tender spirit of his Master, and in that Daniel of Waun-groes*—for by that name he was known—rejoiced and would rejoice. All this, and much more, he confided to John during the short walk they had together. He had serious misgivings about the preacher's exegesis when speaking of the two sheathed swords as being enough, simply because they were sheathed. Daniel held that there was a time when swords ought to be unsheathed; although he agreed with the preacher that Gethsemane was not the place for that. Yet he had a sneaking admiration of Peter for what he did to that servant of the High Priest, who, no doubt, thought a great deal too much of himself, and had made himself intolerable to Peter! Daniel belonged to the Church Militant, and he could never consent to the sword being always sheathed. This would rob life—yea, religious life—of much of its piquancy and relish. There were times, indeed, when he thanked God most fervently because He had taught his hands to war, and his fingers to fight; for was not every Christian to "fight the good fight of faith"?

But whatever might be said about swords sheathed or unsheathed, Daniel greatly admired the remark of the preacher concerning the words, "Let not the sun go down on your wrath," namely, that the sun ere it sets should witness the funeral of all wrath. He believed that we should fight for the truth, and wound its foes, too, with a will, while we are at it; and then have done with it. Daniel was a typical John Bull in the religious sphere: fond of a row, but not bearing a grudge long. He was a muscular Christian, who believed that religion was nothing if it had no backbone; but it must be confessed that Daniel was apt to estimate anyone's moral backbone by his readiness to break it rather than compromise any point of doctrine or element of truth.

That night the tenderness of the preacher's theme exerted a gracious influence over the honest, transparent, but not always

* This was the name of a former house in which this worthy had lived.

MAES-Y-GAER

gentle, spirit of this brave man; and had moreover appealed to his grand emotional nature by the thrilling tale of betrayal and unspeakable anguish. Thus Daniel's talk with John was unusually subdued and tender; and occasionally the great tears trickled down his cheeks as he expressed his increasing wonder at the patience and restraint of Christ, even in the presence of Judas, who had sold Him for thirty pieces of silver, and betrayed him with a kiss!

The company at length arrived at the parting of the ways, and John and Shadrach were left to pursue their course together while the greater number turned to the left, along the more modern and level turnpike.

The rain had now quite passed away; and every cloud had been dispersed; and, as the moon was up, and at its full, a rich silvery light flooded the land. Along the road which John and Shadrach had to walk there were spots—and notably one—where the overhanging trees cast deep shadows upon their way. As the two friends looked into the wood which skirted the road, they could understand how, if the trees in Gethsemane cast as heavy a shadow as those trees did—and there could be little doubt of that—there was more need of lanterns than would at first appear, though the full Paschal moon doubtless shone that night into the valley of Jehoshaphat, and glinted upon the golden roof of the Temple on Moriah. Altogether the walk home impressed upon their minds more than ever the events which the preacher had already so vividly brought before them that night. They spoke a little, but thought more, of the Lord Jesus on a similar night, and amid surroundings not altogether different, agonizing in prayer beneath the shadows of the trees, while already Judas and his band were emerging out of the gate of the city, and marching down the slope of Moriah, to cross the Kidron and enter Gethsemane. What a prayer that was!

"Thank God," exclaimed Shadrach earnestly, "that prayer is recorded."

"Yes," replied John, "we should have been far poorer if His prayers in the Upper Room and in Gethsemane had not been recorded for us; and observe," he added, "those prayers are repeated which were offered by Him amidst the most trying circumstances. Prayer is never so glorious as in our upper rooms and our Gethsemanes. God's saints, like their Lord and Master, sing and pray best in sorrow and in darkness. Indeed, I remember Mr. Morgan once dwelling upon that fact when speaking about Paul and Silas singing in prison—the cold, damp prison, at midnight too, and withal after cruel scourging. 'Why,'

"A RICH SILVERY LIGHT FLOODED THE LAND."

he said, 'they had been beaten with many stripes (v. 23). Those who had scourged them were accustomed to do so, and were skilled in the art. When such men scourged, every stripe cut deep. The Jews were cruel in their scourging, but the Romans more so. There was a limit to the stripes of the Jews. There was a recognised number. Paul writes: "Of the Jews five times received I forty stripes save one." These on each occasion were his thirty-nine articles, which he had to sign with his blood. But there was no limited measure to the stripes of the Romans. Paul, evidently referring to their treatment, says: "In stripes above measure." Paul and Silas had now received stripes without stint. The pain they suffered must have been great. The hospital would have been a far more suitable place for them than a prison cell. Those who are scourged, as a rule, can only groan at such times; but these made the midnight air and the old prison walls ring with their praises. It is wonderful what rich harmonies some of the people of God have sent forth in the midst of all their anguish. Pain has only added to the richness of their melody.' Yes, Shadrach, the grandest prayers and the sweetest songs are those in the night. Never did Christ pray as He did on the night of parting, and never did He and His disciples sing as they did when, before they went out to Gethsemane, they sang a hymn."

"Ah," said John suddenly, after a brief pause, as he looked around, "this place is associated with two of the most memorable events of my life. You will remember when one happened. It was a day in summer when I was passing this spot on my way to Carmarthen. A thunderbolt shot suddenly out of the heart of a heavy cloud, and darted down into the quarry here on the left. I instantly ran into the quarry, and found half a dozen men lying unconsciously on the ground; while one had been struck by the bolt, and lay dead with his head cleaved in two. It was one of the most solemn sights I ever witnessed."

"Yes, I remember that well, John; you were not yourself for months after that," replied Shadrach. "But what was the other event, John?"

"You have heard me talk about that, too, Shadrach," responded John. "It was many years before, when we were young. It happened one of those nights that I went courting yonder.

"My father, as you know, was far too fond of drink, and would, at times, come home at night the worse for it. On that night, a bitterly

cold night in December—I can even now seem to feel its biting wind—
I was coming down this road, and my father was walking just about
the same spot and in the same direction as we are walking now. I saw
him and recognised him instantly. I saw, too, that he was worse for
liquor, although I little realised he was as bad as he proved to be; and,
fearing what he might say to me if he recognised me, I took long strides,
and walked past him on the other side of the road; and then flattered
myself that I had done a clever thing. I took a very different view of
the matter the following morning, when I found that he lay down by
the roadside a very short distance on, and slept there for an hour or
more that awful night, and then awoke well-nigh frozen to death. That
walk was his last long walk on earth. He went home marked for the
grave, although he lingered on for a while; and I shall never feel the
same as if I had not passed my father thoughtlessly by on that dark
night"—John's voice quivered; there was a lump in his throat, and
another in Shadrach's, as John added, "I will say no more."

Shadrach instinctively took his cousin by the arm, and walked
closely by his side: he could do no more, and would do no less. The
moon shone brightly upon the road and imparted a weird aspect to
the scene while the two friends walked in silence, since the shadow
of a bygone memory rested upon them, and the thought of "what
might have been" saddened their spirits.

Gradually, however, relief came. The thought that the responsibility
of an act is not always to be measured by its tragic results, and that
there was One in heaven who knew that often "Evil is wrought for
want of thought, as well as want of heart," brought light and
consolation to the hearts which for a moment had been darkened and
saddened.

"Ah, John," interjected Shadrach in a half-consolatory tone,
"perhaps you would never have hated the drink as you now do were
it not for what it did for your father?"

"There is no doubt about that," replied John, as if realising that
there was some compensation, however small, in that fact.

Soon John and Shadrach had reached Peniel Chapel, and were met
by Jenkin, who had strolled so far in order to accompany them home.

"How did you get on at the service to-night?" inquired Jenkin.

"Gloriously," replied Shadrach. "You lost a treat, Jenkin. You
might as well have brought Margaret with you, instead of telling

her all the soft things you have told her a hundred times before, and getting yourself as white as a miller in walking among her father's sacks and flour bins—but there," he added, "I *will* say that you do not often miss a service for Margaret or anybody else."

"Come that's good," replied Jenkin, glad to escape further chastisement for his courtship. "I am glad you have had a good service to-night, father; and that you are coming home in a charitable mood as the result."

The moon had now risen above the eastern hills and bathed even the valleys in its silvery light. The undulating country, bearing everywhere the signs of harvest in its different stages of progress, lay peacefully around. It was a calm, restful scene, amid which John, Shadrach, and Jenkin continued to talk. As they passed along the road, most of the cottagers had retired to rest. Not a sound was heard save the footfall of the three, relieved by a constantly recurring remark from one or other of them. The birds were at rest, with their heads safely sheltered under their wings, and all nature seemed asleep. John and Shadrach, too, were wearied with their journey, and even Jenkin was slightly tired with the day's events for he had been busy most of the day, and the mill where Margaret lived was a long distance from the village. As the three, therefore, at length came within sight of the village, and dipped into the hollow where it nestled, they were ready for the night's rest and as John's house was reached, the companions hastily separated—John to his house, while Shadrach and Jenkin proceeded a little further, glad that the journey was over, and home near at hand.

CHAPTER XII

John Vaughan and his friends on the Eisteddfod

A FORTNIGHT passed before Llewelyn Pugh returned, and a meeting at John Vaughan's workshop was arranged, at which most of John's intimate friends could be present to hear the account which Llewelyn and Caleb had to give about the Eisteddfod in particular, and their experiences during their visit "to the hills" in general. Indeed, Caleb as we have seen, had given at the preceding meeting some interesting reminiscences of his journey; but had reserved what he had to say about the Eisteddfod until Mr. Pugh could be present, for the latter was an "Eisteddfodwr" and bard of more than ordinary repute, and was, therefore, better versed than Caleb in the details of Eisteddfodic ceremonial and procedure.

The delay in the return of Llewelyn Pugh was due to the fact that a few of his former pupils at the village school, who had since their school days removed "to the hills," had invited him to spend a few days with them. In two instances he had accepted their invitations. They announced far and wide to their friends the anticipated visit of their old schoolmaster, who, in addition to being an excellent Welsh writer and bard, was supposed to be one of the best scholars in Wales; for he had been educated at Oxford, and had enjoyed a distinguished career there. Indeed, they affirmed that he was intended for a bishop, and not a village schoolmaster, and would have been a bishop had he not become a Nonconformist. In one of the places which he visited, a local Eisteddfod had been arranged, and Llewelyn Pugh had been appointed adjudicator of all the compositions in poetry and prose. He had also at their request spoken at the fellowship meetings, prayed at the prayer meetings, and taken the men's Bible-class in the Sunday-school. In addition to this, he had met most of the leading lights in the places which he visited. Altogether Llewelyn Pugh was much lionised, and a fortnight soon passed under such favourable circumstances.

The first places at which he called after his return home were Shadrach Morgan's smithy and John Vaughan's workshop. Shadrach, at whose smithy he first called, told him of the arrangement to meet as soon as possible at John Vaughan's workshop to hear all the news that Caleb and he had to give about their visit to the great National Eisteddfod. Thus, before he arrived at John's house he partly knew what to expect. When he called, therefore, the night and hour were soon fixed.

The news soon spread abroad among John's friends, and Jenkin Morgan, Shadrach's son, was the only one, except Theodore Augustus Swaish—who was barely one of the company, but generally hanged on its outskirts—who did not look forward with great interest to the forthcoming meeting. Not that they were all adherents of the Eisteddfod, or even looked upon it with unqualified approval; but they were favourably inclined towards it, and believed that it possessed far greater possibilities for the future than even its past successes would lead men to expect.

Jenkin, however, had a "crank" in this direction. He had only seen local Eisteddfods, and as these in many instances, and especially those which Jenkin had witnessed, were but caricatures of the great National Eisteddfod, it is not surprising that he, with his ready tendency to be cynical, was reckless in his criticism, and sweeping in his condemnation, of Eisteddfods.

Knowing that Swaish, as an Englishman, would largely sympathise with him, and remembering, too, that Samson Lloyd, the village tailor (who only occasionally favoured the friends with his presence), had once tried for a prize in an Eisteddfod and failed, and since then had formed a low opinion of its merits, though it was by no means as low as that which Jenkin had formed of him, Jenkin urged them to attend. Swaish was interested in the subject, and promised to attend; while Samson Lloyd, flattered by Jenkin's special attention on this occasion, and with the memory of his unsuccessful attempt to secure a prize some years before still rankling in his breast, immediately consented.

On the appointed night the friends arrived at John Vaughan's workshop with commendable punctuality. Old Hugh Roberts, however, was the first to arrive. His early arrival was characteristic of the man, and in harmony with the habit of a lifetime. The farmhouse in which he was born, and where he had lived all his life, was a considerable distance from the village; yet he was always one of the first to arrive at every service and meeting he attended in the village. He attached great importance to avoiding undue hurry, holding that one of the most painful diseases from which the present generation suffered was chronic haste. People, he affirmed, did nothing calmly: not to say leisurely; the result being that nothing was done well. They came up breathlessly to every task, as well as to every meeting.

Reprehensible as this rush was with regard to the ordinary duties of life, it was, he held, still more to be deprecated with reference to meetings for Divine worship. He had often seen men come late to Christian services, to the distraction and annoyance of punctual worshippers: and, when they had arrived, they had done little but mop their faces, and made desperate efforts to subside into the habit of natural breathing, for the first quarter of an hour, or more, after their arrival. He held that such people were but little benefited by coming, and that the little benefit they possibly got was at the cost of distracting the minds and trying the patience of those who had come in time to wait upon God. He said all these things with emphasis, but yet with his wonted grace and gentleness, so that no one could take offence.

These convictions, however, were so strong, and had been held for so many years, that in everything good, old Hugh Roberts observed the same promptness and punctuality. His day's duties were mapped out with unerring precision, a reasonable pause being provided for between each engagement. To this calm and deliberate method of meeting the obligations of life, next to the exceptionally fine constitution which Hugh Roberts had inherited, may be attributed his splendid physique in extreme old age.

It was nearly half an hour before the appointed hour when Hugh passed Shadrach's smithy. Jenkin, looking out through the open door, saw the veteran advance with measured step, and leaning now and then upon his staff in such a way as to suggest the old man's growing need of that friendly support. "Here comes dear old Hugh," said Jenkin, as much out of affection for the aged saint, as out of a desire to say something funny at his expense. "He is like the shadow of good things to come, is he not? We all know it will be time to get ready by and by for some meeting whenever he passes by."

"Ah, my boy!" exclaimed Shadrach, who could never tolerate even the faintest shadow of a reflection upon his, and even his father's, old friend, "the utmost I can hope for you is that you will be as punctual and as good a man as Hugh Roberts, and that you will be as useful and beloved in your day and generation as he has been throughout life. This part of the world will be much poorer than it is when he is gone; and, Jenkin, I am afraid it will not be very long before that happens."

By this time dear old Hugh had reached the smithy door. "Now then, boys," said he, "it's time you should allow the bellows and anvil to rest for the night. Besides it is time you should be stirring, or you will be late."

"Very well, Hugh," exclaimed Shadrach, as the old man smiled, and proceeded on his way.

Tender were the words which Shadrach spoke to his son Jenkin about Hugh Roberts when the good saint had left the smithy door. Old memories came back to him in battalions of those days when he, too, worked with his father at that very smithy, as Jenkin did now with him. Shadrach could never think of those early days, and of the friendship that then existed between Hugh and his father, without brushing away a few tears that involuntarily trickled down over his cheeks. Jenkin, although full of fun and mischief, had much of his father's tenderness, and was touched to the heart when he witnessed those signs of emotion. Pretending, however, that he had not observed anything, he no sooner finished the task that he had in hand than he said: "Father, I think I will now get ready, so as to emulate Hugh Roberts in one of his excellences at least—namely, punctuality." Jenkin himself was so conscious of his habitual lack of that virtue, that he was tickled by his own suggestion; and Shadrach, who thought much of his son, but who was familiar with his failing, smiled as Jenkin hurried to the house.

It was not long before John Vaughan's friends had gathered in goodly numbers in anticipation of hearing what Llewelyn Pugh had to say about the Eisteddfod. Additional interest was imparted to the gathering from the fact that Jenkin and Samson Lloyd, the village tailor, for reasons already hinted at, were for once agreed, and were by no means prepared to admit that the Eisteddfod was all that Llewelyn Pugh and Caleb would have it be. Theodore Augustus Swaish, the only Englishman who lived in the village, was also naturally sceptical about the excellence of an institution so distinctly Welsh.

Thus the friends had arrived with a punctuality, which, apart from the exceptional interest awakened, would have been phenomenal. Hugh Roberts was soon followed by Llewelyn Pugh; and afterwards, in quick succession, by Caleb Rhys, Shadrach Morgan, and David Lewis; and last of all, as giving additional proof that mischief was brewing, Jenkin Morgan (who on this occasion loitered behind his father), Theodore Augustus Swaish, and Samson Lloyd came in a group.

The subject was immediately uppermost. John Vaughan in a friendly style questioned Llewelyn Pugh about the enjoyment and benefit he had received at the National Eisteddfod. Llewelyn spoke most highly about the Eisteddfod and all its arrangements, and was proceeding with his description of the competitions, when Mr. Swaish interrupted.

"Pardon me, Mr. Pugh, but having the misfortune of not being a Welshman, much of this is utterly unintelligible to me. I have never quite understood what the Eisteddfod is, and what purposes it is intended to fulfil."

This at once gave Llewelyn Pugh an opportunity of which he was never slow to avail himself. "I shall be very glad, Mr. Swaish," he replied, "to tell you all I can in order to make you familiar with the Eisteddfod. When I was at Oxford I found that the English people experienced a great difficulty in understanding the character of our great national institution. I am not therefore in the least surprised to hear you speak as you have just done. Indeed, it is only natural that those of other nationalities should feel the same difficulty, as there is no institution similar to it among any other people. It dates back into the distant past, its origin being lost in antiquity. The first Eisteddfod of which there is any record was held in the town of Carmarthen about a thousand years ago. Since then we know that it has been a great national institution, and has been instrumental to a very exceptional degree in fostering a patriotic feeling among us. Unlike most ancient institutions, moreover, it lends itself readily to such developments as the growth of knowledge and the spread of modern civilisation demand.

"The strong patriotic feeling so characteristic of us as a nation is, doubtless, partly due to our emotional nature: but it is equally evident that the Eisteddfod has been largely instrumental in maintaining it at the point of white heat. The old national airs sung in ancient times by bards, and in later times by competing choirs, have kept alive the flame of patriotism in our hearts as a people who have suffered much at the hands of our conquerors but whose sufferings have only brought us the nearer to each other, and inspired our bards to sing songs set in the minor key, and throbbing with pathetic cadences and tender notes—as the songs of a suffering race alone can—and yet ever and anon bursting into glowing predictions of a high destiny and a glorious future."

"Yes, Mr. Pugh," said Jenkin as deferentially as he could, "but patriotic feeling, while very good in its way, is not much by itself. Here are the bards and enthusiastic Welshmen shouting, 'Oes y byd i'r, iaith Gymreig'—('The world's age to the Welsh language')—and yet we know that English is stealing upon it every year in Wales, although Mr. Swaish is the only specimen of an Englishman we have in our neighbourhood. What we want, surely, Mr. Pugh, is something which shall more effectually help to keep the Welsh language as a language of the people, than merely shouting about it in Eisteddfods."

"I see your point, Jenkin," responded Llewelyn Pugh; "but you must remember that the Eisteddfod has not merely kept alive the national sentiment; it has encouraged the study of the Welsh language and the growth of Welsh literature by the prizes which it has offered for the best essays and poems on subjects which have covered a wide range; but in the choice of which the best interests of the nation have been kept well in view. The result has been that, notwithstanding the inroads which the English language has made into the Welsh, owing to English rule and commercial intercourse our national feeling is as distinct and as assertive as ever, and our literature grows to-day by leaps and bounds. Next to the pulpit of Wales, the Eisteddfod has been the most important factor in the maintenance of the Welsh language and the marvellous progress of Welsh literature during the last fifty years.

"The Eisteddfod, too, has given birth to institutions for the fostering of national feeling, the preservation of ancient Welsh literature, and the maintenance and scientific study of the Welsh language. The Cymmrodorion Society and the society bearing the name of Dafydd Ap Gwilym are striking instances of this.

"The proverbs of Wales, largely, too, owe their origin and still more their preservation, to the Eisteddfod. One of the leading Welsh authorities, Dafydd Morganwg, once called attention to the fact that a large proportion of Welsh proverbs are alliterative, and thus supply unmistakable proof of their poetic origin. They are bardic utterances snatched from otherwise forgotten 'Englynion,' or other forms of poetry. A striking instance of this was inscribed upon the walls of the Eisteddfod last month—'Môr o gân y'w Cymru i gyd' ('A sea of song is the whole of Wales')."

"But while the Eisteddfod has been, no doubt, a fine national institution in past ages," said Mr. Swaish, "for maintaining the Welsh language, and for fostering a strong patriotic feeling, is it not rather out of date now in view of the progress of arts and sciences? and do not the bards exaggerate their own importance, and attach too much sacredness to old druidic ceremonials?"

"There would be a great point in what you say," replied Llewelyn Pugh, "were it not that a very interesting feature of more recent Eisteddfods has been their ready adaptation to the special needs of the times. The ancient ceremonial is largely maintained; but the too rigid conservatism of early days, and the rude eccentricities and vaunting assumptions of the bards, who were wont, like the Athenians, to believe that they had sprung out of the earth separate from all others, like a crop of holy vegetables, have given way to the more enlightened views of later days. Thus, this ancient institution, so full of inspiring traditions and precious lore, is now extending its ramifications, and touching the life of the nation at new and important points of contact. It is no longer confined to literary, bardic, or musical effusions, but increasingly, year by year, takes in art in its different branches, and lends valuable aid to technical education. Thus, as the years pass, it becomes increasingly evident that the Welsh people have inherited a national institution which possesses boundless possibilities for the best development and education of the race."

"Well, what is your opinion of the last Eisteddfod?" asked John Vaughan, "as compared with those you have attended in former years, Mr. Pugh?"

Llewelyn Pugh paused, and then emphatically said: "The last Eisteddfod was probably the most remarkable ever held: certainly the most successful within the memory of man, and, there can be little doubt, the most largely attended. The place in which the Eisteddfod was held was typical. Pontypridd is very near one of our ancient rocking-stones, an important seat of old druidic bards, and the haunt of the late eccentric, self-titled arch-druid, Dr. Price. This eccentric man spent most of his life in the immediate neighbourhood, and, garbed in scolloped coat and trousers of green, brought into relief by a red waistcoat, and, withal, having the summit of his being crowned with a fox's skin, whose legs and tail hung profusely down over the old Druid's shoulders, was the admiration and wonder, if not the terror, of boys. There is no spot in Wales where all that is quaint in Druidism has lingered more persistently than there, and where, therefore, there are more, if as many, traditions which would gather as a halo around an eisteddfodic gathering. It was, there, too, that the noted one-arched bridge was erected, early in the last century, over the rushing Taff, by William Edwards, the self-taught architect; and ever since has remained as a monument of his great genius, and the wonder of succeeding generations.

"Pontypridd is also situated on the junction of the Taff and Rhondda rivers, and at the junction of the two valleys which hear these respective names and only a few miles higher another valley diverges from the Vale of Taff. These three valleys—especially the

Rhondda—are densely populated by colliers and iron-workers, to whom the week of the national Eisteddfod is the most important of the year. From each of these vales, as well as from all parts of Wales, eager competitors—especially rival choirs, in many instances numbering hundreds of voices—came and entered the lists for one or other of the numerous prizes offered. Others who did not compete were delighted to hear the best music, and were, moreover, intensely interested in the success of the choir which represented their own district. Thus, large crowds of people repeatedly thronged the huge pavilion at Pontypridd, far exceeding in number any which have hitherto been witnessed at such gatherings."

"I suppose, Mr. Pugh," ejaculated Jenkin, "you had the usual fuss at the Gorsedd, where the old bards clutch at the sword and shout 'peace.'"

"Ah! by-the-bye," exclaimed Swaish, anxious to avoid any unpleasantness that might arise from Jenkin's irreverent allusion to the Gorsedd, and, moreover, desirous of learning something about that ceremony; "let us hear something about the Gorsedd, Mr. Pugh, as I have, unfortunately, never seen it."

"I will gladly tell you what I can," responded Llewelyn Pugh, "Jenkin evidently requires no instruction in the matter—at least, he does not think so, and for all purposes of learning that is equivalent." Here Jenkin winced visibly, as Llewelyn Pugh, with a schoolmaster's instinct, had intended he should. "'Gorsedd,' as you may know, means 'throne.' As usual, the ceremony of the Gorsedd was fully observed, and on this occasion very appropriately on the old rocking-stone which is surrounded by the mystic serpent, consisting of stones pitched at intervals, and in such positions as to form the shape of that typical reptile. The arch-druid held shoulder high and horizontally the sword, while other bards held the scabbard in which it was placed; and as he drew the sword about a fourth of the way out of its scabbard, cried, 'Is there peace?' The answer came in the thrice-repeated 'Peace.' This challenge had to be given by the arch-druid, and favourably responded to by the bards before the Eisteddfod could be proceeded with, as, according to druidic teaching, it is not lawful for druid, bard, or ovate to speak of high things in the presence of a drawn sword. Great teaching belongs to peace, and has no association with war.

GORSEDD—THE BARDS SHEATHING THE SWORD UPON THE
DRUIDIC ROCKING STONE

"It was on this rocking stone, too, that a bard and singer of the
ancient type sang out on the opening day his original rich and racy
stanzas, then heard for the first time, to the accompaniment of the
national harp, and thus, on sacred druidic ground, observed a time-
honoured custom amid an enthusiastic and applauding throng.

"During the week." continued Llewelyn Pugh, numerous meetings
were held, competitive and otherwise. Welcome was also given to those
who had in any striking manner distinguished themselves in different
pursuits during the year. The speeches delivered, too, dwelt upon
subjects closely associated with the life and welfare of the nation.
Indeed, it would be difficult to enumerate, even if our time permitted,
the many ways in which the Eisteddfod must prove conducive to the
highest interests of the nation. Well may the Welsh be proud of their
Eisteddod! What the Derby Day is in England the Eisteddfod is in

Wales. The Welshman may, therefore, be pardoned for his pride. The adjudicator, an eminent Englishman, was amazed at what he saw and heard. It was such a new experience for him to see working colliers, tin-plate workers, and slate quarrymen, leading great choirs, consisting also of the sons and daughters of toil, in competitions which revealed such high-class renderings of the most difficult choruses, as to draw forth from him the criticism that in the works they had undertaken they had reached the highest pitch of refinement, and that their over-refinement was their only defect in their rendering of the masterpieces submitted to them.

"And now, Mr. Swaish, while I am speaking," continued Llewelyn Pugh, as he evidently warmed up to his subject, "I should like to refer to a very characteristic incident which occurred one afternoon. Amid the pauses which necessarily took place between the competitions there was naturally a difficulty in interesting the audience till the next important event came on. The great pavilion was far too large for anyone to command attention by a racy speech, and one pause became slightly tedious. But it was not long before the audience, with that instinct which is very often found in the crowd, solved the problem. A voice began to sing an old familiar sacred tune, and in an instant the vast throng, consisting of 20,000 people, joined in the grand old melody; and like the voice of mighty thunderings and the sound of many waters, but all balanced and blended in one perfect harmony, the song of praise went up from a nation's heart to God. In quick succession 'Aberystwyth,' 'Twrgwyn,' and other familiar tunes were sung to equally well-known hymns. The hearts of all were stirred, and many wept. It was no music-hall song that came as an impromptu; but the songs of the sanctuary.

"The Eisteddfod will not condescend to other than choice music in its great competitions; the result is that comic songs have no place within its precincts."

"I confess" replied Swaish, "that Welsh psalmody has always impressed me most favourably, and I have often wondered how to account for its excellence. I have never been to an Eisteddfod, because I have felt that it is distinctly Welsh, and is not likely to interest any but Welsh people: indeed, I have looked upon it as a national fad, accompanied by a good deal of noise and nonsense; but since you have been speaking I have wondered whether after all the Eisteddfod fosters the love for music in the Welsh people, who are evidently musical whatever else they may be."

"That's exactly it," responded Llewelyn Pugh, enthusiastically, "and that brings us to the last point—namely, that much of the excellence of Welsh psalmody is attributable to the encouragement which the Eisteddfod gives to the cultivation of the purest and best music. The English people, Mr. Swaish, do not know what congregational singing means. It cannot be heard in England as it is to be found in hundreds of places in Wales. Here, as you know, the rule is for every member of a congregation to sing his distinct part; the result is that the hymn is sung with such a richness and flexibility of voice, and fulness of harmony, as to impart a thrilling effect to it. The impetus which the Eisteddfod has given to the knowledge and practice of the best music, among a people naturally gifted with the sense of harmony, and with the power of expressing it, largely accounts for the inspiring congregational singing that is to be heard to-day throughout Wales. If the Eisteddfod had done no more than this, it would have rendered an incalculable service to the cause of Christ. When in addition to that we remember that some of the finest productions in the Welsh language, in poetry and prose, bearing upon Christian truth and practice, have been the direct outcome of the Eisteddfod, we rejoice, and will rejoice, in our glorious national institution."

Jenkin looked and spoke as respectfully as he could—especially as he remembered the quiet rebuke he had received from Llewelyn Pugh—in spite of the distrust he had in Eisteddfods from his knowledge of local ones. Thus in addressing Llewelyn Pugh, he said: "The Eisteddfod, I have no doubt, would be a very excellent thing if it were all that you would like it to be, or even what it is on those grand occasions when the National Eisteddfod is held; but when John Jones, the tailor, calls himself by some mysterious bardic name, conveniently forgetting the name he has inherited from his parents, and forthwith is elected as the adjudicator of poetry for a local Eisteddfod: when James Williams, the local preacher, becomes a great authority on singing, Thomas Hughes, the tax-collector, is made adjudicator of prose compositions, and William Thomas, the weaver, the adjudicator of the recitations, things are not quite so imposing or satisfactory, are they?"

"After making due allowance for your exaggerated way of stating things, Jenkin, you must remember," replied Llewelyn Pugh, in suggestive tones, and with a look that was evidently significant, "that the competitors on such occasions are as different from the competitors at the National Eisteddfod as the adjudicators can be from the National adjudicators. It is all in keeping. I have no doubt the adjudicators in the local Eisteddfods are quite equal to the task of deciding justly upon the relative merits of the competitions submitted to them on such occasions."

"I cannot accept that!" shouted Samson Lloyd, the village tailor, as he lifted himself up from the chair on his crutch, and stood his full length, which was about five feet. Samson's indignant look added meaning to his words, as be proceeded I competed once at a recitation, and have no doubt whatever that I deserved the prize; but it was awarded another, who by universal consent was by no means equal to me as a reciter. There is a great deal of favouritism, or ignorance, or both, I think, about the adjudications in local Eisteddfods. Most of those who have competed in them are thoroughly convinced of this."

"That's only an illustration, Samson Lloyd," said Llewelyn Pugh politely, "of the necessity of having adjudicators. Every man stands nearer to his own performances than he does to his neighbour's; the result is that his own naturally loom more largely upon his vision than anyone else's. Then, again, when a man seeks the opinions of others, he is most likely to ask his friends who have a bias in his favour; and even when they have no such bias, they, in many instances, are tempted to say more than they mean in their estimate of his merits. It is not pleasant, to say the least, to give an opinion against the man himself. Besides, there are numerous flatterers who adapt themselves to circumstances, and express themselves favourably to both sides. An adjudicator is far more likely to be right as to the relative value of any performance at an Eisteddfod than either the competitors or their friends. There is nothing more unbecoming, I think, than it is for a man who has competed to protest, as he does occasionally, against the decision of the adjudicator, and to enlarge upon his own excellences to the depreciation of other competitors." There was a subtle meaning in Llewelyn Pugh's tones and looks, in spite of all his politeness, as he said this, that could not have escaped an ordinary sensitive man.

Even Jenkin, notwithstanding his agreement with Samson Lloyd

on the question of Eisteddfods, was amused with the cause of
Samson's offence, and rather enjoyed the rubbing down he was
quietly getting from Llewelyn Pugh. His eyes twinkled with mischief
as the old schoolmaster proceeded, and as soon as there was a pause,
said: "That was a lively time when Will Thomas, of Pant-gwyn, got
up at a recent Eisteddfod, and complained bitterly because the
adjudicator did not agree with him as to the excellency of his choir's
singing. Everybody on the platform, and many of those in the
audience, did their best to persuade him to be quiet. The more they
tried the more he persisted. At last the chairman said to him
impatiently, 'My dear sir, do not make a fool of yourself.' 'Oh, there's
no danger of that, sir,' interjected Mr. Davies, of Login, who was
sitting near, 'Nature has already done that for him.' They told me
that poor Will soon collapsed: the remark was so pointed."

"There are many who attend Eisteddfods, and compete for prizes,
whom Nature has accommodated in that direction," replied Llewelyn
Pugh naïvely. "The fact is that the competitions, and the publicity
given to successful competitors, appeal strongly to ambition; and,
unfortunately, ambition is not only an infirmity—and in one sense,
certainly, an excellence—of noble minds; but it is also a chronic
disease from which many incapables seriously suffer."

There was a painful silence at the close of these words. No one
cared to venture a remark. Meanwhile Samson grew visibly shorter,
and looked vacantly at his crutch.

At length David Lewis broke upon the silence, and said: "I am
personally a great admirer of the Eisteddfod, Mr. Pugh; but I think
it would be greatly improved if there were less *Englynion*, with their
endless and often meaningless alliterations, and especially if, in the
competition for the Bardic Chair, a bard was not expected to adopt
all the extraordinary metres of the ancients. I have heard many of
our leading bards say that some of those metres are so complex that
it is well nigh impossible for the muse to breathe freely in such fetters.
Anything that tends to make poetry mechanical ought to be
discouraged, I think."

"You are quite right in the principle you lay down," replied
Llewelyn Pugh, "but you are barely right as to fact. Now it perhaps
would surprise you that the bard who won the chair this year only
adopted three metres."

"It is certainly news to me to know that he only wrote in three metres," answered David Lewis, "but I knew that he had not slavishly adopted all the old bardic metres, and that this was the reason why one of the three adjudicators protested against his being chaired."

"Yes, it was so," said Pugh; "but two out of the three insisted that it should be no disqualification, and the vast assembly upheld the two against the third. That just illustrates what I have already said, that the silly defects and bardic pretensions in connection with ancient Eisteddfods are rapidly passing away, while all that is valuable in our grand national institution is carefully preserved and adapted, with increasing success, to the new conditions amid which we, as a nation, find ourselves."

"It strikes me there is a lot to be done yet in that direction, Mr. Pugh," replied Jenkin, half timidly, as if mindful of recent rebuffs. "If we were to take some of our small rhymesters ('Talcenau Slip') at their own estimation we should purchase them at a fancy price."

"But, happily," replied Llewelyn Pugh, "that is precisely what the Eisteddfod teaches us not to do. Every man is judged, not according to his own estimate of himself, but according to the judgment of competent adjudicators; and it would be well if this kind of thing could prevail more generally in life. There is no place where a man finds his proper level sooner than the Eisteddfod; and if an incompetent man can, after the sifting he gets at an Eisteddfod, remain conceited, I am afraid that nothing will cure him. Conceit must be the warp and woof of his being. His case is hopeless."

It was now late, and Mr. Hugh Roberts, upon whom the infirmities of old age had come apace of late, and who had nearly a mile to walk along a lonely country lane, began to make signs of starting for home. Before he did so, however, he thanked Llewelyn Pugh, with a tenderness and grace which were characteristic of the old man, for all that he had told them about their national institution. He said that he remembered the days when the ancient Eisteddfod had apparently become obsolete; but he rejoiced that the interest in it had been so thoroughly revived during the last generation, and that, rid of much that was not worth preserving, the Eisteddfod promised to become an increasing power in the life of the Welsh people.

He added that they could well afford to dispense with a few old foolish customs which were once connected with the Eisteddfod but that they could not dispense with the Eisteddfod itself as an institution, without becoming much poorer as a nation for it. One thing, he said, that filled his heart with profound gratitude and joy at the close of a long life was the conviction that Wales, during the last seventy years, had made immense strides in every sense, but especially in spiritual enlightenment and mental culture. Whenever the hour would come when he should be called hence, he affirmed that he should die with bright hopes, yea, joyous anticipations, concerning the future of his people and country.

All felt that it would be sacrilege to add anything to Hugh's solemn words. Thus a meeting, which at the commencement threatened to be slightly discordant, closed with the tenderest and most united feeling, owing in part to Llewelyn Pugh, but chiefly to the patriarchal Hugh Roberts, whose closing words had descended like a benediction upon all present.

CHAPTER XIII

Kitty Vaughan at Llanstephan

KITTY Vaughan had not taken a summer holiday, for, when John and Shadrach went to Llandrindod Wells, she had remained at home with her children, and superintended the little that had to be seen to in connection with the trade, while the apprentice attended to the most urgent jobs. The harvesting, too, had further delayed her departure with her little son for a brief change to her favourite resort, Llanstephan. At length, now that the autumn had come, John insisted upon her going without further delay. Thus on the morning of one Saturday, the market day at Carmarthen, Hugh Roberts and his man John took Kitty and her lad as far as Carmarthen, whence she proceeded by another conveyance that was returning from market to Llanstephan—which being interpreted, is "Stephen's Church."

This is one of the most picturesquely situated little watering places in Wales. Nestling under the shadow of the ruins of an ancient castle, built probably in the twelfth century, and in the wooded hollow of the hill, at the extreme southerly summit of which the castle stands, it presents from Ferryside, on the other side of the estuary of the Towy, a charmingly pretty aspect. Beyond it, and around the next promontory, is the fishing village of Laugharne, reached by a sheltered road, which as it passes over the hill, lets in occasional glimpses of the sea, that add very greatly to the beauty of the surroundings. Beautiful as Llanstephan is in summer, it is, we think, still more charming in autumn—on account of the infinitely varied tints upon the wooded slopes.

"The Sticks,"—apparently so called by its early inhabitants, in their endeavour to translate into English the Welsh word "Coed," which should have been rendered "The wood," or "Trees,"—is one of the glories of Llanstephan. It is a small wood at the foot of the promontory upon the highest point of which the castle stands, and is between the castle and the Towy. It consists for the most part of high fir-trees, which present those cathedral-like features of high columns and fretted roofs, and which are supposed by some to have given the first conception of Gothic naves, aisles, and transepts. Here during the summer months the visitors congregate daily, at certain hours, to hold unconventional "Eisteddfods," the details of which are extemporised day by day. Periodical collections, among those specially interested in the success of these entertainments, supply means for the unpretentious prizes which are given to successful competitors in songs, recitations, and impromptu speeches. This feature of holiday life at Llanstephan has made it famous throughout South Wales as a favourite resort.

The wood, commencing with "The Sticks," extends along the slopes of the hill up to its summit, and beneath the shadow of the old castle, except where the village has encroached upon it, and where great gaps still reveal the devastating work of "Rebecca and her Children" in the solitary Welsh rising of the past two centuries, when the stateliest trees were stripped of their bark and thus left to wither as they stood. The open space in front of the "Plâs," still tells the tale of devastation, although Nature with its healing touch has removed all signs of disfigurement, and has made the open gap add to the beauty of the otherwise thickly wooded scene.

The prospect from the beach as the spectator looks over to Ferryside, and sees in the distance that palace surrounded by noble trees, from which General Picton went forth to fight and die for his country, is very beautiful and restful. The appearance of the passenger trains on the Great Western Railway, as they sweep along the edge of the water, adds to the charm of this rustic scene.

Kitty Vaughan, however, was not only drawn by the beauty of the surroundings; but she also felt a strong attraction toward Llanstephan, because Mary Price, who was one of the greatest friends of her girlhood, and had been closely attached to her ever since, lived there. She had lodged with her in former years; but that was impossible now, as Mary Price was in the last stages of consumption. Kitty took apartments very near, on "The Green," so that she might often see, and do the little she could in serving her dear friend. Early and late, and repeatedly throughout the day, Kitty was to be found near Mary's bedside, or busily preparing some delicacy for her. As the result of her constant presence and helpful and comforting services, Mary Price seemed to have vastly improved during the first week of Kitty's stay at Llanstephan.

Mary had married a fisherman who possessed many of the noble characteristics of those brave toilers. As he returned periodically he was quick to note the change in Mary, and with beaming face used to tell Kitty that he verily believed there was a chance of recovery yet; and that she herself had never in her life done a nobler thing than come to Llanstephan just then.

When a week had passed, and another happy Sunday had been spent by the villagers in their different places of worship, the fishermen from Llanstephan and the neighbouring Laugharne went out on Monday before noon in pursuit of their vocation, with wind and tide in their favour, and, long ere the sun had set, their sails had dipped beneath the horizon. With the setting sun and the returning tide the wind gathered force and vehemence, until at length it assumed the proportions of a hurricane. The channel was lashed into fury, and with darkening night there came the deepening moan of the wild storm that raged far out at sea. Mary Price, after a brief evening visit from Kitty, lay upon her bed pale and wan. For many months she had struggled with her relentless disease, and in spite of growing weakness, and for the love she had for husband and

children, had attended to her household duties, and, whenever
exhausted, had rested a while. Gradually but certainly her strength
had ebbed away, and she became daily less able to cope with the
growing claims of her family. Her children would soon be the better
able to cope with the world, she thought. If only her life were
preserved for their sakes a few years: that was all she wanted; though
even then it would be hard to leave them, as well as the man she so
much loved, and who had toiled hard on the great deep for the sake
of wife and children.

On this night, however, her thoughts took a different turn, for
the storm was terrible without. It was an awful night. The children,
save the infant who slept in the cradle close to the fire, were playing
in that subdued way in which sympathetic children learn to play
when the mother is ill. But her thoughts were far away; and yet not
so distant, for her loved one, she felt sure, had only gone far enough
to enter into the very heart of the storm, and feel the terrible throb
of its mighty pulsations. Thus she lay, and

> "listened to the raging sea,
> And heard it thunder, lunging at the cliffs,
> As like to tear them down."

As the night advanced the gale increased in violence. It beat rudely
at the window; howled dismally in the chimney; while at times it
paused and sighed; and then roused itself to renewed effort as it
shook the house to its foundations, and hurled the angry waves
against the rocks with deafening crash, to subside in a seething, angry
mass of waters that snarled and hissed as they sneaked back again
into darkness and the great deep. The wild elements were in dire
conflict, and woe betide the sailor or fisherman who found himself
involved in their powerful embrace!

Every sound reached the ear of the patient and loving wife in
that small cottage. She knew too well the import of all. At best her
husband was in peril, and she inwardly sighed as she thought of the
possibilities of the hour, and the hardships of a fisherman's life. If
aught befell her loved one, what would become of the children, who
had, indeed, already dropped their play to listen to the howling storm
and the raging sea? They, too, thought of their father, and hoped all

THE CASTLE AND "THE STICKS" FROM "THE GREEN"

was well but the mother had more anxiety and less hope than they. She thought of the dangers of a fisherman's lot, and uttered to herself a translation, by a local poet, of Kingsley's stanzas, which she had often repeated before that night; but never, perhaps, with such a conception of their meaning as now, as she looked once more at her three children by the table and the babe in the cradle:—

> "Men must work, and women must weep,
>   And there's little to earn, and many to keep,
>   Though the harbour bar be moaning."

She bethought herself again of the experiences of that evening; of her foreboding fear when she saw the sun set; "and then the night-rack come rolling up ragged and brown;" and wondered whether her husband had time to note the ominous signs, and escape for safety; but still she fell back upon the old refrain, which gained additional pathos from its varying form:—

> "But men must work, and women must weep,
>   Though storms be sudden, and waters deep,
>   And the harbour bar be moaning."

And then, as a wave of desolation momentarily passed over her soul, she thought of the plaintive close of Kingsley's song:—

> "For men must work, and women must weep,
>   And the sooner it's over the sooner to sleep,
>   And good-bye to the bar and its moaning."

Yes, these words were sweet; but there were better words than even Kingsley's: and she would ask her eldest boy to read them from the Bible, which rested on the table by her bedside; and bid his sister and brother sit by the table, too, as he read, so that they might learn the same lesson of trust together; though the storm raged furiously without. That Book she largely knew by heart, especially those parts that spoke of storms, for she had been in need of them before that night. She, therefore told the lad to read Psalm cvii. 24-31: "These see the works of the Lord and His wonders in the deep. For He commandeth, and raiseth the stormy wind, which lifteth up the waves thereof. They mount up to the heaven; they go down again to the depths; their soul is melted because of trouble. Then they cry unto

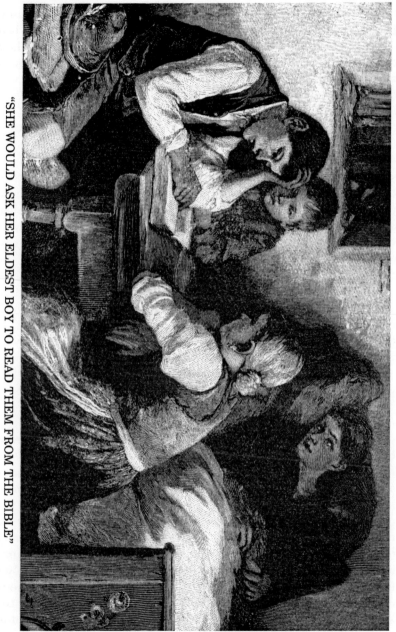

"SHE WOULD ASK HER ELDEST BOY TO READ THEM FROM THE BIBLE"

the Lord in their trouble, and He bringeth them out of their distresses.
He maketh the storm a calm, so that the waves thereof are still. Then
are they glad because they be quiet; so He bringeth them unto their
desired haven. Oh that men would praise the Lord for His goodness
and for His wonderful works to the children of men." "Yes, that will
do, Jack," exclaimed his mother. "We can leave your father there. He
is safe in his Lord's keeping; and we will trust God for him and for
ourselves; and He will not disappoint." And then, as if inspired by a
faith that defied all storms, she sat up in her bed, and, looking upward,
she exclaimed, as the children listened, "'God is our refuge and
strength, a very present help in trouble. Therefore will not we fear,
though the earth be removed, and though the mountains be cast into
the midst of the sea; though the waves thereof roar and be troubled,
and though the mountains shake with the swelling thereof.' There,"
she added, "it hasn't come to that yet. We can leave your father and
ourselves in His keeping, and sleep." The children slept until the
fisherman knocked at his own door in the early dawn, when they awoke
to find their mother sleeping still; and when the rugged fisherman
drew near the bedside, and looked at those placid features, upon which
had been stamped in the watches of that night an unearthly beauty,
he learned that she had "crossed the bar," and entered that haven,
where winds never blow and storms never rage.

During the night as the storm grew more furious, and the restless
waters of the Towy, in full tide, heaved and with increasing frequency
broke upon the beach with a heavy thud, while from the heart of the
frowning clouds the lightning darted in its zigzag course, Kitty
thought much of Mary Price upon her sick bed, and of her brave
husband out at sea in the midst of the conflicting elements.

She slept but little amid the brief pauses of the storm, and soon
after daylight she arose from her bed and hastened to render some
loving service to her friend. She, however, arrived to find that the
only service she could now offer was to prepare that frail body for
the burial, and to speak some comforting words as opportunity
offered to the bereaved husband, and the children who were stunned
by the suddenness of their great loss, and the memory that, only a
few hours before, their mother had fondly caressed and kissed them,
ere she bade them her last "Good Night." In the early morning the
storm gradually subsided; and while Kitty was busily employed in

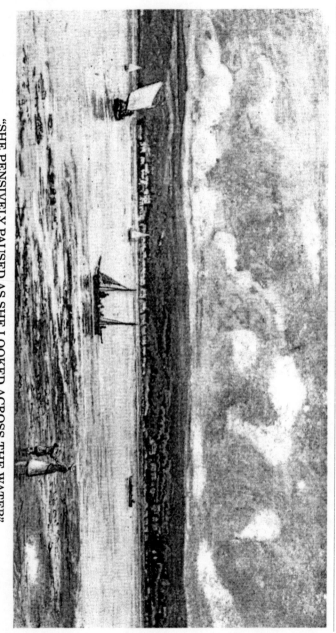

"SHE PENSIVELY PAUSED AS SHE LOOKED ACROSS THE WATER"

attending to her self-imposed duties in the darkened home of her
old friend, the sun shone forth; fleecy clouds hung over the opposite
hills; while right above Llanstephan the parting clouds revealed an
infinite depth of sky, and the broad river reflected upon its calm
surface the blue serenities that arched over it.

In the afternoon Kitty having done all she could, took her little
son for a walk along the sands. She pensively paused as she looked
across the water. On the opposite side a train rushed along the line.
It was the first that the child had ever seen. He was full of
wonderment as he asked his mother what that living thing was that
was running away from the smoke. She scarcely heard the question;
for a far greater mystery—the sudden withdrawal of her friend from
those who needed her so much—perplexed her heart. She imagined
her wondering lad without a mother! and John at home without his
Kitty! and then hastily brushed off a tear.

The little fellow looked up into his mother's face, and was
perplexed by the unwonted expression upon it. She noted this, and
planted a kiss upon his brow. She then returned to Mary Price's
cottage to bestow a kiss upon each of the motherless children left
there, and especially the little babe in its cradle, all too unconscious
of its loss; and then her heart was relieved.

A few days passed and the funeral was over. The brave fisherman
went out to sea again, although the shadow of a great sorrow rested
upon his heart; and the elder children received their first lesson from
Kitty how best to shift for themselves, with the parting injunction
to try to do as their mother had taught them, and the request that
if, at any time, they wanted help to be sure to send to their mother's
friend and theirs.

The last morning she spent with them, ere she returned home,
was full of pathetic incidents. She felt keenly the parting, and left
Llanstephan with the depressing consciousness that life was much
poorer now to her, than it had ever been before.

CHAPTER XIV

John Vaughan on "The Lad with the Barley Loaves"

JOHN Vaughan was pre-eminently a Bible Class Teacher but occasionally he would take a Cottage Service and then it was an occasion to be remembered. He was as quaint and racy in his sermons and addresses as he was in his lessons. About two and a half miles from the village there were twin cottages, at one of which a cottage

243

service was held once a week. John's turn to conduct the service arrived, and during the whole of that day he had little to say to callers, and even to his apprentice; but he hammered the leather on the lapstone with keener zest, and pulled the stitches with greater vigour than usual; and now and then he would hum a fragment of a familiar hymn tune, and occasionally take up his well-thumbed Bible that was always within reach, and eagerly consult it.

The apprentice well knew John's emphatic opinion about the evil of disturbing men, when they were preparing their sermons. Had John dogmatized upon the unpardonable sin, he would probably have given that as one of the few things which he thought would be a near approach to it. In his more jocular mood, too, he had often repeated a story about Dr. William Rees (Gwilym Hiraethog), who, after a very busy week, was in great consternation on Saturday evening with regard to the morrow. At such times Dr. Rees got very depressed and almost desperate. On that particular Saturday evening he had an unbroken succession of callers; and yet he could not refuse to see any one of them. It was nine o'clock when he dismissed the last. He returned to his study, and groaned and sighed with anxiety. Once more a knock at the study door brought him to his feet in utter despair! A poor woman was announced. She at once pleaded with him to intercede for her son, who had "just joined the soldiers." She was sure, if anyone could succeed, Dr. Rees would. Dr. Rees had a tender and responsive heart for such a plea; but he could not take in its significance. He only just managed to catch the words that the poor woman's son had joined something; and, arousing himself to a supreme effort, he sympathetically asked, "What did you say your son had done?" "Joined the soldiers, sir," responded the woman. A ray of hope seemed instantly to enter his soul, as he exclaimed with all his well-known emphasis and earnestness, "Well, as I live, *I'll join the soldiers, too!*" He evidently thought there was one chance left even for him!

John Vaughan's apprentice did not want him to "join the soldiers;" he was therefore silent and unobtrusive all that day. Besides, Thomas, as already stated, was preparing for the Presbyterian College, at Carmarthen, and was frequently engaged in local preaching; thus, with a fellow-feeling which made him wondrous kind, he did as little as possible to disturb his master in his meditations. Long before the time for starting John became very uneasy, and proportionately impatient to start. Shadrach, who was as inseparable from him as Jonathan was in ancient days from David, accompanied him. To hear John discourse on any subject was a treat which he would on no account miss.

The two friends started in good time, passing by Pontresais, and "The Stag and Pheasant," and arrived in good time at the cottages, called "The Quarries," because they were built in what had at one time been small quarries by the wayside. In one of these the meeting was to be held. Gradually the congregation assembled and filled the little cottage. Among them was John's father-in-law, who lived about half-a-mile distant. He was the oracle of the neighbourhood, especially in Greek, which he had learnt, as we have seen, after the age of sixty, by the aid of students from a neighbouring college, who lodged at his house. He had not the gifts of John Vaughan in speaking, and in clear and quaint exposition; but he was a careful Bible student, and, as such, John paid him great deference.

The meeting began with a hymn: then reading: again a hymn; and then a few prayers, followed by another hymn. Then John gave out his text: "There is a lad here which hath five barley loaves and two small—('small' is rightly omitted from the Welsh Version)—fishes; but what are they among so many?" (John vi. 9.)

He began by saying, "Our subject this evening is—'The discovery of obscure gifts, and the use Jesus can make of them.' I suppose I must divide my subject into three heads, like all great preachers; but, if I cannot keep them quite separate, you must forgive me. We have here:—

"1. A lad overlooked. None of us like to be overlooked. We feel instinctively that we are not made to be lost sight of. One of the glories of home is that no one is overlooked there—not even the smallest. Indeed, the smaller he is, the bigger the place he occupies, as a rule. There's a place there for everyone round the table and the hearth, and a place in the hearts of the dear ones who form the family circle. And it is this that we miss when we cross the threshold of our early home. The cold world outside does not readily supply a place for us: thus we feel desolate and lonely when for the first time we go into it from the warmth and brightness of the home of our childhood.

"This lad must have felt very lonely. He was where it was most easy to feel lost—in a crowd. In a crowd, too, where no count was taken—no, not even by the Evangelists—of women and children. He was, moreover, a *little* lad (bachgenyn*). He was very young, or at least small for his age, and on that account it was easier for him to be overlooked in so great a multitude.

"Then again, there was no one to take care of him. Other lads had their parents or their friends with them. This lad had evidently no one. Indeed, I am inclined to think that he scarcely belonged to the crowd. The other day one of my children came home from school, and said that the teacher had told the class that these five barley loaves and two small fishes were the boy's dinner. I did not care to shake my child's confidence in the infallibility of the teacher. But now that I am at a little distance, I venture to say that I cannot agree with that statement. I do not believe that this interesting little lad had such an unconquerable appetite as all that; or, if he had, he would not have kept his dinner so long. Boys in Palestine are very much the same as boys in Wales: and I have never yet seen a boy who has gone to the country for a day, and has taken his dinner with him, who has not consumed it two hours, at least, before dinner time; and yet this lad had his store by him at even.

"No, I do not agree with that teacher. I venture to think that this lad was one of those camp-followers, who were accustomed in those days to hang on the outskirts of the crowds, vending their wares as best they could. I fancy—mind, it is only imagination; and yet I think there is much reason for it—that this poor lad was one of those who had to earn his living in that way; and thus was elbowed and pushed aside by those who belonged to the crowd.

"Now, of all the thousands who were assembled on this occasion, no one was more likely to be ignored, and less likely to be specially noticed, than this lad. But—

"2. This lad was specially noticed. Who was the first to notice him? Andrew. How much the world and the Church owe to the Andrews of history—men who have found promising lads! How indebted we are to men who have eyes in their heads, and know when they see an interesting youth! Andrew was great at finding. We read in the first chapter of this Gospel—'One of the two which heard John speak, and followed him, was Andrew, Simon Peter's

---

* Here the Welsh translation, as in many other instances, excels the English, in using the diminutive term.

brother. He first *findeth* his own brother Simon, and said unto him,
We have found the Messias.' True to his character, he *found* what
others had overlooked on this occasion."

Here Shadrach nodded vigorously, while his face was all aglow
with an approving smile. John's father-in-law also gave an emphatic
response to this. He had noted the word in the Greek; and he now
put his *imprimatur* on John's remark, as only a Greek scholar could!
John proceeded:—

"Why was this lad found? First, because he had something which
no one else had: not even the disciples—and, I say it reverently, not
even Jesus! It was not much; yet it was something peculiarly his
own. Not two of us, any more than two leaves in the forest, as we
have often heard, are exactly alike. If we were, the second would
have no reason to give for his existence and God sends nothing into
this world without giving it a reason for its existence. Thank God,
everyone of us has a gift distinctly his own; and there our opportunity
and our responsibility lie. So was it with this lad. He had only five
barley loaves and two fishes; but no one else had even those.

"Then, again, this lad had something which the multitude needed.
When that became the case the lad could not be long hidden. A hungry
crowd must sooner or later find the lad with five barley loaves and
two fishes. This was the lad's opportunity; and this comes sooner or
later to all who wait patiently; and who have something that this great,
but poor, world needs—and who hasn't, if he but waits his time!

"Again, this lad had something which Christ was willing to use
and bless. This cannot be said of every store which men possess.
The first question we ought to ask is, Whether Jesus would be willing
to bless those things which we treasure? They are of very little good
to us, if He would not touch them.

"Even more, this lad had something that he was willing to place
in the hands of Jesus Christ. Ah, that was important! If he had clung
to his little store we should not have heard anything of him, except
it be by way of reference to a lost opportunity. It was his placing all
in the hands of Christ that made this miracle possible. It is then
that we, too, get miracles wrought in our lives; and it is by
withholding this that we limit the Holy One of Israel.

"Now I have another word to say:—

"III. This lad was used and honoured. He was used in spite of his being so little. Although Andrew was the first to notice him, he talked about him after all in rather patronising tones. If I were an artist I would represent Andrew as a tall man, six feet at least in height, and proportionately broad. Why! Because he talks in such a patronising way about this *"little"* lad. You never hear men of my size talk about *little* people. We have so often been referred to in that depreciating term that we are heartily weary of hearing the word. But notice that Jesus did not patronise the lad, even when Andrew did; but said at once, 'Make the men sit down.'"

Here a smile stole over the countenances of those present, and a blush over the faces of one or two men, who were taller than the rest.

"He was also used, although his store was so small and poor. Notice that these were barley loaves. I heard Llewelyn Pugh say, the other day, that the Romans would not eat barley in any form; but gave it to their horses. That is the reason, I suppose, why their horses were finer than they were in the latest days of ancient Rome. One thing I know, that the grandest men Wales has ever known— especially its mightiest preachers—have been fed on barley bread. Christmas Evans thrived well, and preached gloriously, on barley bread and butter-milk. Some of you, too, have done well on the same fare. The other day my little son came up to see his grandfather— who is here with us now—and did not much relish the barley bread that was put before him. His grandfather evidently noticed it, and said to the boy: "David, the bread that was good enough for Jesus to eat, when He was here on earth, ought to be good enough for you.'"

"Daniel, Waungroes," John's father-in-law, smiled and blushed as his saying was repeated, while those present cast admiring side-glances at him. John continued "That boy was full of it when he returned home; and I pray God he may never forget it."

This called forth murmurs of cordial approval from all directions. John proceeded: "Besides, there were only five barley loaves, and two fishes, which had been dried, and were used as a relish to make the barley bread more palatable. Why, if the lad had five thousand loaves within reach, there would have been no miracle wrought, for no miracle would have been necessary; and Christ never wrought a miracle when there was no need of it.

"Thus the very smallness of the boy's store became Christ's opportunity. He looked into that little basket: saw in it the germ of a miracle; and then out of it fed the multitude. It is out of our poverty that He makes us rich.

"Now just think of the effect all this would have upon the lad. I can imagine how during the day, as he carried his burden under the burning sun, he would often think of his trying lot, as compared with other boys in the crowd, who had their parents and friends with them. Now, I imagine that the little fellow was the son of a widow—if so there would be a special point of sympathy between Jesus and him. If he had a father, he would, probably, not have had to go out to earn his living so early. Thus the little fellow's mother would make the loaves, and he would go out to sell them. You can readily see how such a lad, as he saw other boys accompanied by their parents in that crowd, would think that his lot was hard, and his chances few. But what think you were his thoughts now, when Jesus fed the hungry multitude out of his basket? Again, of all the people, who had passed him by with disdain during the day, who would not gladly have acknowledged him, now that Jesus had so honoured him?

"And then think of him returning home, and bounding over the threshold into his mother's presence; and how she would say to him, 'Well done, Benjamin, you have been a good boy to-day—sold everything!' Then imagine what he would have to say to her—'Oh, mother, I wish you had been with me to-day! Five thousand men, besides women and children, have been fed out of my basket.' Then he would let out the secret as he added how Jesus of Nazareth took the basket, and having thanked God for the loaves,—'the very loaves you made mother!' broke them with His own hands, and gave them to His disciples, and they to the multitude. Then he would conclude, 'and Jesus would not have a crumb lost; and when all was gathered there were twelve basketsful; and all in the first place out of my little basket, mother!' What a new view of the possibilities that opened up before her and her lad the mother would now have! How she would rebuke herself for ever thinking that her lot, and her child's, were too poor to admit of any possible honour, since now Jesus had touched her lad's life, and made it glorious. Whenever she made barley cakes after that, and whenever her lad had to carry his basket, it was with a heart free from all murmur, or even doubt, and with the feeling that their humble task had been transfigured once for ever by the touch of Christ.

"Again, I have often wondered whether this lad, when he grew up, ever became a disciple of Jesus. That, surely, is almost certain. Having entered into this memorable partnership with Jesus Christ, he would long to be associated with Him in a still more glorious partnership in giving to men the Bread from heaven, having partaken of which they would never hunger."

Here there were numerous responses from all parts of the room.

"And when this lad became a man, and had a family of his own, if his children were at all like yours and mine, they would at times gather round him, and say, 'Father, tell us a story.' I can imagine that on such an occasion he would look lovingly at them, and say: 'Yes, I'll tell you a story,' and then would proceed to tell them what occurred on that ever-memorable occasion when he, as a poor lad, who had to earn his living early in life, was honoured by Christ as probably no other lad ever had been. How graphically he would relate the details, and how the children would open their eyes, yea, and their mouths, as they took all in. Before very long they would come to him again, and ask for a story, and when he told them that he had none to relate, they would answer earnestly, 'Tell us the story about when you were a little boy with the basket and the five barley loaves and two fishes'! Then he would once more tell the same tale, and pointing to the basket that hung on the wall, would say, 'and that is the very basket which I carried, and Jesus took, and out of which He fed the hungry thousands.' And he would add, 'I have no wealth to leave you, my children; but I will leave that basket. Treasure it as an heirloom, and think of Jesus—and your father—when you look at it.'

"My dear friends, do you think this story would be forgotten by those children, or their children after them? Do you think it was important enough for John to record, and that it was not important enough for this lad's descendants to remember? Would *you* forget it if he had been *your* father, or grandfather or great grandfather?—and remember, Jewish parents were specially careful to repeat the sacred memories and traditions of the past to their children. Depend upon it, this story was told hundreds of times in that family, and it would generally be brought to a close by the proud addition, 'And that lad was our grandfather—or great grandfather.'

"Oh! how blessed are such traditions! And these are some of the kind, surely, which we have inherited from our fathers, who, in poverty, and amid much hardship, were greatly honoured in being permitted to be fellow-workers with Christ. Jesus has been many a time in this very cottage, and in many other thatched cottages in our neighbourhood, and we will tell the story to our children. How many humble gifts he has honoured, and obscure services He has blessed; and He who has done so in the past, will do so still. Who is there here who has but a poor store, which the world would consider of little value; who nevertheless will place it, as it is, in the hands of Christ? I for one will place this little barley-loaf of a sermon, just as it is, in His hands; and, who knows, perhaps He will make it enough to satisfy your hunger, great as it must be; and that shall indeed be reward and honour enough, yea, and more than enough, for me. God grant it."

There were loud and repeated responses from all present, and a consciousness of having been abundantly fed out of John Vaughan's basket, by the hands of Christ, when the preacher, in the closing prayer following the sermon, asked Him who blessed the lad's little store to bless his. Another hymn brought the meeting to a close, and all present, like those who witnessed the ancient miracle, exclaimed with grateful hearts: "We have seen strange things to-day."

On their homeward journey Shadrach said to John admiringly, "Well, John, you made a great deal of that lad. I never thought he was such an interesting little fellow before to-night."

"I hope I have not made of him more than the narrative justifies," replied John. "I must say that I have been disgusted with the way in which commentators talk about the six barley loaves and fishes; but nothing about the lad. Andrew found him, and Jesus Himself made a great deal of him and his basket; but commentators have since then done their little best to bury him out of sight. The Gospels have brought him into prominence; and we should keep him there."

"Quite right John," responded Shadrach. "I do not think those who were present to-night are likely to overlook that lad again. And yet I suppose we often overlook boys quite as promising; until they are fairly thrust before our eyes by Providence, on account of the gifts they possess, and the honour that the Master would place upon them."

"Yes," said John "that has been true about almost all our grand preachers in Wales—Christmas Evans: Williams, of Wern; and in later times John Jones, of Talsarn, and similarly gifted men. I thought of John Jones as I spoke to-night. He, as I suppose the lad

THE BIRTH-PLACE OF REV. JOHN JONES, OF TALSARN,
AS IT WAS—FRONT VIEW

in the Gospels must have been, was the son of a widow very early in life. But he had a noble mother; and that is generally the case with sons who grow up to be great men."

"I never knew that before about John Jones, of Talsarn," said Shadrach. "Where was he born?"

"He was born," replied John, "at Tan-y-Castell ('Beneath the Castle'), in the parish of Dol-y-ddelen, Carnarvonshire, on March 1st,

THE BIRTH-PLACE OF REV. JOHN JONES, OF TALSARN,
AS IT WAS—BACK VIEW

1796. Caleb Rhys has often passed the house in which John Jones was born. He was the eldest of many children; and yet he was only ten years old when his father died. That was a dark day to the family. John was just old enough to sympathise with his mother; and in after years he helped her to the utmost of his powers to bring up the family. He never forgot his father. To the end of his life he could never refer to him, except with great emotion. The house in which he was born is now uninhabited and sadly dilapidated; but a worthy grandson of John Jones is, I hear, thinking of restoring it, in loving memory of his great ancestor. But John Jones is not the only one in Wales, as I have said, who has been raised from obscurity and poverty, to great honour and usefulness. It is true, of almost every great preacher Wales has ever had. More than that, this is largely true of all great men in the world's history. The world owes most to lowly cradles and obscure huts. From the lowliest circumstances, great and holy men, inspired with great thoughts and laden with solemn messages from God to man, have arisen in all ages. Outward circumstances have never yet constituted the greatness or the smallness of a life. Men may rise above them, or fall below them. True greatness has never been confined to any locality or people: and there is no reason why it should to-day. The Divine One came out of Nazareth, and not out of Jerusalem; out of the carpenter's shop, and not out of the Temple."

This, and much more, John said to Shadrach in the silvery moonlight, as they returned to their homes. He had warmed up to his subject, and, when that was the case, all that was required of his companion was to listen; and this Shadrach was always glad to do when John was the speaker. They at length arrived at the village, and separated for the night; but the memory of that service, and the walk homeward that night, long abode with Shadrach as an inspiration and joy.

CHAPTER XV

The Closing Scenes in Hugh Roberts' Life

ABOUT a quarter of a mile from the smithy was Pentre-mawr Farm, the home of Hugh Roberts. Eighty years had passed away since he was born in that old farmstead, and ever since then his life had been closely identified with it. The old house had been the scene of all his domestic joys and sorrows during those long and changeful years. Indeed even its interior arrangements were much the same now as when Hugh was born; with the one exception that the tenants had changed! Hugh's father had early in life been brought under the influence of the Calvinistic Methodist revival during its later period: namely, the closing decades of the eighteenth century; and notwithstanding the unwise ejection of Rev. Peter Williams, of Carmarthen, for a supposed leaning toward Sabellianism—an event which Hugh's father keenly felt, as a devoted

255

admirer of that gifted man—he continued to be the pillar of the little Methodist community in the village till the close of life.

Thus Hugh had been brought up from his childhood—in accordance with the custom of the Calvinistic Methodists—in the fellowship meetings of the Church. Often had he, in his early days, knelt on the hearth by the old settle in the open chimney, while his father led the devotions of the family; and while he was yet young he was called upon, by the death of his father, to take his place at the head of the household, and in the conduct of family worship. For many years he continued to be a dutiful son to his mother, and after her death brought his bride into the old home, amid the rejoicings of friends and neighbours. Since then his experience had been chequered with alternating joys and sorrows. He had buried his wife, and then his daughter, who, after his first great loss, had been his sole stay in the home. His son had settled in a neighbouring farm. Meanwhile, Hugh Roberts remained in the old home: surrounded, indeed, by devoted servants; but yet alone as the sole representative of the family, and of a generation that had passed away.

Yet he was not self-involved, nor in any sense out of touch with the changed condition of things in which he found himself. Sanctified sorrow and trial had, during the long years through which he had passed, matured his spirit, and imparted a rare charm to what always was a beautiful and impressive countenance; nor had these taken away from him aught of the buoyancy of hope, or of interest in the activities of life, or of sympathy with the young, which had always characterised him.

He seldom missed the market at Carmarthen on Saturdays. John, his head servant ("gwas mawr,") used to drive him to the market and back, starting in the morning, and returning early in the afternoon. The noble veteran, who had traversed the road thousands of times, never lost his interest in the surrounding country, as he proceeded on his way; but in passing one farm after another, he would repeat tender reminiscences connected with them, as he recalled friend after friend who had lived there long ago.

Hugh, however, unlike most old men, readily formed new acquaintances, and entered sympathetically into new relationships and friendships. Hence his presence was ever welcome to the children of his former friends. He loved them for their fathers' sake, and was quick to trace in each some striking similarity to the old friend he loved in former days. Thus Hugh's interest in life, and hopefulness concerning the rising race, were perennial; and everywhere his presence was welcome. All agreed he was the youngest in sympathy, as well as the most mature in experience, they knew. The old man and the young man were blended in wondrous fashion in him.

The last Saturday upon which Hugh Roberts went to market was a beautiful autumn day. As he proceeded on his way, and neared Carmarthen, the sun shone forth brightly, while the trees, which skirted the highway, and stretched along the river side toward Abergwily, had been touched by the subtle glories of the skies, and reflected almost all the colours of the spectrum in the brilliant sunshine. It was a scene of surpassing glory in decay: of the leaf putting on the image of the heavenly as its earthly life was ebbing. Hugh was in harmony with his surroundings. The outward man in his case was doubtless perishing—although the process was very gradual—yet the inward man was renewed day by day. If the leaf could present such a glorious proof of its kinship with the heavens, even in the hour when earth was fast claiming it as its own; how much more ought he to be adorned with heavenly graces, the predictions of a fuller and diviner life, just at the time when earth withdrew from him those physical gifts, which were essentially transient; but which had fulfilled their purpose in his earthly existence. Thus, as a rule, the old man was in sympathy with his surroundings, and, from almost everybody and everything, drew material for the highest thoughts and devoutest yearnings.

Yet he was not a dreamer or mystic; for he no sooner entered the market than he conversed freely about the price of butter and cheese, wheat and barley, and expressed his opinion in genial fashion about the prospects of agriculture, and the probable rise or fall of the markets. All who saw Hugh Roberts on this occasion, however, were struck more than usually with the refined and well-cut features, as well as the mellowed tones and sweet alluring smiles, of the aged man. The noise of buying and selling, and the discord of competing voices, subsided by mutual consent as Hugh drew nearer. His very presence quickened people's delicacy of feeling, and made them realize the incongruity and vulgarity of anything approaching disputation or blatant bargaining. Greed and selfishness seemed to

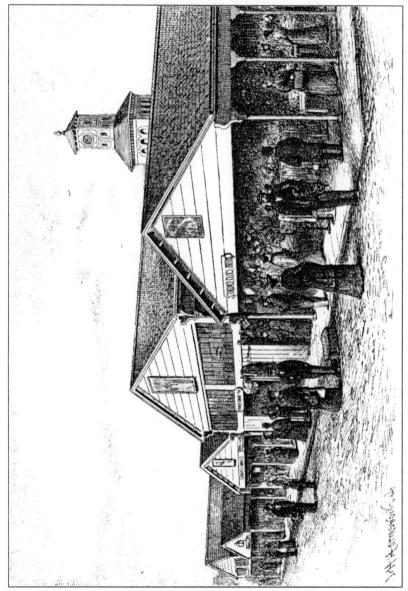

THE MARKET PLACE, CARMARTHEN

lose their grip of their victims for the time being; and anyone who watched Hugh Roberts' movements among the stalls, and consequent silencing of touting dealers, could better understand how Hugh's Lord and Master, when the zeal of God's house consumed Him, swept the sacred floor of the stalls and tables of unholy traffickers, and restored to a house of prayer, what men had turned into a den of thieves. Had there been similar need Hugh Roberts would have done much the same thing. As it was, the market at Carmarthen was a far nobler thing for his presence on that day.

As the day wore on Hugh Roberts became more weary than he usually did on market days. There was a growing transparency about his features, and a faraway look about his eyes that impressed all who saw him. Some shook their heads, and said that the other world was alluring Hugh Roberts away, and that soon his marketing days would be over. It appeared, too, as if Hugh himself had some such presentiment; for he urged upon his man John to see that all his little liabilities were squared up that day; "because," he significantly added, "we never can tell what may take place."

And yet never had Hugh been more cheerful than now. It was not that he loved the earth less, but heaven more. To the last he was an intense admirer of nature. On the way home on this occasion he seemed at times to be in a joyous reverie; at other times he was in a pleasant chatty mood, talking freely about the loveliness of the scene on every hand. As they ascended the hill from Glangwily the glow of the westering sun had transformed the landscape. Soon the shadows began to lengthen, and in the slanting rays everything was brought into vivid relief. Gradually the clouds, which gathered in the distant west to bid the sun adieu, reflected its gorgeous crimson and brilliant golden hues; while beyond all was an infinite depth of blue, shading off into a trembling paleness on the dim, feathery outskirts of the transfigured clouds. "Who would not set like that sun?" asked Hugh, half in soliloquy, and half in converse with John. "I like sunset better than sunrise, when it can be seen like this. It is so mellow, and yet so rich. It was in the cool of the day that the Lord walked among the trees in paradise; and I often think He still walks among the trees of this earth of ours in the cool of the evening. The light is never so charming as it is when it darts across the landscape, and flits among the boughs and leaves of the trees, ere the great sun sinks beyond the hills. Strange that earth and sky should put on such glowing colours as they do in autumn, when the leaves decay, and the sun is setting among the gathering clouds of an October evening. There is wonderful meaning in those words, 'At even time it shall be light'— yea, and such light! There is silver in the morning light; but it becomes more golden as the day advances; until at last there is nothing but molten gold in its beams, when it sinks in the distant west. So is it with the leaves. In spring and summer they are rich in living green; but as they fade, the treasures of light, which they have gathered during bright days, shine out of them as they never did in days of greater vigour. They are like the saint who on his death-bed reveals those hidden glories, which only come to light when his strength is failing, and heaven is claiming him as its own."

John listened with amazement; but simply nodded assent. He had never heard his master speak quite like that before; and he had a grave suspicion that he would not hear the same again.

At length they arrived at the village, and passing by the smithy, proceeded to Pentre-mawr. Hugh Roberts was glad to retire early that night; and, being exceptionally weary the following morning, did not rise with the dawn, as was his wont; but got up in time for the morning service that commenced at ten o'clock. About a quarter of an hour before the time for service, Hugh Roberts passed through the village, on his way to the chapel, leaning more heavily than usual upon his staff.

Still there was a calm, restful, although abstracted, look about his countenance. He sat as usual in one of the corner seats of the big pew, and listened with intentness to the sermon. John, his head-servant, was present at the service: but paid little heed to the proceedings; being anxiously bent upon watching his master, in whom he had traced a great change. At the close of the service he went to Hugh, and suggested that he might give him his arm, as he looked weary, and appeared to need just a little help. Hugh Roberts eagerly accepted the offer, and at once started homeward without the usual conversation with his friends at the close of the service.

John Vaughan and Shadrach Morgan, who had just come from the service at Horeb, met Hugh and his servant at the smithy corner, and, after exchanging a few words with him, bade him "Good Morning."

"He is going to the better country, John," whispered Shadrach as soon as he left them. "Yes," replied John, "and he looks as if he is in

HUGH ROBERTS RETURNING FROM MARKET

haste to be gone. I have never before seen his face look quite so
heavenly, or his body quite so frail, as to-day. The earthly house is
evidently breaking up; and through the chinks we can catch better
glimpses than usual of the bright spirit within, as we can the light
in blind Betty's house at night through the gaping mud walls of her
humble dwelling."

Just as they were talking Caleb Rhys hurried to the spot. He had
suddenly missed Hugh Roberts, and now inquired if he had passed by.
They replied that he had just gone with John, the head-servant. "Then
that is all right," replied Caleb, "it strikes me it will be the last time he
will pass the smithy corner; he is bent upon another journey now."

Kitty Vaughan and Mary Morgan, who had walked quietly after
their husbands on the way from the service, came up just as Caleb
was speaking. They at once eagerly inquired what the reference to
Hugh Roberts could mean, and on hearing the news, Kitty grew pale
and in her quiet, thoughtful, yet emphatic manner, said, "Well, when
he is gone, we shall not see his equal again."

"That is to doubt God's power, Kitty," said John, in tones which
betrayed as much admiration for Kitty, as they did reproof of her
pessimism.

"No," replied Kitty quietly, "I do not doubt God's power, I only
remember how He acts. He sets great value on such men as Hugh
Roberts. Depend upon it He does not send saints of Hugh's type every
day. They are not among his commonplace gifts, but His
extraordinary blessings and we have no right to expect God to be
always, or even once in a generation, sending his very best men into
our neighbourhood. There are other neighbourhoods to think of; and
we must put up with more ordinary saints now; but thank God we
can to our dying day remember the time when one of God's princes
was in our midst."

All this was said in calm and deliberate tones; but with the
emphasis of moistened eyes, and saddened and mellow countenance.

Early in the afternoon Kitty Vaughan proceeded along the village
highway, and then turning along the by-road walked toward Pentre-
mawr. She was dressed in her little swallow-tail flannel gown, and
striped apron to match; and wore her tall silk hat, the surface of which
was so carefully preserved as to reflect the light, and even passing
objects, almost like a mirror; while underneath was a neat cap of

unblemished whiteness, with its narrow ribbons worked into rosettes at each side of her comely face, and broad loops under her chin.

On her left arm was suspended a small basket containing a few delicacies for Hugh Roberts, while on the other side, with his tiny hand placed confidingly in his mother's, was her little son, seven years old. Kitty in earlier years had been an intimate friend and companion of Hugh Roberts' only daughter. Next to Kitty herself, she had in bygone days been the best rider in the whole neighbourhood; and when Kitty was married she had flown through the air upon her Arab steed, on the homeward gallop to the bride's house after the wedding; but all too late to welcome the bride, since Kitty herself was the first to arrive, amid the enthusiastic plaudits of the villagers. Those days of high glee and youthful mirth had passed by now; and the memory of them only added to the pathos of the circumstances in which Kitty at this time visited the home, which a few years ago was ever made bright and musical by the presence and song of her old companion; but from which she had since passed away on a dark wintry night, to which there had been no dawn to her aged father.

Yet Hugh Roberts had never murmured. He had been enabled to sing songs in the night; and thus made even the darkness harmonious. Giving the literal translation to the words of the Psalmist, he used to say that "Weeping came in to lodge at even; but Joy in the morning." He therefore welcomed Weeping in her sombre garb and with pensive countenance; for he knew that she had something to teach him, before Joy would come, and ere the day dawned, and the shadows fled away.

Kitty well knew how calmly and patiently; yea, at times, even joyfully, Hugh Roberts bore his losses, and trod his lonely path; yet for the love that she once had for his daughter, and the reverent regard that she had for him, she had often sought an opportunity of gladdening his heart by some gentle deed of thoughtful service.

It was not an accident that she took her little son with her on this occasion. She had a suspicion that it might be the last opportunity; and she wanted her child to remember Hugh Roberts when he was gone. Among the greatest blessings she could wish for him in future years, when the world and its trials and temptations would press upon him, was the recollection of having seen a saint like Hugh Roberts. Besides, the lad himself, partly from his mother's estimate of Hugh, which he caught with a child's unerring precision, unawares to her, was charmed by the personality of the saintly old farmer. Indeed, his childish fancy cast more than a saintly halo round that aged man's head. He had asked his mother in wonderment one day, as she talked to him of the angels, whether they were *almost* as good and as lovely as Hugh Roberts; and how it was that *he* wasn't among them? And now that his mother had told him that perhaps Hugh Roberts was going to leave Pentre-mawr, to live with the angels, the little lad's eyes opened even wider than usual as he asked her whether he could see him once more before he went, so that he might send his love to his little brother; who two years before had taken the same journey. Kitty's eyes moistened as she listened to her child's request, scarcely liking to accede to it, and yet not daring to deny him the favour. "It will please him," she thought, "and when he sees Hugh, he will forget the message. These things weigh lightly upon the child's heart."

When they arrived at Pentre-mawr, Hugh Roberts had, owing to great exhaustion, retired to bed—one of those old-fashioned oak cupboard-beds, which were then universally used in farmhouses, and which may still be seen far inland in Wales. Kitty and her little son were asked into the room. They drew near the bed; when Hugh, who ever loved little children, having shaken hands with Kitty, patted the lad on his head, and asked him if he was going to be a preacher.

It was the first time the suggestion was made to him, and it was recalled after this with overpowering force; but now he replied, "No, I want to be an angel, and go with you." Kitty blushed, and felt uneasy; but Hugh was touched and pleased; and putting his arm fondly round the child's neck, said, "You are too young for that now, David, you'll grow up yet to be a Christian man, I hope."

"No, I am not too young to be an angel," replied the little lad eagerly, "I am not too young, for my little brother has been with the angels long since, and"—here the child paused—"mother says you are going; and we'll come, won't we, mother?"

Kitty sat behind the child, and was greatly confused. She wished she had not told her child quite so much. Children were such tell-tales.

But Hugh was drawn more and more to the lad. It was a touching sight. Both extremes of life had met, and there was a touch of tender sympathy between them. The old man and the child—one looking into life full of wonderment; and the other looking out of it full of eager expectancy—were in one another's embrace. The childhood of innocence was linked to the childhood of life-long and matured trust. And Kitty looked on in bewilderment; and yet with delight. Her child she thought, would never be the same as if Hugh Roberts had not embraced him.

Suddenly she got up to confer with the servant as to whether Hugh had better have, just then, one of the little delicacies she had brought, glad meanwhile to leave him and the child together. She soon returned to induce Hugh to take a little nourishment; but all the while he and the child looked lovingly at each other.

At length Kitty, after many good wishes and offers of service, bade Hugh good-bye, and took her little son by the hand to go. But the little fellow gently resisted. He did not want to leave; but expressed his intention to go with Hugh to the angels, and to his little angel brother. It was the first time that a power mightier than his mother's love had possessed the child; and Kitty noted it. The tears trickled down her countenance as she looked at the eager face of her child, and then at the pale, etherealised, yet infinitely tender face of the aged saint.

Hugh observed all, and said to the little lad: "My blessing be upon thee, my child. May the Lord direct and uphold thee, and make thee a joy to thy father's and mother's heart." Then turning to Kitty he said: "Take care of him Kitty; let him be thy Samuel whom thou shalt consecrate to the service of God and His house and the Lord will accept thine offering, and fill thy life with brightness, and thy heart with peace."

Kitty thanked Hugh, and finally departed as the aged patriarch's blessing still rang in her ears, and thrilled her soul. Life to her would never be the same again, for having heard that blessing uttered over her child and herself. It was a benediction from an aged saint in the midst of death's river, ere he set his foot on the other side.

On the way home the little lad had many questions to ask his mother as to how Hugh Roberts would go to be with the angels. Would he have to go up by the same staircase as her friend Mary Price, who had so recently gone from Llanstephan? He wondered, too, how she got there that dark and stormy night. Did an angel fetch her; and did he bring a light with him? Would Hugh Roberts know the way, and be strong enough to walk it; or would Jesus come to meet him, and perhaps—here the child paused—carry him. How

was it that none ever came back? Had they forgotten the way; or
didn't they love their friends after they were gone; or did they love
Jesus and the angels more, and didn't like to leave them?

These and many other questions, eagerly asked, and for which
answers were as earnestly and impatiently demanded, well-nigh
bewildered poor Kitty Vaughan. She answered her child as best she
could, and once more looked tenderly into that little face, so full of
eager inquiry, and into those eyes, through which an immortal spirit
peeped out, and claimed relationship with all that was mysterious
in life, and sacred in its closing scenes.

On her arrival at the smithy, the Sunday Schools being over, John
and Shadrach were about to start for Pentre-mawr. Having heard from
Kitty how Hugh was, and concluding that he must be fast nearing his
hour of departure, they proceeded along the narrow road toward the
old farmstead, which for more than fifty years had been closely
associated with the name of Hugh Roberts. They soon arrived at the
house, entered, and approached the cupboard-bed upon which he lay.

There was a heavenly look about the old saint, which greatly struck
them as they entered the room, and met his glance. John spoke tenderly
as he addressed him, and said: "Well, Hugh, Shadrach and I thought
we would like to come and see you, for we guessed you would be alone."

"Thank you much," responded Hugh, with his sweet dulcet voice,
"I am alone now; although, thanks to Kitty Vaughan and her little
son, I have been anything but alone this afternoon. I could not go to
my Sunday School as usual; but I did not lose anything, for the little
lad and I had sweet talk about the angels; while Kitty—angel that
she is—brought some of the good things you have at home, John, to
tempt the failing appetite of an old man, who is not likely to want
anything here much longer." John was touched by this allusion to
Kitty and his little son, and replied, "I am glad to hear it, Hugh. My
little lad will have a nobler conception of the angels, for having seen
a saint as ripe for heaven as you are." There was no note of flattery
in all this; but the emphasis of a powerful and solemn conviction.

"Ah," responded Hugh, "I fear that it was but little of the saint
that the little fellow saw in me; except it be that I have grown
patriarchal enough to love little children with an intensity which I
did not in my younger days, although I was always fond of them. I
can now better understand the feelings of Jacob, when he blessed

both the sons of Joseph, and exclaimed, 'God, before whom my fathers Abraham and Isaac did walk, the God which fed me all my life long, unto this day, the Angel which redeemed me from all evil, bless the lads.' This is a time when one can link the past to the future—our fathers to our children—and feel that there is a glorious continuity in history, when the same faith joins together succeeding ages. All we can grasp of the future is to be found in our lads; and what they can grasp of the past is largely to be found in us. We bid them look to the past, and accept the blessings which come from it to them; while they, in their simple way, bid us look forward, and believe that it shall yet be well with the world."

"Very true, Hugh," responded Shadrach. "What wonderful feelings Simeon must have had when he held the Child Jesus in his arms, and said, 'Now lettest Thou Thy servant depart in peace.'"

"Ah, Shadrach, life could have no further attraction to Simeon after that," exclaimed Hugh Roberts. "Once having had the Holy Child in his arms, any other experience to him would be a terrible 'come down.' His motto was 'See Christ, and die.' Nothing but heaven could be tolerated by an old Testament saint after that. And I too, John, have the last few hours seen enough of Jesus not to desire to go back to farming; one glimpse of heaven spoils one for earth."

"Let us read the story of Simeon and the Child Jesus, Hugh," said John, as he opened the Bible; and then read very tenderly the story from Luke. (Luke ii 25-38.) "I once heard a very striking sermon about Simeon, by Rev. G. Griffiths, Rhymney," added John. "He said among many excellent things that men as a rule, plead for the extension of the lease of life; but Simeon longed to surrender it. He did not wish to wait longer, to pollute his vision with anything after seeing Jesus Christ. He had now seen enough to fit him for dying; then the preacher added with greater power, 'No one has seen enough for dying till he has seen the Christ.'"

"Thank God," exclaimed Hugh, "that's true. It is wonderful how true religion pays, even in this life. It grows upon you wonderfully. Your last visions are your best; and it is marvellous how genuine faith bears a man up at last. For a time he has patiently to carry his cross; but by-and-bye the carrying is done for him—indeed, he *is* carried: he has simply to trust and wait."

"That reminds me," said Shadrach, "of what I heard Rev. John

Evans, (Eglwys-bach) once say. He spoke of the fishermen on the
rivers of Wales, who still use the old British coracle; and said: 'You
have seen the fisherman carry his coracle mile after mile along the
dusty road, or rugged by-way; but the moment he comes to the river
the coracle carries him. So is it with true religion. My friends, carry
it on the highway of life, and beneath the heat and burden of the
day; by-and-bye when you come to the River it shall carry you.'"

"Oh, how gloriously true!" exclaimed Hugh Roberts. "That is
precisely what it is doing for me now for I am fairly in the River,
Shadrach; but Jesus upholds me; and that is enough. You, John, can
pitch St. Garmon; let us sing it to Islwyn's hymn.

> "Gwel uwchlaw cymylau amser,
>   O fy enaid: gwel y tir,
>   Lle mae'r awel fyth yn dyner,
>   Lle mae'r wybren fyth yn glir;
>   Hapus dyrfa
>   Sydd yn nofio yn ei hedd."
> (See above Time's cloudy regions,
>   See, my soul, that land in green;
>   Where the air is ever balmy;
>   Where the sky is e'er serene.
>   Happy myriads
>   Who are buoyant in its peace.)

"Yes, Hugh," replied John, "that is one of the few I can pitch; but
I fear the singing will try you."

"No, my son," responded the veteran, "I shall not do much of the
singing, personally; I am always helped by hymn singing, especially
when Islwyn's hymn is sung to St. Garmon. They seem to be made
for each other."

"Yes," said John, "and yet St. Garmon was composed for the well-
known hymn of William Williams, of Pant-y-celyn. You know the
circumstances?"

"No, I always thought that the hymn and tune were made for
each other," replied Hugh Roberts. "Tell us the circumstances, John."

"The author of St. Garmon," responded John, "is Mr. Edward
Meredith Price. He composed the tune amid extraordinary
circumstances. He was at that time engaged as a conductor of public

psalmody at Dolau, Nantmel, Radnorshire. A missionary meeting was about to be held there, and Mr. Price was anxious to have a new tune for the well-known hymn of Williams, of Pant-y-celyn—'O'er the gloomy hills of darkness.' He had spent some thought over the matter; but apparently in vain. One day, however, he was trimming the hedges on his farm close to a mountain stream, and near the spot where it leapt over the precipice in a wild cataract. As the wind played upon the falling waters, they sent forth rich and varied strains to the ear that was trained for their reception. Wafted by the passing breeze, they resolved themselves into an air which entered the soul of the rustic musician; and what had come as an inspiration to him— with such force that he assured me that he never composed the tune; but caught it from the passing breeze—has taken possession of us as a nation, so that now it is often sung in every chapel in Wales."

John and Shadrach then joined in singing, and Hugh struck an occasional note; but ere they came to the close he had joined the heavenly choristers, and had exchanged St. Garmon for the Hallelujah Chorus. He had passed away in song. The strains of St. Garmon had lifted him up so high, that he was caught in the eddies of the rapturous praises of the redeemed.

The two friends returned with slow steps and pensive spirits, and told the villagers of Hugh Roberts' death. Kitty Vaughan was greatly affected by the strange, and yet attractive features, that death had presented to her, in the two instances in which she had so recently been brought face to face with it. In the first case it had been a sleep: in the last case, a song. What terror could it have, if it came in either form? Death to the saint after all, she concluded, had no terror, for it had no sting.

The day of Hugh Roberts' funeral was one of universal mourning for many miles round. Hundreds came to pay him their last loving homage; and to the villagers in after days came the keen and growing consciousness that "he was not, for God took him."

THE END

A COMPANION TO THIS VOLUME

By REV. DAVID DAVIES.

ECHOES FROM THE WELSH HILLS;

OR, REMINISCENCES OF THE PREACHERS AND PEOPLE OF WALES.

Illustrated by T. H. THOMAS, R.C.A.

☞ Extract from a letter from the Right Hon. W. EWART GLADSTONE:—"It is, Mr. Gladstone thinks, a want of knowledge which causes the scant measure of justice to Wales, and he heartily rejoices in the appearance of a work like yours, which aims at giving the requisite information."

The Rev. C. H. SPURGEON, in the *Sword and Trowel,* says of this work:— "Mr Davies, whose sermons we well remember, has produced a remarkable book, full of fine specimens of Welsh oratory... One is made by these 'Echoes to fall in love with Welsh piety and to long for its like in our English villages... We shall not be surprised to hear that Mr. David Davies's books obtains a high meed of praise from his own countrymen, and that it interests many readers in other lands. We know of no volume which gives so good an idea of the power of the living ministry of Wales."

Extract from a letter from DEAN HOWELL, of St. David's.—"The best delineation of Welsh social and religious life that ever appeared in English to my knowledge. I have often spoken of it as brimful of interest, humour, quaintness, and the characteristics which are peculiar to the Wales of 1840-70 ... Your books will serve to crystallize many of the quainter features of our immediate fore-fathers as no other books in English do. Such a delineation could never be the result of mere observation; only an actual experience of the life itself could qualify for such a work."

Dr. ANDREW A. BONAR writes:—"'Echoes from the Welsh Hills' is a most readable book. May the Master put His seal upon it."

Dr. CULROSS writes:—"I have greatly enjoyed your book, It is capital; and the vein you have struck has gold in it."

"A book well worth looking into, and one that will open to many of our readers quite a new region of religious life."—*Guardian.*

"Mr. Davies is in very hearty sympathy with his subject, and evidently writes upon it with the advantage of an intimate acquaintance with the past and present history of the preachers and people of Wales... We do not know of a book which, in the general scope of its treatment, gives so full a conception of Welsh religious life and character as this book does."—*Christian World.*

"It is a work which will enhance Mr. Davies's already high reputation as a writer... It will do for Wales what Dean Ramsay's work has done for Scotland... His description of the village is really worthy of Goldsmith... A really charming and edifying work, for which we thank Mr. Davies."— *Freeman.*

"This is a bright book... A most alluring volume."— *Homiletic Magazine.*

"It deserves, and we have no doubt will have, a wide circulation."— *Literary World.*

"The Rev. David Davies's 'Echoes from the Welsh Hills' ought to be read by all tourists to the Principality... We must say a word about the illustrations; they are excellent and full of character, as we should expect from their author, Mr. T. H. Thomas."— *Graphic.*

"Mr. Davies, in this volume, which is the result of the closest intimacy, and loving sympathy as the offspring of it, has made us free of Welsh village life. Every phase of it is here represented to us with a kind of graphic simplicity, which produces such effects as the writer could hardly have expected... Altogether the volume deserves to be highly commended as a faithful picture of a most interesting phase of life. The illustrations are well conceived and well executed in view of the author's purpose."—*Nonconformist and Independent.*

"There was genuine need of a book of this kind on the religious and social life and customs of the Welsh people... The gap has not been adequately filled until now... The author neither overdraws nor caricatures his country nor people, but places before the reader a beautiful and charming picture of the customs of the Welsh nation. We shall be disappointed if this book does not secure a wide circulation in England, and an honourable position for its author among its contemporaries."—*Seren Cymru (Star of Wales).*

"Mr. Davies displays, to an unusual degree, all the best temperamental, intellectual, and spiritual characteristics of the Welsh mind. His heart is large; his imagination is vivid, vigorous, and refined his humour is quick, pure, and genial; he can think closely, and can express his thoughts in clear, terse, and impressive language; and his spiritual tone is pervaded by a richly Evangelical faith, hope, and gladness. This new publication is unique... We have enjoyed these 'Echoes' so much that we should be very grateful for another and equally large collection of a similar kind, and we have no doubt that every reader of the present collection would promptly make the same acknowledgment. The talks of the villagers at the smithy about the characteristic preachers of the Principality, the tit-bits, gems, and larger quotations from their sermons which the many conversions produce from tenacious memories and appreciative hearts, the pictures we have of great field services, and the vivid illustrations supplied to us of almost every phase of Welsh life combine to invest the book with a power of fascination which comparatively few books possess."—*Baptist Magazine.*

List of Tentmaker Publications

Biography

Charles Graham: Apostle of Kerry	W G Campbell	hb	£11.95
Countess of Huntingdon (2 vols)	Aaron Seymore	hb	£47.50
Griffith Jones of Llanddowror	David Jones	pb	£6.95
Irish Worthies	Thomas Hamilton	hb	£12.50
Journals of William Clowes	William Clowes	hb	£13.95
Life & Labours of Hugh Bourne (2 vols)	John Walford	hb	£36.95
Life of Howell Harris the Welsh Reformer	Hugh J Hughes	hb	£15.95
Life of John Kennedy	Alexander Auld	hb	£13.95
Life of Samuel Miller DD, LLD (2 vols)	Samuel Miller	hb	£36.95
Lives of the Early Methodist Preachers (3 vols)	T Jackson (Editor)	hb	£47.95
Memoirs of the Life & Labours of Hugh Bourne (2 vols.)	John Walford	hb	£36.95
Some Great Preachers of Wales	Owen Jones	hb	£17.95
Wesley's Designated Successor: John Fletcher	Luke Tyerman	hb	£17.95

History

A History of the Plymouth Brethren	William B Neatby	hb	£13.95
Days of Revival (6 vols)	C H Crookshank	pb	£39.95
Echoes from the Welsh Hills	David Davies	hb	£15.95
History of Dissenters (3 vols)	Bogue & Bennett	hb	£47.95
History of the Earlier & Later Puritans (2 vols)	J B Marsden	hb	£37.95
History of the Presbyterian Church in Ireland (3 vols)	James Seaton Reid	hb	£49.95
History of the Puritans (3 vols)	Daniel Neal	hb	£64.95
Revivals in Highlands & Islands in the C19th	Rev A Macrae	pb	£5.95
Sweet Singers of Wales	Elvett Lewis	bkt	£2.95

Commentaries

Analytical Exposition of Romans	John Brown	hb	£19.95
Christ and His People in the Book of Psalms	Andrew Bonar	hb	£15.95
Critical and Exegetical Commentary on Exodus	James G Murphy	hb	£15.95
Jonah, His Life, Character, and Mission	Patrick Fairbairn	hb	£13.95
Lectures on the Prophecy of Zechariah	Ralph Wardlaw	hb	£15.95
Nichol Puritan Commentary Series: 1 John	Nathanael Hardy	hb	£24.95
Nichol Puritan Commentary Series: Ephesians	Paul Bayne	hb	£24.95
Nichol Puritan Commentary Series: Individual Psalms	Pierson, Gouge & Smith	hb	£24.95
Nichol Puritan Commentary Series: Jonah, Obadiah & Haggai	King & Reynolds	hb	£24.95
Nichol Puritan Commentary Series: Malachi & Ruth	Stock, Torshell, Bernard & Fuller	hb	£24.95

Nichol Puritan Commentary Series: Philippians & Colossians

| | Airay & Cartwright | hb | £24.95 |

Theology

Atonement & the Cross	Octavius Winslow	hb	£11.95
Discourses suited to the Administration of the Lord's Supper			
	John Brown	hb	£14.95
Expository Lectures	John Kennedy	hb	£12.95
Glimpses in the Inner Life of Christ	W. Blaikie & Robert Law	hb	£9.95
Expository Lectures	John Kennedy	hb	£12.95
The Spiritual Life	Octavius Winslow	hb	£9.95
Theology of the Old Testament	Gustave F Oehler	hb	£17.95
Works of Henry Smith (2 vols)	Henry Smith	hb	£39.95
Works of Rev. Thomas Boston (12 vols)	Thomas Boston	hb	£195.00

Devotional

Hymns of W Vernon Higham	W Vernon Higham	hb	£9.95
Meditations at the Table	Jim Waring	pb	£4.95
Work & Conflict	John Kennedy	hb	£13.95

Issues

Character of Freemasonry	Charles G Finney	hb	£7.95
Current Trends in Roman Catholicism	J D T McCauley	bkt	£1.25
Do Gypsies Speak in Tongues ...?	Gary Nixon	pb	£4.95
Freedom & Discipleship	Jerram Barrs	bkt	£2.95
From Spiritual Powers to Liberating Grace	Torbjörn Swartling	pb	£6.95
Gift of Tongues	Phil Roberts	bkt	£1.95
Letters on the Masonic Institution	Jn Quincy Adams	pb	£5.95
Women in Ministry	Phil Roberts	bkt	£1.95

Reference

| The Finder (Index) | Michael Keen | hb | £9.95 |

Prices correct for summer 2002

Tentmaker Publications
121 Hartshill Road
Stoke-on-Trent
Staffordshire
UK
ST4 7LU
☎ 01782 416119
Email: Sales@tentmaker.org.uk

Tentmaker Publications

Tentmaker Publications is a family operation. It was originally set up when we were church-planting in Ireland with the aim of supporting the work there. This it still does, but we are now involved in establishing a new church here in the Potteries area of Staffordshire and rely to some degree on Tentmakers to support our own work in pioneering. Besides producing books and booklets, we use the equipment to produce a regular evangelistic magazine for the area in conjunction with a number of local churches.

The method of production we employ uses a high-volume laser printer to produce the books individually. We then have them bound in batches of 100 or so. This enables us to maintain low stocks and publish books that would otherwise never be reprinted. It does mean that our costs are higher yet we try to keep the retail price at about the same as other publishers of similar material.

We sell direct to the customer where possible but also supply shops. Some titles are only available to customers purchasing direct.

Full details of the titles we publish can be found on our website at www.tentmaker.org.uk

Phil & Joy Roberts